MW01422346

Tom Rettig's Clipper Encyclopedia

Tom Rettig's Clipper Encyclopedia

Tom Rettig
Debby Moody

BANTAM BOOKS
TORONTO • NEW YORK • LONDON • SYDNEY • AUCKLAND

Clipper is a registered trademark of Nantucket Corporation
Tom Rettig's HELP is a trademark of Tom Rettig Associates

TOM RETTIG'S CLIPPER ENCYCLOPEDIA

A Bantam Book / July 1989

All Rights Reserved
Copyright © 1989 by Tom Rettig Associates
This book was produced by Tom Rettig Associates, Beverly Hills, CA

No part of this book may be reproduced or transmitted in any form or by any means, electronic or mechanical, including photocopying, recording, or by any information storage and retrieval system, without permission in writing from the publisher. For information address: Bantam Books.

ISBN 0–553–34798–5

Published simultaneously in the United States and Canada

Bantam Books are published by Bantam Books, a division of Bantam Doubleday Dell Publishing Group, Inc. Its trademark, consisting of the words "Bantam Books" and the portrayal of a rooster, is Registered in U.S. Patent and Trademark Office and in other countries. Marca Registrada, Bantam Books, 666 Fifth Avenue, New York, New York 10103

PRINTED IN THE UNITED STATES OF AMERICA

0 9 8 7 6 5 4 3 2 1

For Leonard "C-Wizard" Zerman whose skill and determination in writing Tom Rettig's HELP software made this project possible.

Contents

A

B

C

D

E

F

G

H

I

J

K

L

M

N

O

P

Q

R

S

T

U

V

W

Y

Z

_ (Underscore)

Introduction

This book introduces concepts that ease the learning curve of new programming languages and speed the reference process of familiar ones. These concepts were born with Tom Rettig's HELP software where they are an integral part of its design.

The concepts cover categorizing individual language elements by both grammar and functionality, stating explicit data type and representation in syntax metavariables, breaking up very long commands into functional groups, and providing the source code diskette in the form of a complete pop-up reference. These are each explained below. Other conventions are explained under the alphabetic entry "Conventions."

Language Categories

Each language element is categorized two ways, by its functional action and by its grammatical type in the language. We use the names "Category" to refer to functional actions and "Type" to refer to grammar. For example, some functional Categories are Database, Input, Menu, Numeric, and Search. Some grammatical Types are Command, Function, Operator and Procedure.

When Category and Type are combined, they make a phrase descriptive of each language element. For example, Database Command, Character Function, Numeric Operator, and Error Procedure. Associating these names directly with each keyword helps you better understand and use the language. All alphabetic entries identify their keyword by both Category and Type.

↙*Keyword* *Category*↘ *Type*↘

ACHOICE() **Menu Function**

You can look up language elements by either functional Category or grammatical Type when you are unsure exactly what feature you want to use. For example, if you are interested in searching a database, you would look in Appendix A: Category Cross Reference under "Search" and there you would see everything in the language you could use for searching. If you wanted to see a list of all the operators in Clipper, you would look in Appendix B: Type Cross Reference under "Operator."

Syntax Metavariables

We have extended metavariables (items within angle brackets) to explicitly state both their data type and representation. This allows you to know everything you need by looking at the syntax without having to refer to the text to discover what the parameters represent.

Syntax metavariables usually contain the data type in the form <expN> with the representation explained elsewhere. Sometimes only their representation is shown like <position>, leaving the data type to be explained later. We put both in every metavariable, using an uppercase letter to indicate data type followed by the lowercase functional representation, <N position>.

For example, Clipper's complex MEMOEDIT() function is often shown like this:

Syntax: MEMOEDIT([<expC1> [, <expN1> [, <expN2> [, <expN3>
[, <expN4> [, <expL1> [, <expC2> [, <expN5>
[, <expN6> [, <expN7> [, <expN8> [, <expN9>
[, <expN10>]]]]]]]]]]]]])

As you can see, it is necessary to refer elsewhere to find out exactly what any parameter means. With our model, you have all the information you need in the place it belongs.

Syntax: MEMOEDIT([<memo field> | <expC>
[,<N top row> [,<N left col>
[,<N bottom row> [,<N right col>
[,<L edit> [,<C UDF name>
[, <N line length> [, <N tab size>
[, <N start row> [, <N start col>
[, <N relative row> [, <N relative col>]]]]]]]]]]]]])

Where we omit the data type, as in the first parameter of the previous example, the parameter is a "literal" rather than an expression. See the alphabetic entries "Conventions" and "Expression" for more information.

We remained more traditional with our C syntax, using modern C function prototypes. But, we placed representation metavariables inside angle brackets instead of in italics. C syntax usually looks like this:

Syntax: _exmback(unsigned char * *address*, unsigned *bytes*)

To retain consistency and familiarity for Clipper programmers, our C looks like this:

Syntax: _exmback(unsigned char * <address>, unsigned <bytes>)

Long Commands

When the syntax gets too long, it becomes confusing and difficult to reference which parts go together. For example, the syntax of @...GET and @...SAY is usually documented like this:

Syntax: @ <expN1>, <expN2> [SAY <exp> [PICTURE <expC>]]
[GET <variable> [PICTURE <expC>]
[RANGE <expN1>, <expN2>]
[VALID <expL>]]

We break up the SAY part from the GET part—they actually are two separate commands. We group GET under Input and SAY under Output.

Syntax: @ <N row>, <N column> [SAY <expression>
[PICTURE <C template>]]

Syntax: @ <N row>, <N column> GET <variable>
[PICTURE <C template>]
[RANGE <N | D minimum>, <N | D maximum>]
[VALID <L condition>]

We then provide an additional entry for the special combination which is unique among all the @... commands.

Syntax: @ <N row>, <N column> SAY <@...SAY options>
GET <@...GET options>

How would you categorize this combination, Input or Output? You can see which we chose on page 36.

Source Code Diskette

Although code diskettes for books are not a new concept, the form this one takes is. The code in this book is available on disk in Tom Rettig's HELP software, which is a pop-up quick reference tool with the ability to export code directly into your editor while you are programming. It's easier than working with separate source code files and provides additional functionality.

Tom Rettig's HELP is available from your software dealer or directly from Tom Rettig Associates in Beverly Hills, California. See the advertisement in the back of this book for more information.

Tom Rettig's Clipper Encyclopedia

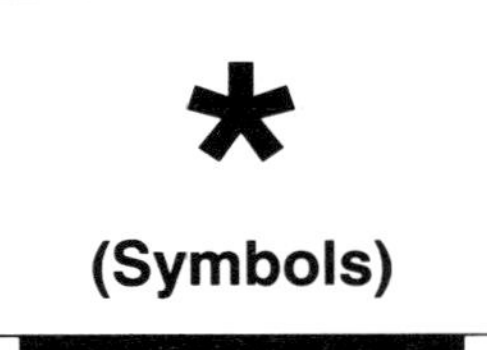

This chapter contains all Clipper language symbols, except for the underscore character (_) which is covered in the last alphabetic chapter following the letter Z.

! (logical) — Logical Operator

Syntax: ! <L condition>

Action: Performs a logical negation of the specified condition.

Return: <expL> true if <condition> is false, otherwise false.

Detail: The exclamation point (!), when it precedes a logical expression, is identical to the logical .NOT. operator. The following example uses ! to test the EOF() function. EOF() returns a value of false (.F.) except when the end of file is encountered, so that the condition, ! EOF(), is true for each record in the file:

```
DO WHILE ! EOF()
   .
   . <commands>
   .
   SKIP
ENDDO
```

Any condition, no matter how simple or complicated, can be negated using ! (or .NOT.) to form a new condition. Using any of the three logical operators, you can make more complicated conditions. Logical operations are performed in the following order unless the order is overridden using parentheses:

1. .NOT. or !
2. .AND.
3. .OR.

Also: !=, .NOT., .AND., .OR., <, <=, >, >=, <>, #, $, ()

! (run) — OS Command

Syntax: ! <OS command> | <com filename> | <exe filename> | <bat filename> | (<expC>)

Action: Executes an external program.

Detail: The ! (bang) command is used to execute external programs. All active memory variables, environment settings, and open files remain intact when control is returned. Note that you must have enough available memory to load the DOS command processor, Command.COM, plus the program that you are attempting to execute. Otherwise, bang results in an error message such as "Insufficient memory."

For example, to change the current directory you could use:

```
! cd\dos
```

You can specify the program name that you want to run as a character expression. To do this, enclose the expression in parentheses. For example, to gain DOS access:

```
cmd_name = "Command"
! (cmd_name)
```

Type EXIT at the DOS prompt to return to the program.

The order of precedence used by the bang command is indicated in the command syntax. For example, if there is a .COM and a .BAT file named Test:

```
! Test
```

executes the .COM file, not the .BAT file.

Bang is functionally identical to RUN.

Do not execute memory resident programs with the bang command.

Also: RUN, CALL

!= Comparison Operator

Syntax: <expression> != <expression>

Action: Compares expressions of the same data type for inequality.

Return: <expL> true if the two expressions are not equal, otherwise false.

Detail: As a comparison operator, != (not equals) forms a logical condition that can be used anywhere in the language where <condition>, <expL>, or <exp> is part of the syntax representation. Character, date, and numeric expressions can be compared to like expressions using the not equals operator. For example:

```
USE Mailing
LIST FOR Zip != "90026"
```

or

```
LIST FOR Age != 13
```

or

```
COUNT FOR Name != "John Doe"
```

Also: ! (logical), .AND., .OR., .NOT., <, <=, >, >=, <>, #, DO WHILE, ()

” ” Character Symbol

Syntax: ”<string>”

Action: Delimits character strings.

Detail: Character string delimiters are:

Delimiter	Example
matching double quotes:	`"string"`
matching single quotes:	`'string'`
left and right brackets:	`[string]`

Use the delimiters that do not occur in the string:

```
"string's 'single' quotes and [brackets]"
'string has "double" quotes and [brackets]'
[string's 'single' and "double" quotes]
```

Also: ’ ’, [ ], Expression

Comparison Operator

Syntax: <expression> # <expression>

Action: Compares expressions of the same data type for inequality.

Return: <expL> true if the two expressions are not equal, otherwise false.

Detail: As a comparison operator, # (not equals) forms a logical condition that can be used anywhere in the language where <condition>, <expL>, or <exp> is part of the syntax representation. Character, date, and numeric expressions can be compared to like expressions using the not equals operator. For example:

```
USE Mailing
LIST FOR Zip # "90026"
```

or

```
LIST FOR Age # 13
```

Also: !=, .AND., .OR., .NOT., ! (logical), <, <=, >, >=, <>, DO WHILE, ()

$ Comparison Operator

Syntax: <C search> $ <C target>

Action: Looks for the search string in the target string.

Return: <expL> true if <search> is found within <target>, otherwise false.

Detail: The substring operator forms a logical condition that tells you whether or not one string is a substring of another. It is convenient for doing keyword searches in character fields. For example, the following shows all of the people in the mailing list who go by the title of Mr. The UPPER() function is used so that entries such as MR. and mr. are not left out:

```
USE Mailing
LIST FOR "MR." $ UPPER(Name)
```

Also: SUBSTR(), LEFT(), RIGHT(), UPPER(), LOWER(), AT(), .AND., .OR., .NOT., DO WHILE

% Numeric Operator

Syntax: <expN> % <expN>

Action: Evaluates the remainder of the first number divided by the second, or the "modulo."

Return: <expN> representing <expN1> modulo <expN2>.

Detail: The modulus operator is used whenever you need to express some number in terms of another. For example, the following routine converts any length expressed in inches, to yards, feet, and inches:

```
PROCEDURE Convert
PARAMETERS length, yards, feet, inches
* yards is the integer portion when you divide the
* length by 36 because there are 36 inches in each yard.
yards = INT(length / 36)

* length mod 36 equals inches remaining after yards
* are removed
feet = INT((length % 36) / 12)

* length mod 12 equals inches remaining after feet
* are removed
inches = length % 12
RETURN
```

To convert the number 1578 and display the result:

```
STORE 0 TO yards, feet, inches
DO Convert WITH 1578, yards, feet, inches
? yards, "Yards", feet, "Feet", inches, "Inches"
```

Also: INT(), /, ()

& Conversion Symbol

Syntax: &<memory variable>[.<string>]

Action: Substitutes the contents of the memvar for itself and the memvar name.

Detail: Macro substitution is used whenever you want the contents of a character memory variable to appear as a literal value (e.g., a file name, variable name, keyword, etc...) in a command or function. For example:

```
ACCEPT "Enter the file name to use" TO file_name
USE &file_name
```

Use the period to indicate where the memory variable ends if you want to concatenate other characters on the end. For example:

```
fmt_file = "EditRecs"
* In the next command, the first period shows where the
* variable name ends.  The second one is part of the
* file name extension.
SET FORMAT TO &fmt_file..FMT
```

Using macro substitution slows down processing so use it sparingly. For example, USE (file_name) is preferable to USE &file_name.

Also: EXTERNAL

&& **Program Symbol**

Syntax: <command> && <text>

Action: Allows you to make a comment on the same line as a command.

Detail: The following program makes liberal use of the && in-line commenting feature:

```
* Over30.PRG
USE MailList                 && Open database file
SET INDEX TO Last            && Indexed on Last_Name
DO WHILE .NOT. EOF()         && Process entire file
   IF Age > 30               && Display record only if
      ? First_Name, Phone    &&   over 30 years of age.
   ENDIF
   SKIP
ENDDO
CLOSE DATABASES
RETURN
```

Essentially, && is an optional keyword for every command in the language and, as such, it respects the semicolon command line continuation character. Do not use a semicolon as the last character of a comment, or the next command line will be treated as part of the comment.

Because true constant definition, such as C's #define, is unavailable in the current incarnation of Clipper, one alternative is to use memory variables:

```
enter = 13
IF INKEY() = enter
```

However, where memory is limited, the no-cost alternative can be as simple as a single in-line comment:

```
IF INKEY() = 13  && Enter key
```

Also: * (comment), NOTE

' ' **Character Symbol**

Syntax: '<string>'

Action: Delimits character strings.

Detail: Character string delimiters are:

Delimiter	Example
matching double quotes:	`"string"`
matching single quotes:	`'string'`
left and right brackets:	`[string]`

Use the delimiters that do not occur in the string:

```
"string's 'single' quotes and [brackets]"
'string has "double" quotes and [brackets]'
[string's 'single' and "double" quotes]
```

Also: " ", [ ], Expression

( ) **Program Symbol**

Action: Changes the order of expression evaluation.

Detail: The parentheses, (), are used to group operators and operands in an expression so that their natural order of precedence can be changed.

The following examples illustrate:

```
 2 *  4 + 1   ::=   9
 2 * (4 + 1)  ::=  10

 2 + 4  * 1   ::=  10
(2 + 4) * 1   ::=   8
```

Extended Expression

Commands that require a literal parameter normally require the use of a macro if the parameter is contained in a variable:

```
file = "Filename"
USE &file                   && macro expansion

old_area = STR(SELECT())
SELECT 0
.
. <commands>
.
SELECT &old_area            && macro expansion
```

In many such commands, parentheses can be used in place of the macro to make an extended expression:

```
file = "Filename"
USE (file)                  && extended expression

old_area = SELECT()
SELECT 0
.
. <commands>
.
SELECT (old_area)           && extended expression
```

Functions

Functions that return database information do so on the currently selected work area. Parentheses can be used with an alias prefix to test unselected areas:

```
USE Foo
? EOF()            && test selected for end of file
SELECT 0
USE Bar
? Foo->(EOF())     && test unselected for end of file
```

Note that the function must be within parentheses, and may be a UDF.

Also: Precedence, Expression, .NOT., .AND., .OR., <, <=, >, >=, <>, #, !=, = (compare), ==, **, ^, /, %, ->, &

* (comment) — Program Command

Syntax: * [<text>]

Action: Used to comment programs. The text is ignored.

Detail: Everything following the asterisk, or comment, command is ignored. As with other commands, a semicolon at the end of a comment line indicates that the comment is continued on the next line, but the best readability is obtained by beginning each comment line with new asterisk instead of using the semicolon.

The three types of comments are prologue, directory, and explanatory.

Prologue

Prologue comments appear at the beginning of every program. Often called the program header, it contains the program name, author's name, copyright notice, revision and other general program notes.

```
* Program: FOO.PRG
* Author : Tom Rettig
* Notice : Copyright 1988 Tom Rettig Associates
*        : All Rights Reserved
* Revised: 12/13/88, 1/29/89, 3/15/89, 6/1/89
* Notes  : Compile in Clipper, Summer '87
*        : Link with Tom Rettig's Library, version 1.1
*
```

Prologue comments also belong at the beginning of every subroutine. They contain the syntax, action, return value if any, and notes regarding its use.

```
FUNCTION err_msg
* Syntax: err_msg( [<C message1> [, <C message2>]] )
* Action: Displays error message(s) on one or two lines
*         in window.
* Return: <expC> null string.
* Notes : Expects global variable 'msg_window' in which
*            to save and restore message windows.
*         Global vars made PUBLIC in ERRORSYS procedure.
PARAMETERS message1, message2
PRIVATE p_count, box_double
.
. <function code>
.
```

Directory

In longer program files, directory comments are added to the program header to list all the file's subroutines with a brief description of their purpose.

```
* Table of Contents:
*  PROGRAM   main          Application entry and exit
*  PROCEDURE act_first     User action the first time
*  FUNCTION  bar           Paint prompt pads and messages
*  PROCEDURE disp_pbox     Display the prompt box
*  FUNCTION  get_file      User enters filename
*  FUNCTION  get_pword     User enters password
*  PROCEDURE main_menu     Top level application menu
*  FUNCTION  msg           Display message in prompt box
*  PROCEDURE not_imp       Display "not implemented yet"
*  FUNCTION  tone_error    Sound an error tone
*  FUNCTION  v_item        Validate item code
*  FUNCTION  v_recno       Validate record number
```

Explanatory

Explanatory comments are interspersed with the code, and their purpose is to convey an understanding of the program that is not obvious simply by reading the code. High level languages are designed to be readable and self documenting, but the program logic is not always apparent. Explanatory comments should provide additional information instead of just paraphrasing the code. This is a useless comment because anyone who knows the language can see that the code performs the action:

```
* CHR(13) exits the loop.
IF INKEY() = 13
   EXIT
ENDIF
```

The following comment is far more useful because it adds information that is not present in the code.

```
* Enter keypress at main menu selects submenu below.
```

Also: NOTE, &&

* (numeric) — Numeric Operator

Syntax: <expN> * <expN>

Action: Multiplies the first number by the second.

Return: <expN>

Detail: The multiplication operator forms a numeric expression that can be used anywhere in the language where you see <exp>, <expN>, or <N...> in the syntax representation. For example:

```
USE Employee
LIST Rate * Hours     && numeric fields
CLOSE DATABASES
```

or

```
* rebate is a numeric memvar.
? (5995.99 - rebate) * 1.065
```

Also: /, ()

****** **Numeric Operator**

Syntax: <expN> ** <expN>

Action: Raises the first number to the power represented by the second number.

Return: <expN>

Detail: The exponentiation operator forms a numeric expression that can be used anywhere in the language where you see <exp>, <expN>, or <N...> in the syntax representation. For example, in order to compute the variance of a random sample of numbers, you must be able to square each number and their average. The following routine uses the exponentiation operator to do just that:

```
USE Numbers
square_sum = 0
DO WHILE .NOT. EOF()
   square_sum = Number1 ** 2 + square_sum
   SKIP
ENDDO

AVERAGE Number1 TO mean
variance = square_sum / RECCOUNT() - mean ** 2

CLOSE DATABASES
RETURN
```

Note that ** is functionally identical to ^.

Also: EXP(), SQRT(), ^, ()

+ (character) — Character Operator

Syntax: <expC> + <expC>

Action: Concatenates the two specified character strings.

Return: <expC>

Detail: The + operator can be used to add, or concatenate, two character strings together. The result of concatenating two or more character strings is a character expression.

Like the + concatenation operator, the – operator concatenates two strings together to form a new one. The difference between these two operators is that the – moves any trailing blank spaces of the first string to the end of the resulting string. The following example illustrates the difference between the two types of character string concatenation:

```
? "Tom     " - "Rettig"  && Result: "TomRettig     "
? "Tom     " + "Rettig"  && Result: "Tom     Rettig"
```

Also: – (character)

+ (date) — Date Operator

Syntax: <expD> + <expN> | <expN> + <expD>

Action: Adds the specified number of days to the indicated date.

Return: <expD>

Detail: In an expression where a number is added to a date value, the number represents a number of days that is added to the date to come up with a new date. For example, to find out the date 5 days from now, you could use the following expression:

```
DATE() + 5
```

or

```
5 + DATE()
```

Also: DATE(), CTOD()

+ (numeric) — Numeric Operator

Syntax: <expN> + <expN>

Action: Adds the two specified numbers.

Return: <expN>

Detail: The addition operator forms a numeric expression that can be used anywhere in the language where you see <exp>, <expN>, or <N...> in the syntax representation. For example, the following routine uses addition in order to accumulate a counter that controls a DO WHILE loop:

```
i = 0
DO WHILE i < 100   && repeat loop 100 times
   .
   . <commands>
   .
   i = i + 1       && increment counter variable
ENDDO
```

Also: SUM, TOTAL, ()

– (character) — Character Operator

Syntax: <expC> – <expC>

Action: Concatenates the two specified character strings.

Return: <expC>

Detail: The + operator can be used to add, or concatenate, two character strings together. The result of concatenating two or more character strings is a character expression.

Like the + concatenation operator, the – operator concatenates two strings together to form a new one. The difference between these two operators is that the – moves any trailing blank spaces of the first string to the end of the resulting string. The following example illustrates the difference between the two types of character string concatenation:

```
? "Tom      " - "Rettig"  && Result: "TomRettig      "
? "Tom      " + "Rettig"  && Result: "Tom      Rettig"
```

Also: + (character)

– (date) — Date Operator

Syntax: <expD> – <expN>

Action: Subtracts the specified number of day from the indicated date.

Return: <expD>

Detail: In an expression where a number is subtracted from a date value, the number represents a number of days that is subtracted from the date to come up with a new date. For example, to find out what the date was 30 days ago, you could use the following expression:

```
DATE() - 30
```

Although you can subtract a number from a date, you cannot subtract a date from a number because it does not make any sense to do so. Such an attempt results in an error.

Also: DATE(), CTOD(), – (numeric)

– (numeric) Numeric Operator

Syntax: <expN> – <expN> | <expD> – <expD>

Action: Subtracts the second expression value from the first.

Return: <expN>

Detail: The subtraction operator forms a numeric expression that can be used anywhere in the language where you see <exp>, <expN>, or <N...> in the syntax representation. For example, to update each customer's balance by subtracting the payments that have been made:

```
USE Customer
REPLACE ALL Balance WITH Balance - Payment
```

Two dates can be subtracted to form a numeric expression. The interpretation of the result is a number of days. For example:

```
USE Mailing
* Display name and number of days old today.
LIST First_Name, DATE() - Birthday
CLOSE DATABASES
```

Also: DATE(), CTOD(), (), – (date)

-> Database Operator

Syntax: <alias> -> <field name> | (<function name>)

Action: Refers to a field or database function in an unselected work area.

Detail: When working with more than one database file, you can access fields in unselected database files without changing work areas. To do this, you attach a prefix to the field name that consists of the database file alias followed by the alias pointer symbol ->. For example, to list fields from two related files:

```
USE Parts INDEX Part_No
SELECT 2
USE Orders
SET RELATION TO Part_No INTO Parts
LIST Cust_No, Part_No, Quantity, Parts->Descrip,;
     Parts->Price
CLOSE DATABASES
```

You can also edit fields in an unselected work area using commands such as REPLACE, and @...GET...READ. For example, the following routine changes a particular part number in both the Orders and the Parts database files:

```
USE Parts INDEX Part_No
SELECT 2
USE Orders INDEX O_Part
SET RELATION TO Part_No INTO Parts
SEEK "B-254"
IF FOUND()
   REPLACE Parts->Part_No WITH "B-264"
ENDIF
DO WHILE FOUND()
   REPLACE Part_No WITH "B-264"
   SEEK "B-254"
ENDDO
CLOSE DATABASES
```

Note that the alias pointer can also be used with any database function or UDF to cause the function to refer to a database file other than the active file. The function must be contained within parentheses, for example:

```
Parts->(EOF())   && end-of-file for the Parts file
```

Also: SELECT, ALIAS(), SELECT()

.AND. — Logical Operator

Syntax: <L condition> .AND. <L condition>

Action: Performs a logical "and" operation between the two conditions.

Return: <expL> true if both conditions are true, otherwise false.

Detail: As a logical operator, .AND. is used to combine two conditions to form a new one. To combine two conditions with .AND. means that both of them must be true in order for the new condition to be true. The new condition can be used anywhere in the language where <condition>, <expL>, or <exp> is part of the syntax representation. For example:

```
SEEK key_value
DO WHILE Key_Field = key_value .AND. (.NOT. EOF())
   .
   . <commands>
   .
   SKIP
ENDDO
```

Any condition, no matter how simple or complicated, can be combined with another using .AND. to form a new condition. Using any of the three logical operators, you can make more complicated conditions. Logical operations are performed in the following order unless the order is overridden using parentheses:

1. .NOT. or !
2. .AND.
3. .OR.

Also: .OR., .NOT., ! (logical), <, <=, >, >=, = (compare), ==, <>, #, !=, $, ()

.NOT. Logical Operator

Syntax: .NOT. <L condition>

Action: Performs a logical negation of the specified condition.

Return: <expL> false if <condition> is true, otherwise false.

Detail: The following example uses .NOT. to test the EOF() function. EOF() returns a value of false (.F.) except when the end of file is encountered, so that the condition, .NOT. EOF(), is true for each record in the file:

```
DO WHILE .NOT. EOF()
   .
   . <commands>
   .
   SKIP
ENDDO
```

Any condition, no matter how simple or complicated, can be negated using .NOT. to form a new condition. Using any of the three logical operators, you can make more complicated conditions. Logical operations are performed in the following order unless the order is overridden using parentheses:

1. .NOT. or !
2. .AND.
3. .OR.

Also: ! (logical), .AND., .OR., <, <=, >, >=, = (compare), ==, <>, #, !=, $, ()

.OR. Logical Operator

Syntax: <L condition> .OR. <L condition>

Action: Performs a logical or operation between the two conditions.

Return: <expL> true if either condition is true, otherwise false.

Detail: Use .OR. when you are concerned with two conditions but do not care which of them is true. For example, to see the names of all people in your mailing list who live in Pennsylvania or in California:

```
USE Mailing
LIST First_Name, Last_Name ;
     FOR State="PA" .OR. State="CA"
```

The two conditions that you connect with .OR. must be complete, logical expressions. For example, it is not correct to use:

```
IF State = "PA" .OR. "CA"
```

because, by itself, "CA" is a character expression. Thus, you use:

```
IF State = "PA" .OR. State = "CA"
```

Any condition, no matter how simple or complicated, can be combined with another using .OR. to form a new condition. Using any of the three logical operators, you can make more complicated conditions. Logical operations are performed in the following order unless the order is overridden using parentheses:

1. .NOT. or !
2. .AND.
3. .OR.

Also: .AND., .NOT., ! (logical), <, <=, >, >=, = (compare), ==, <>, #, !=, $, ()

/ **Numeric Operator**

Syntax: <expN> / <expN>

Action: Divides the first number by the second. The second number must not be zero.

Return: <expN>

Detail: The division operator forms a numeric expression that can be used anywhere in the language where you see <exp>, <expN>, or <N...> in the syntax representation. The following routine uses division to compute a weighted average:

```
USE Numbers
weighted = 0
DO WHILE .NOT. EOF()
   weighted = (Number1 * Weight) + weighted
   SKIP
ENDDO
weighted = weighted / RECCOUNT()
```

Also: %, ()

; **Program Symbol**

Syntax: <command> [;
<command continued> ...]

Action: Allows you to continue a command on subsequent lines in a program.

Detail: The semicolon can be used in programs, procedure, and format files. Use it to break up long command lines in order to make them more readable. For example:

```
REPLACE First_Name WITH M_First,;
        Last_Name  WITH M_Last, ;
        Address1   WITH M_Addr1,;
        Address2   WITH M_Addr2,;
        City       WITH M_City, ;
        State      WITH M_State,;
        Zip        WITH M_Zip
```

< **Comparison Operator**

Syntax: <expression> < <expression>

Action: Compares expressions to determine if the first is less than the second.

Return: <expL> true if the first expression is less than the second, otherwise false.

Detail: As a comparison operator, less-than forms a logical condition that can be used anywhere in the language where <condition>, <expL>, or <exp> is part of the syntax representation. Character, date, and numeric expressions can be compared to like expressions using the less-than operator. For example:

```
LOCATE FOR Age < 30
DO WHILE FOUND()
   ? First_Name, Phone, Age
   CONTINUE
ENDDO
```

or

```
LIST FOR Due_Date < DATE()
```

or

```
? "string" < "string a long"
```

Also: .AND., .OR., .NOT., ! (logical), <=, >, >=, <>, #, ()

<= **Comparison Operator**

Syntax: <expression> <= <expression>

Action: Compares expressions to determine if one is less than or equal to the other.

Return: <expL> true if the first expression is less than or equal to the second, otherwise false.

Detail: As a comparison operator, less-than or equal forms a logical condition that can be used anywhere in the language where <condition>, <expL>, or <exp> is part of the syntax representation. Character, date, and numeric expressions can be compared to like expressions using the less-than or equal operator. For example:

```
i = 1
DO WHILE i <= 100  && Repeat loop 100 times
   .
   . <commands>
   .
   i = i + 1
ENDDO
```

Also: .AND., .OR., .NOT., ! (logical), <, >, >=, <>, #, ()

<> **Comparison Operator**

Syntax: <expression> <> <expression>

Action: Compares expressions of the same data type for inequality.

Return: <expL> true if the two expressions are not equal, otherwise false.

Detail: As a comparison operator, not equals forms a logical condition that can be used anywhere in the language where <condition>, <expL>, or <exp> is part of the syntax representation. Character, date, and numeric expressions can be compared to like expressions using the not equals operator. For example:

```
USE Mailing
LIST FOR Zip <> "90026"
```

or

```
LIST FOR Age <> 13
```

or

```
COUNT FOR Name <> "John Doe"
```

Also: .AND., .OR., .NOT., ! (logical), <, <=, >, >=, !=, #, ()

= (compare) — Comparison Operator

Syntax: <expression> = <expression>

Action: Compares two expressions of the same data type for equality.

Return: <expL> true if the two expressions are equal, otherwise false.

Detail: As a comparison operator, equals forms a logical condition that can be used anywhere in the language where <condition>, <expL>, or <exp> is part of the syntax representation. For example, the following DO WHILE loop processes all records with a given key value:

```
SEEK key_value
DO WHILE Key_Field = key_value
   .
   . <commands>
   .
   SKIP
ENDDO
```

Character, date, and numeric expressions can be compared to like expressions using the equals operator. For example:

```
LIST FOR Due_Date = DATE()
COUNT FOR Age = 27
AVERAGE Age FOR Last_Name = "Smith"
```

The single equals operator (=) is subject to the setting of SET EXACT, the double equals operator (==) is not.

Also: .AND., .OR., .NOT., ! (logical), <, <=, >, >=, <>, #, ==, SET EXACT, !=, ()

= (store) **Memory Command**

Syntax: <memory variable> | <array element> = <expression>

Action: Assigns the value of the expression to the memvar or element. Creates the memvar if it does not exist.

Detail: The assignment statement, <variable> = <expression>, is equivalent to STORE <expression> TO <variable>. Use the assignment statement when you want to assign a different value to each variable and the STORE command to assign the same value to many variables. For example:

```
STORE SPACE(20) TO m_first, m_last, m_city
m_state = SPACE(2)
m_zip   = SPACE(5)
m_phone = SPACE(13)
* Character variables can be up to 64K long:
m_memo  = Memo_field
```

Since individual array elements are treated just like individual memory variables, the assignment statement can also be used to initialize them. The following example fills an array with values from a database file:

```
DECLARE names[10]
USE Mailing

FOR i = 1 TO 10
   names[i] = First_Name + Last_Name
   SKIP
NEXT
CLOSE DATABASES
```

Note that you cannot have an array definition and a memory variable with the same name. For example:

```
DECLARE names[10]    && defines array names[]
names = "Joe Smith"  && wipes out array names[]
```

As a general rule, you should not use command, function, or keyword names for naming memory variables, fields, and files. With the assignment statement, you cannot use command names as memory variable names without causing an error.

You can initialize a logical variable directly from a logical result of a comparison. For example:

```
exp1 = 45
exp2 = 17

* The long way.
IF exp1 > exp2
   is_bigger = .T.
ELSE
   is_bigger = .F.
ENDIF

* The short way.
is_bigger = exp1 >= exp2
* Adding parentheses make the code more easily readable.
is_bigger = (exp1 >= exp2)
```

Also: STORE, DECLARE, AFILL()

== Comparison Operator

Syntax: <expression> == <expression>

Action: Compares two expressions of the same data type for equality.

Return: <expL> true if the two expressions are exactly equal, otherwise false.

Detail: The double equals operator (==) works differently depending on the data type of the expressions that you are comparing. It compares character strings for an exact match including trailing blank spaces, and ignoring the status of SET EXACT altogether. For example:

```
SET EXACT OFF
? "TEST" == "TEST    "   && .F. - blanks are significant
? "TEST"  = "TEST    "   && .F. - blanks still significant
                         *        when SET EXACT is OFF
```

```
SET EXACT ON
? "TEST" == "TEST   "  && .F. - blanks are significant
? "TEST"  = "TEST   "  && .T. - blanks are ignored
```

Thus, with the == operator, the only way for two character strings to compare favorably is if they are exactly the same.

When comparing two numeric expressions, the == operator compares only the 12 most significant digits of the number instead of the entire number. Using this operator instead of = to compare numbers helps to avoid rounding errors.

With all other data types, the == operator performs the same operation as the = operator.

Also: =, SET EXACT, ()

> **Comparison Operator**

Syntax: <expression> > <expression>

Action: Compares expressions to determine if the first is greater than the second.

Return: <expL> true if the first expression is greater than the second, otherwise false.

As a comparison operator, greater-than forms a logical condition that can be used anywhere in the language where <condition>, <expL>, or <exp> is part of the syntax representation. For example:

```
LIST First_Name, Phone FOR Age > 20
```

Character, date, and numeric expressions can be compared to like expressions using the greater than operator. For example:

```
LOCATE FOR Zip > "90026"
SUM Amount FOR Due_Date > DATE()
```

Also: .AND., .OR., .NOT., <, <=, >=, <>, #, ()

>= **Comparison Operator**

Syntax: <expression> >= <expression>

Action: Compares expressions to see if one is greater than or equal to the other.

Return: <expL> true if the first expression is greater than or equal to the second, otherwise false.

Detail: As a comparison operator, greater-than or equal forms a logical condition that can be used anywhere in the language where <condition>, <expL>, or <exp> is part of the syntax representation. Character, date, and numeric expressions can be compared to like expressions using the greater-than or equal to operator. For example:

```
SEEK 21
DO WHILE Age >= 21
   ? First_Name, Phone, Age
   SKIP
ENDDO
```

Also: .AND., .OR., .NOT., <, <=, >, <>, #, ()

[ ] **Character Symbol**

Syntax: [<string>]

Action: Delimits character strings.

Detail: Character string delimiters are:

Delimiter	Example
matching double quotes:	`"string"`
matching single quotes:	`'string'`
left and right brackets:	`[string]`

Use the delimiters that do not occur in the string:

```
"string's 'single' quotes and [brackets]"
'string has "double" quotes and [brackets]'
[string's 'single' and "double" quotes]
```

Note that square brackets also are used to denote array elements and are used in syntax representations to denote optional parameters.

Also: " ", ' ', Expression

---

^ Numeric Operator

Syntax: <expN> ^ <expN>

Action: Raises the first number to the power represented by the second number.

Return: <expN>

Detail: The exponentiation operator forms a numeric expression that can be used anywhere in the language where you see <exp>, <expN>, or <N...> in the syntax representation. For example, in order to compute the variance of a random sample of numbers, you must be able to square each number and their average. The following routine uses the exponentiation operator to do just that:

```
USE Numbers
square_sum = 0
DO WHILE .NOT. EOF()
   square_sum = Number1 ^ 2 + square_sum
   SKIP
ENDDO

AVERAGE Number1 TO mean
variance = square_sum / RECCOUNT() - mean ^ 2

CLOSE DATABASES
RETURN
```

Note that ^ is functionally identical to **.

Also: EXP(), SQRT(), **, ()

? **Output Command**

Syntax: ? [<expression list>]

Action: Evaluates an expression list, and displays the results on the next line.

Detail: The following example shows how the ? command evaluates different types of expressions:

```
m_first = "Alan"
m_age   = 24
USE MailList
? First_Name = m_first
? First_Name, Age
? First_Name, Age, m_first, m_age
? "Two names:  ", TRIM(First_Name) + " " +;
                  Last_Name, m_first
CLOSE DATABASES
```

Note that the ? command evaluates and displays Memo fields as well as other expressions.

The ? command always outputs a carriage-return/line-feed pair before it outputs the expression. With no parameters, ? displays a blank line.

Also: ??, SET PRINTER, @...SAY

?? **Output Command**

Syntax: ?? [<expression list>]

Action: Evaluates an expression list, and displays the results on the current line.

Detail: For the people who live in California, the following example prints the First_Name and Phone on the same line. For the others, it prints the message “Out of state” beside the First_Name:

```
USE MailList
SET PRINTER ON
DO WHILE .NOT. EOF()
   ? TRIM(First_Name)
   ?? IIF(State = "CA", " " + Phone, " Out of state")
   SKIP
ENDDO
SET PRINTER OFF
CLOSE DATABASES
```

The ?? command does not output a carriage-return/line-feed pair when it outputs the expression. Thus, ?? is often used with CHR() to send control characters to the printer so that the paper does not advance a line unnecessarily.

Also: ?, SET PRINTER, @...SAY, CHR()

@...BOX — Output Command

Syntax: @ <N top row>, <N left col>, <N bottom row>, <N right col>
BOX <C border definition>

Action: Draws a box using the specified screen coordinates and border.

Detail: The @...BOX command is designed for drawing boxes on the screen. It is a more powerful version of the @...TO command, and like @...TO, it ignores the status of SET DEVICE (i.e., the boxes cannot be printed).

The coordinates represent the upper-left and lower-right corners of the box.

The border definition can be up to nine characters in length. Starting with the upper-left corner and moving clockwise, the characters in the border definition string are used to draw the box. If included, the ninth character is used to fill the box. If any of the first eight characters are omitted, the one before it in the border definition string is used in its place. For example:

```
@ 10, 0, 15, 79 BOX "*"  && draws a box with * as border
```

The following example draws a shaded box with a double line on the top and bottom and a single line on the sides:

```
@ 10,0, 15,79 BOX CHR(213)+CHR(205)+CHR(184)+CHR(179)+;
                  CHR(190)+CHR(205)+CHR(212)+CHR(179)+;
                  CHR(178)
```

Also: @...TO, @...CLEAR, CHR(), SCROLL()

@...CLEAR — Output Command

Syntax: @ <N top row>, <N left col> CLEAR
[TO <N bottom row>, <N right col>]

Action: Erases a designated rectangular portion of the screen.

Detail: @...CLEAR is often used in conjunction with @...TO to erase the interior portion of a box. For example:

```
@ 5,10 TO 12,30 DOUBLE  && draw box border
.
. <commands to fill in the box>
.
@ 6,11 CLEAR TO 11,29   && erase interior, not border
```

If the TO coordinates are omitted, the extreme lower, right corner (e.g., 24, 79 on a 25 x 80 screen) of the screen is assumed.

Also: @...BOX, @...TO, CLEAR, SCROLL()

@...GET — Input Command

Syntax: @ <N row>, <N column> GET <variable>
[PICTURE <C template>]
[RANGE <N | D minimum>, <N | D maximum>]
[VALID <L condition>]

Action: Used with READ to edit a field or memvar at a specific screen location.

Detail: The following example displays several fields from a mailing list file on the screen for editing. Examples of PICTURE are illustrated:

```
USE MailList
@ 3, 5 GET First_Name
@ 4, 5 GET Last_Name
* State uses the PICTURE function ! that must be
* preceded by the @ character.  This forces uppercase.
@ 5, 5 GET State PICTURE "@!"
* Zip uses PICTURE to insure only numbers are entered.
@ 6, 5 GET Zip PICTURE "99999"
READ  && allow editing of GET fields
CLOSE DATABASES
```

Note that if more than one is used, the PICTURE, RANGE, and VALID clauses must come in that order in the @...GET command syntax. See PICTURE, RANGE, and VALID for more information and examples.

Also: @...SAY...GET, @...SAY, READ, ACCEPT, INPUT, WAIT, SET FORMAT TO, PICTURE, RANGE, VALID

@...PROMPT — Menu Command

Syntax: @ <N row>, <N column> PROMPT <C prompt>
[MESSAGE <C message>]

Action: Displays a menu prompt at the specified screen location.

Detail: The following example illustrates the use of @...PROMPT and MENU TO in constructing and activating a lightbar menu:

```
* Menu messages are displayed on line 2.
SET MESSAGE TO 2  && turn on messages

* Allow left/right arrow keys to wrap around.
SET WRAP ON
```

```
DO WHILE .T.   && infinite loop for menu display
   CLEAR
   @ box_home, 0, 3, 79 BOX box_double
   @ 1, 5 PROMPT "Customer" MESSAGE;
          "Add/search/edit customers and transactions."
   @ 1,17 PROMPT "Invoice"  MESSAGE;
          "Print invoices from customer transactions."
   @ 1,28 PROMPT "Label"    MESSAGE;
          "Print labels from customers or transactions."
   @ 1,37 PROMPT "Report"   MESSAGE;
          "Print reports."
   @ 1,47 PROMPT "Shipping" MESSAGE;
          "Browse ship-to names and companies."
   @ 1,59 PROMPT "Maintain" MESSAGE;
          "File and system maintenance utilities."
   @ 1,71 PROMPT "Quit"     MESSAGE;
          "Quit to the operating system."

   MENU TO action

   DO CASE   && make decision based on option selected
      CASE action == 1
         DO Customer
      CASE action == 2
         DO Report WITH "INVOICES"
      CASE action == 3
         DO Report WITH "LABELS"
      CASE action == 4
         DO Report
      CASE action == 5
         DO Shipping
      CASE action == 6
         DO Maintain
      CASE action == 7
         SET MESSAGE TO   && turn off messages
         SET WRAP OFF     && turn off menu wrap
         RETURN
   ENDCASE
ENDDO
```

Also: MENU TO, SET MESSAGE TO, SET WRAP

@...SAY **Output Command**

Syntax: @ <N row>, <N column> [SAY <expression>
[PICTURE <C template>]]

Action: Displays an expression at a particular screen location.

Detail: The following example displays information from the mailing list file on the screen with each field preceded by a label:

```
USE MailList
CLEAR
@ 3, 5 SAY "Name:     " + TRIM(First_Name) + " " +;
                          Last_Name
@ 4, 5 SAY "Address: " + Address1
@ 5, 5 SAY "          " + Address2
@ 6, 5 SAY "          " + TRIM(City) + ", " + State +;
                                      "  " + Zip
CLOSE DATABASES
```

The result of @...SAY commands are printed if SET DEVICE TO PRINTER is in effect when they are issued. You can send to a text file instead by using SET PRINTER TO <file>.

Also: ?, ??, SET DEVICE TO, SET FORMAT TO, PICTURE

@...SAY...GET **Input Command**

Syntax: @ <N row>, <N column> SAY <@...SAY options>
GET <@...GET options>

Action: Combines @...SAY and @...GET to display a label beside the field or memvar.

Detail: This form of the @ command is more common than using @... SAY and @... GET as separate commands. It allows you to combine a prompt and an edit field using a single command. For example:

```
@  5, 4 SAY "First Name     " GET First_Name
@  6, 4 SAY "Street Address" GET Address1
@  7, 4 SAY "Apartment #    " GET Address2
@  8, 4 SAY "City           " GET City
@  9, 4 SAY "State          " GET State
@ 10, 4 SAY "Zip Code       " GET Zip
READ
```

The GET field edit area is automatically placed one space to the right of the SAY prompt. Both the SAY and GET portions of the command can have any clause that is allowed in individual @... SAY and @... GET commands. For example:

```
@ 7, 15 SAY First_Name PICTURE "!AAAAAAAAAAA";
        GET Age PICTURE "999" RANGE 0, 150
READ
```

Also: @... SAY, @... GET, READ, PICTURE, RANGE, VALID

@... TO — Output Command

Syntax: @ <N top row>, <N left col> TO <N bottom row>, <N right col> [DOUBLE]

Action: Draws a box with the specified upper left and lower right screen positions.

Detail: @... TO is used to draw a single or double bordered box on the screen. For example:

```
@ 5, 10 TO 12, 30 DOUBLE  && draw double bordered box
@ 6, 12 TO 11, 28  && draw a single bordered box inside
```

Boxes can be used in conjunction with @... SAY to bring attention to instructional messages on the screen. For example, to place a message inside the boxes drawn above:

```
@ 7, 14 SAY "Press PgDn to"
@ 8, 14 SAY "edit the next"
@ 9, 14 SAY "record."
```

Unlike the @... SAY command, the output of @... TO cannot be sent to the printer.

Also: @... BOX, @... CLEAR

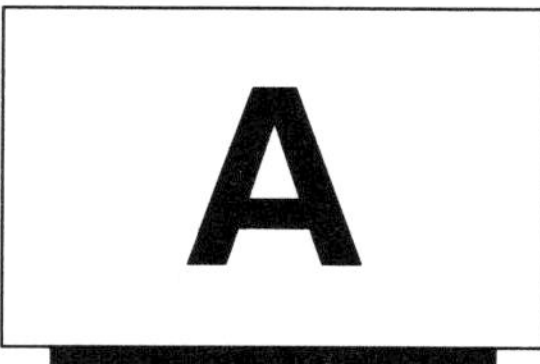

ABS() **Numeric Function**

Syntax: ABS(<expN>)

Action: Evaluates the absolute value of the specified number.

Return: <expN> representing the absolute value as a positive number.

Detail: Suppose that a particular field value should always contain a negative value, but you are not sure whether all of the fields were entered correctly. You could use:

```
LIST -ABS(<field>)
```

to show the correct values, or:

```
REPLACE ALL <field> WITH -ABS(<field>)
```

to update all values so that they are correct.

Note that data like this should be checked during entry to prevent incorrect data from going into the file.

ACCEPT — Input Command

Syntax: ACCEPT [<C prompt>] TO <memory variable>

Action: Waits for keyboard input and saves it in a character memvar that it creates.

Detail: To prompt the user for a name and repeat the name to the user:

```
ACCEPT "Enter your first name" TO m_first
?
?
? "Hello " + m_first
```

If Enter is pressed without typing any other characters in response to the ACCEPT command, the TO memory variable will have a null value.

```
IF "" < m_first
   RETURN
ENDIF
```

Also: INPUT, WAIT

ACHOICE() — Menu Function

Syntax: ACHOICE(<N top row>, <N left col>,
<N bottom row>, <N right col>,
<array of choices>
[, <array of available choices> [, <C UDF name>
[, <N first choice> [, <N window row>]]]])

Action: Defines and activates a menu using an array of choices.

Return: <expN> representing which menu choice was selected.

Detail: ACHOICE() defines and activates a menu using an array of choices that you DECLARE. The following example illustrates the function in its simplest form:

```
DECLARE choice[4]
choice[1] = "Exit"
choice[2] = "Add Records"
choice[3] = "Edit Records"
choice[4] = "Reports"
DO WHILE .T.
   CLEAR
   userchoice = ACHOICE(8, 10, 12, 25, choice)
   DO CASE
      CASE userchoice = 1 .OR. userchoice = 0
         QUIT
      CASE userchoice = 2
         DO Add_Recs
      CASE userchoice = 3
         DO EditRecs
      CASE userchoice = 4
         DO Reports
   ENDCASE
ENDDO
```

The second array in the function syntax is an array of logical values that you can use to make certain menu choices unavailable to the user. Borrowing from the above example, the next example arbitrarily makes the "Edit Records" option unavailable. To make the menu visually appealing, a SET COLOR TO command is added to brighten the available menu options and dim the others:

```
SET COLOR TO W+/N, , , , W/N
DECLARE choice[4], avail[4]
choice[1] = "Exit"
choice[2] = "Add Records"
choice[3] = "Edit Records"
choice[4] = "Reports"

STORE .T. TO avail[1], avail[2], avail[4]
avail[3] = .F.
```

```
DO WHILE .T.
   CLEAR
   userchoice = ACHOICE(8, 10, 12, 25, choice, avail)
   DO CASE
      CASE userchoice = 1 .OR. userchoice = 0
         QUIT
      CASE userchoice = 2
         DO Add_Recs
      CASE userchoice = 3
         DO EditRecs
      CASE userchoice = 4
         DO Reports
   ENDCASE
ENDDO
```

The user-defined function name in the ACHOICE() syntax is a UDF, called a "user function," that tells how to process keystrokes for the menu. This option is useful if you do not agree with the automatic processing of keys by ACHOICE(). When the UDF is called, ACHOICE() passes three numeric parameters to it. In order, these are ACHOICE() mode, current choice number, and current row number relative to the menu window. The possible modes are:

Mode	**Meaning**
0	Idle
1	Past first menu choice
2	Past last menu choice
3	Keystroke exception
4	No item selectable

To capture these parameters in the user function, use a PARAMETERS command with three parameters. To determine the keypress that triggered the user function, use LASTKEY().

Note that if you use a user function, it is specified as a character expression without the parentheses. For example, if the function is called Keys(), use "Keys" as the ACHOICE() parameter. The user function should return one of the following numeric values to tell what to take in the menu:

Return Value	Meaning
0	Cancel menu selection
1	Make menu selection
2	Continue selection process with current selection
3	Go to the next menu choice with a first character that matches the last key pressed

The next parameter, following the user function name, is used if you want the menu selection to begin with a choice other than the first one, the default.

The final parameter specifies where you want the current menu selection to appear in the menu relative to the top of the ACHOICE() window. This parameter is useful if you have a scrolling menu (i.e., more choices than will fit in the menu). You could highlight option 2 and put that option at the top of the menu with:

```
ACHOICE(8, 10, 11, 25, choice, .T., .F., 3, 0)
```

Any optional parameter can be omitted using a logical value in its place. For example, to make the initial menu choice the third array element without specifying a UDF or the available choices array, you could use:

```
ACHOICE(8, 10, 12, 25, choice, .T., .F., 3)
```

Also: DECLARE, SET COLOR TO, @...PROMPT, MENU TO, SET MESSAGE, FUNCTION, LASTKEY(), PARAMETERS, AFIELDS()

ACOPY() — Array Function

Syntax: ACOPY(<source array>, <target array>
[, <N source start> [, <N elements> [, <N target start>]]])

Action: Copies the contents of one array to another.

Return: Nothing.

Detail: The following example illustrates how to copy the contents of one array to another:

```
DECLARE names[12], friends[25]

* Copy the entire array.
ACOPY(names, friends)

* Copy only 5 elements beginning with the 3rd.
ACOPY(names, friends, 3, 5)

* Copy all elements from names so that elements 14 - 25
* are filled in the target array.
ACOPY(names, friends, 1, 12, 14)
```

ACOPY() compensates for any size difference between the two arrays without causing any errors.

Also: DECLARE

ADEL() — Array Function

Syntax: ADEL(<array>, <N position>)

Action: Deletes the indicated array element.

Return: Nothing.

Detail: When an array element is deleted, elements in the positions following that element are each moved up one element, leaving the last element undefined. The following example illustrates:

```
USE Mailing
DECLARE names[10]
FOR i = 1 TO 10
   names[i] = Last_Name
   SKIP
NEXT
CLEAR
```

```
FOR i = 1 TO 10
   @ i, 0 SAY STR(i) + ": " + names[i]
NEXT
choice = 0
@ 23, 5 SAY "Enter a number to delete or zero for none";
        GET choice RANGE 1, 10
READ

* Delete user's choice.
ADEL(names, choice)

* Display new array elements.
CLEAR
FOR i = 1 TO 9  && Element 10 is undefined
   @ i, 0 SAY STR(i) + ": " + names[i]
NEXT
```

Also: AINS(), DECLARE

ADIR() Array Function

Syntax: ADIR(<skeleton>, [<filename array> [, <size array>
[, <date array> [, <time array>
[, <attribute array>]]]]])

Action: Stores the file attributes of files matching the skeleton in arrays.

Return: <expN> representing the number of files that match the skeleton.

Detail: The following example uses ADIR() to fill an array with database file names, sorts the array, and displays them on the screen:

```
num_files = ADIR("*.DBF")
DECLARE dbf[num_files]
ADIR("*.DBF", dbf)
ASORT(dbf)
CLEAR
@ 0, 8 TO 10, 23 DOUBLE
```

```
@ 12, 5 SAY "Press Esc for more files"
FOR i = 1 TO num_files
   @ ((i-1)%9)+1, 10 SAY SPACE(12-LEN(dbf[i])) + dbf[i]
   * When the box is filled with file names,
   * wait for user to press Esc.
   DO WHILE ((i-1) % 9) + 1 = 9 .AND. INKEY() != 27
      * This loop just waits for user to press Esc.
   ENDDO
NEXT
```

In the next example, ADIR() is used twice. The first time, it counts the database files in order to DECLARE an array of the correct size. The second time, it stores only the file names in the array. If you want, you can also save the other directory attributes in different arrays. The following examples saves them all and lists them:

```
CLEAR
num_files = ADIR("*.DBF")
DECLARE dbf[num_files], size[num_files],;
        date[num_files], time[num_files],;
        attribute[num_files]
ADIR("*.DBF", dbf, size, date, time, attribute)
FOR i = 1 TO num_files
   ? SPACE(12 - LEN(dbf[i])) + dbf[i], size[i],;
     date[i], time[i], attribute[i]
NEXT
```

The file name, time, and attribute arrays contain character data types. The date array contains date values, and the file size array contains numeric values. The file attributes are listed below:

Attribute	Meaning
R	Read Only
H	Hidden
S	System
D	Directory
A	Archive

Also: DECLARE, DIR, AFILL(), AFIELDS()

AFIELDS() Array Function

Syntax: AFIELDS([<fieldname array> [, <type array>
[, <length array> [, <decimals array>]]]])

Action: Fills one or more arrays with the field attributes of the active file.

Return: <expN> representing the number of fields processed.

Detail: The following example uses AFIELDS() to present the fields in the Mailing list as a menu. The user can select the fields to display from the menu:

```
USE Mailing
num_fields = FCOUNT()
* choices[] and i are used by the UDF for ACHOICE().
DECLARE fields[num_fields], choices[num_fields]
i = 0
* Fill the fields[] array with Mailing list field names.
AFIELDS(fields)
SET COLOR TO W+/N,,,,W/N
CLEAR
@ 24, 0 SAY "Press Enter to select fields, Esc to list."
userchoice = ACHOICE(1,10,23,35, fields, .T., "Save_It")
* Display fields that user selected.
CLEAR
DO WHILE .NOT. EOF()
   FOR x = 1 TO i
       temp = choices[x]
       ?? &temp
   NEXT
   ?
   SKIP
ENDDO
RETURN
```

```
FUNCTION Save_It
PARAMETERS mode, element, row_num
key = LASTKEY()
DO CASE
   * If Enter pressed, field name is marked and saved.
   CASE key = 13
      i = i + 1
      choices[i] = fields[element]
      @ row_num + 1, 9 SAY CHR(175)
      RETURN 2
   CASE key = 27
      RETURN 0
   OTHERWISE
      RETURN 2
ENDCASE
```

In this example, only a single array was used with AFIELDS() to capture the field names. The next example utilizes all of the function parameters to capture all field attributes and list them. The field name and type arrays hold character data, and the length and decimals arrays hold numeric values:

```
USE Mailing
num_fields = FCOUNT()
DECLARE fields[num_fields], fld_type[num_fields],;
        fld_len[num_fields], fld_dec[num_fields]
* Fill the arrays with Mailing list field attributes.
AFIELDS(fields, fld_type, fld_len, fld_dec)
CLEAR
? "Mailing Database File Structure"
?
? "Field Name Type  Length   Decimals"
FOR i = 1 TO num_fields
    ? fields[i] + SPACE(10 - LEN(fields[i])),;
      fld_type[i], fld_len[i], fld_dec[i]
NEXT
RETURN
```

Also: DECLARE, USE, FCOUNT(), ADIR(), AFILL(), ACHOICE()

AFILL() Array Function

Syntax: AFILL(<array>, <fill expression> [, <N start> [, <N elements>]])

Action: Fills an array with a specified value.

Return: Nothing.

Detail: The following example illustrates how to initialize all the elements in an array to the same value:

```
DECLARE numbers[30]
* Fill entire array with zeros.
AFILL(numbers, 0)
* Change last 5 elements to a logical .T.
AFILL(numbers, .T., 26, 5)
```

Also: DECLARE, AFIELDS(), ADIR(), STORE

AINS() Array Function

Syntax: AINS(<array>, <N position>)

Action: Inserts a single element into an array.

Return: Nothing.

Detail: When an array element is inserted, elements in the positions following that element are each moved down one element, losing the last element. The following example illustrates:

```
USE Mailing
DECLARE names[10]
FOR i = 1 TO 10
   names[i] = Last_Name
   SKIP
NEXT
CLEAR
```

```
FOR i = 1 TO 10
   @ i, 0 SAY STR(i) + ": " + names[i]
NEXT
new_name = SPACE(15)
choice = 1
@ 22, 5 SAY "Enter number to delete" GET choice;
                                     RANGE 1,10
@ 23, 5 SAY "Enter a new name      " GET new_name
READ

* Delete and insert user's choice.
ADEL(names, choice)
AINS(names, choice)

* Display new array elements.
CLEAR
FOR i = 1 TO 10
   @ i, 0 SAY STR(i) + ": " + names[i]
NEXT
```

Also: ADEL(), DECLARE

ALIAS() Database Function

Syntax: ALIAS([<N work area>])

Action: Evaluates the alias name of the database file in the specified work area.

Return: <expC> alias name in uppercase letters.

Detail: The following example illustrates the ALIAS() function:

```
USE Orders
SELECT 2
USE Customer ALIAS CustFile
? ALIAS()      && returns "CUSTFILE"
? ALIAS(1)     && returns "ORDERS"
? ALIAS(3)     && returns "" null string
```

If there is no open database file in the specified work area, ALIAS() returns a null string.

Also: FILE(), SELECT(), SELECT

ALLTRIM() — Character Function

Syntax: ALLTRIM(<expC>)

Action: Trims all leading and trailing blanks from the character string.

Return: <expC> a character string with no leading or trailing blanks.

Detail: The following example uses the ALLTRIM() function to make sure there are no leading and trailing blank spaces in the first and last name fields:

```
USE Mailing
? ALLTRIM(First_Name), ALLTRIM(Last_Name)
CLOSE DATABASES
```

Note that ALLTRIM() is equivalent to the composite function LTRIM(RTRIM()).

Also: TRIM(), LTRIM(), RTRIM()

ALTD() — Debug Function

Syntax: ALTD([<expN>])

Action: Invokes the debugger and controls the use of Alt-D for that purpose.

Return: Nothing.

Detail: Normally, the debugger is not available while a program is running. To be able to invoke the debugger at any time during your application by pressing Alt-D, you need to use the ALTD() function at the beginning of the main program. The possible function parameters are listed below:

Parameter	Meaning
None	Invokes debugger, enables Alt-D
0	Disables Alt-D
1	Invokes debugger, enables Alt-D
2	Invokes debugger at View Privates screen, and enables Alt-D

Note that specifying no parameter is equivalent to specifying a parameter of 1. Debug.OBJ must be linked to use the debugger.

Also: SETCANCEL()

APPEND BLANK — Database Command

Syntax: APPEND BLANK

Action: Adds a blank record to the database file.

Detail: The following routine uses APPEND BLANK with REPLACE to enter information into a database file. This allows you to check the data for accuracy before it goes into the file:

```
USE Mailing
* Mem_Vars.FMT has @...GET commands to edit
* the memvars below.
SET FORMAT TO Mem_Vars.FMT
* Initialize memvars that correspond in type and size
* to the fields in the database file.
DO WHILE .T.
   STORE SPACE(20) TO m_first, m_last, m_city
   m_state = SPACE(2)
   m_zip   = SPACE(5)
   READ       && Activate format file
   DO Verify  && check memvars for accuracy
```

```
      IF okay    && Verify.PRG sets okay to .T. or .F.
         APPEND BLANK
         REPLACE First_Name WITH m_first,;
                 Last_Name  WITH m_last,;
                 City       WITH m_city,;
                 State      WITH m_state,;
                 Zip        WITH m_zip
      ENDIF
   ENDDO
   CLOSE DATABASES
```

Also: REPLACE, @...GET, SET FORMAT TO

APPEND FROM — Database Command

Syntax: APPEND FROM <dbf filename> | (<C dbf filename>)
[FIELDS <field list>] [<scope>]

Action: Adds records from another database file to the end of the active one.

Detail: When records are added to the active file from another database file, only those fields that have the same name in both files are included. If a scope is used, it applies to the FROM file and can involve field names that do not occur in the active file. The following example splits your mailing list into two files — one for those people who live in California and the other for everyone else:

```
USE Mailing
COPY STRUCTURE TO Mail_CA  && California mailing list
COPY STRUCTURE TO Mail_OS  && Out-of-State mailing list
USE Mail_CA
APPEND FROM Mailing FOR UPPER(State) = "CA"
USE Mail_OS
APPEND FROM Mailing FOR UPPER(State) # "CA"
CLOSE DATABASES
```

If you prefer, the database file name can be a character expression. To accomplish this, enclose the expression in parentheses. For example:

```
filename = "Mail_OS"
APPEND FROM (filename) FOR UPPER(State) # "CA"
```

Also: COPY TO

APPEND FROM (text) Database Command

Syntax: APPEND FROM <txt filename> | (<C txt filename>)
[FIELDS <field list>] [<scope>]
SDF | DELIMITED [WITH BLANK | <delimiter> |
(<C delimiter>)]

Action: Adds records from a non-database file to the active database file.

Detail: When records are added to the active file from a foreign file format, the fields are added positionally to the active file. The scope applies to the FROM file, but must involve a field name that occurs in the active file. For example, suppose that you add new employees from a standard ASCII text file according to a code that is in the first position. Assuming that this first position is the first character in the Emp_Code field:

```
USE Employee
APPEND FROM Master FOR ISALPHA(Emp_Code) SDF
```

To express the file name as a character expression rather than a literal value, simply enclose the expression in parentheses. For example:

```
USE Employee
txt_file = "Master"
APPEND FROM (txt_file) FOR ISALPHA(Emp_Code) SDF
```

SDF or "System Data Format" is a standard ASCII text (.TXT) file with fixed length fields and records, no field delimiters or separators, and records are separated by a carriage-return/line-feed pair.

DELIMITED [WITH BLANK | <delimiter> | (<C delimiter>)] is a standard ASCII text (.TXT) file with fields separated by commas and character fields enclosed in delimiters. The delimiter can be expressed either as a literal value or as a character expression. If a character expression is used, it must be enclosed in parentheses. DELIMITED WITH BLANK is a special format where each field is separated from the next by a blank space and no other field delimiters are used. In either case, the records are separated by a carriage-return/line-feed pair.

ASC() — Conversion Function

Syntax: ASC(<expC>)

Action: Evaluates the ASCII value of the first character in the specified string.

Return: <expN> representing the ASCII decimal number of the character.

Detail: You can use ASC() in conjunction with INKEY() to determine when a particular key has been pressed. The relationship between these two functions is that INKEY() returns the ASCII numeric equivalent of a key that is pressed and ASC() returns the ASCII numeric equivalent of the letter you specify as the function parameter. Usually, it is more convenient to use ASC() with a letter instead of looking up the ASCII code for that letter. The following routine displays a clock on the screen until you press the S key:

```
@ 24, 0 SAY "Type S to stop the clock display."
DO WHILE .T.
   @ 0, 72 SAY TIME()
   * Could have used the numbers 83 and 115, but the
   * code is more readable with ASC("S") and ASC("s")
   keypress = INKEY()
   IF keypress = ASC("S") .OR. keypress = ASC("s")
      EXIT
   ENDIF
ENDDO
CLEAR
```

ASC() and CHR() are inverse functions.

Also: CHR(), INKEY()

ASCAN() Array Function

Syntax: ASCAN(<array>, <C scan expression> [, <N start> [, <N elements>]])

Action: Scans the named array for an element that matches the scan expression.

Return: <expN> number of the matching array element, or zero if there is none.

Detail: ASCAN()'s search is subject to the setting of SET EXACT.

The following example uses ASCAN() to search an array for a value that is input by the user:

```
USE Mailing
DECLARE names[10]
FOR i = 1 TO 10
   names[i] = Last_Name
   @ i, 0 SAY names[i]
   SKIP
NEXT
STORE SPACE(15) TO old_name, new_name
@ 22, 5 SAY "Enter name to replace" GET old_name
@ 23, 5 SAY "Enter a new name     " GET new_name
READ

* Find the old name and insert the new one.
position = ASCAN(names, old_name)
IF position > 0
   ADEL(names, position)
   AINS(names, position)
   names[position] = new_name
ENDIF
```

In this example, ASCAN() was used to scan the entire array. Using the optional parameters, you can limit the array elements that the function scans. For example, to check only the first five elements, you could use:

```
ASCAN(names, old_name, 1, 5)
```

Also: SET EXACT

ASCII Codes

TRHELP Info

Detail: These are the 128 lower or "standard" ASCII codes, of which the first 32 are printer and communication controls shown with IBM characters.

Dec	Hex	Char	Code	Name	Dec	Hex	Char	Dec	Hex	Char	Dec	Hex	Char
0	00		^@	NUL	32	20		64	40	@	96	60	`
1	01	☺	^A	SOH	33	21	!	65	41	A	97	61	a
2	02	☻	^B	STX	34	22	”	66	42	B	98	62	b
3	03	♥	^C	ETX	35	23	#	67	43	C	99	63	c
4	04	♦	^D	EOT	36	24	$	68	44	D	100	64	d
5	05	♣	^E	ENQ	37	25	%	69	45	E	101	65	e
6	06	♠	^F	ACK	38	26	&	70	46	F	102	66	f
7	07	•	^G	BEL	39	27	’	71	47	G	103	67	g
8	08	◘	^H	BS	40	28	(	72	48	H	104	68	h
9	09	○	^I	HT	41	29	)	73	49	I	105	69	i
10	0A	◙	^J	LF	42	2A	*	74	4A	J	106	6A	j
11	0B	♂	^K	VT	43	2B	+	75	4B	K	107	6B	k
12	0C	♀	^L	FF	44	2C	,	76	4C	L	108	6C	l
13	0D	♪	^M	CR	45	2D	–	77	4D	M	109	6D	m
14	0E	♫	^N	SO	46	2E	.	78	4E	N	110	6E	n
15	0F	☼	^O	SI	47	2F	/	79	4F	O	111	6F	o
16	10	►	^P	DLE	48	30	0	80	50	P	112	70	p
17	11	◄	^Q	DC1	49	31	1	81	51	Q	113	71	q
18	12	↕	^R	DC2	50	32	2	82	52	R	114	72	r
19	13	!!	^S	DC3	51	33	3	83	53	S	115	73	s
20	14	¶	^T	DC4	52	34	4	84	54	T	116	74	t
21	15	§	^U	NAK	53	35	5	85	55	U	117	75	u
22	16	▬	^V	SYN	54	36	6	86	56	V	118	76	v
23	17	↨	^W	ETB	55	37	7	87	57	W	119	77	w
24	18	↑	^X	CAN	56	38	8	88	58	X	120	78	x
25	19	↓	^Y	EM	57	39	9	89	59	Y	121	79	y
26	1A	→	^Z	SUB	58	3A	:	90	5A	Z	122	7A	z
27	1B	←	^[	ESC	59	3B	;	91	5B	[	123	7B	{
28	1C	∟	^\	FS	60	3C	<	92	5C	\	124	7C	|
29	1D	↔	^]	GS	61	3D	=	93	5D	]	125	7D	}
30	1E	▲	^^	RS	62	3E	>	94	5E	^	126	7E	~
31	1F	▼	^_	US	63	3F	?	95	5F	_	127	7F	⌂

These are IBM's 128 higher or "extended" ASCII codes. The characters represent math, language, box, arrow, and block symbols.

Dec	Hex	Char	Dec	Hex	Char	Dec	Hex	Char	Dec	Hex	Char
128	80	Ç	160	A0	á	192	C0	└	224	E0	α
129	81	ü	161	A1	í	193	C1	┴	225	E1	β
130	82	é	162	A2	ó	194	C2	┬	226	E2	Γ
131	83	â	163	A3	ú	195	C3	├	227	E3	π
132	84	ä	164	A4	ñ	196	C4	─	228	E4	Σ
133	85	à	165	A5	Ñ	197	C5	┼	229	E5	σ
134	86	å	166	A6	ª	198	C6	╞	230	E6	μ
135	87	ç	167	A7	º	199	C7	╟	231	E7	γ
136	88	ê	168	A8	¿	200	C8	╚	232	E8	Φ
137	89	ë	169	A9	⌐	201	C9	╔	233	E9	θ
138	8A	è	170	AA	¬	202	CA	╩	234	EA	Ω
139	8B	ï	171	AB	½	203	CB	╦	235	EB	δ
140	8C	î	172	AC	¼	204	CC	╠	236	EC	∞
141	8D	ì	173	AD	¡	205	CD	═	237	ED	ϕ
142	8E	Ä	174	AE	$\ll$	206	CE	╬	238	EE	$\in$
143	8F	Å	175	AF	$\gg$	207	CF	╧	239	EF	$\cap$
144	90	É	176	B0	░	208	D0	╨	240	F0	$\equiv$
145	91	æ	177	B1	▒	209	D1	╤	241	F1	$\pm$
146	92	Æ	178	B2	▓	210	D2	╥	242	F2	$\geq$
147	93	ô	179	B3	│	211	D3	╙	243	F3	$\leq$
148	94	ö	180	B4	┤	212	D4	╘	244	F4	⌠
149	95	ò	181	B5	╡	213	D5	╒	245	F5	⌡
150	96	û	182	B6	╢	214	D6	╓	246	F6	$\div$
151	97	ù	183	B7	╖	215	D7	╫	247	F7	$\approx$
152	98	ÿ	184	B8	╕	216	D8	╪	248	F8	^{o}
153	99	Ö	185	B9	╣	217	D9	┘	249	F9	•
154	9A	Ü	186	BA	║	218	DA	┌	250	FA	·
155	9B	¢	187	BB	╗	219	DB	█	251	FB	$\surd$
156	9C	£	188	BC	╝	220	DC	▄	252	FC	^{n}
157	9D	¥	189	BD	╜	221	DD	▌	253	FD	^{2}
158	9E	₧	190	BE	╛	222	DE	▐	254	FE	■
159	9F	ƒ	191	BF	┐	223	DF	▀	255	FF	

ASCII Special **TRHELP Info**

Detail: These ASCII characters are grouped by their graphical appearance, and only their decimal values are shown.

Boxes

```
     218 196 194 191              201 205 203 187
      ┌   ─   ┬   ┐                ╔   ═   ╦   ╗
179   │                      186   ║
195   ├   197 ┼   ┤ 180      204   ╠   206 ╬   ╣ 185
      └       ┴   ┘                ╚       ╩   ╝
     192     193 217              200     202 188

     214 196 210 183              213 205 209 184
      ╓   ─   ╥   ╖                ╒   ═   ╤   ╕
186   ║                      179   │
199   ╟   215 ╫   ╢ 182      198   ╞   216 ╪   ╡ 181
      ╙       ╨   ╜                ╘       ╧   ╛
     211     208 189              212     207 190
```

Arrows

24	↑	18	↕	30	▲	174	«
25	↓	23	↨	31	▼	175	»
26	→	29	↔	16	►	60	<
27	←			17	◄	62	>

Blocks

176	░	178	▓	220	▄	221	▌	22	▬
177	▒	219	█	223	▀	222	▐	254	■

Language

131	â			136	ê			147	ô			150	û		
132	ä	Ä	142	137	ë			148	ö	Ö	153	129	ü	Ü	154
133	à			138	è			149	ò			151	ù		
160	á			130	é	É	144	162	ó			163	ú		
134	å	Å	143												
145	æ	Æ	146	140	î			135	ç	Ç	128				
				139	ï							152	ÿ		
				141	ì			164	ñ	Ñ	165				
				161	í										

19	‼	155	¢	158	₧	167	º
20	¶	156	£	159	ƒ	168	¿
21	§	157	¥	166	ª	173	¡

224	α	alpha		
225	β	beta		
231	γ	gamma	Γ	226
235	δ	delta		
233	θ	theta		
230	μ	mu		
227	π	pi		
229	σ	sigma	Σ	228
237	ϕ	phi	Φ	232
		omega	Ω	234

Math

170	¬	238	∈	244	⌠	250	·
171	½	239	∩	245	⌡	251	√
172	¼	240	≡	246	÷	252	^{n}
174	≪	241	±	247	≈	253	^{2}
175	≫	242	≥	248	∘		
236	∞	243	≤	249	•		

ASORT() Array Function

Syntax: ASORT(<array> [, <N start> [, <N elements>]])

Action: Sorts the elements of the named array in ascending order.

Return: Nothing.

Detail: The following example uses ASORT() to sort an array of database file names:

```
CLEAR
num_files = ADIR("*.DBF")
DECLARE dbf[num_files]
ADIR("*.DBF", dbf)
ASORT(dbf)
@ 0, 8 TO 10, 23 DOUBLE
@ 12, 5 SAY "Press Esc for more files"
FOR i = 1 TO num_files
   @ ((i-1)%9)+1, 10 SAY SPACE(12-LEN(dbf[i])) + dbf[i]

   * When the box is filled with file names, wait for
   * the user to press Esc.
   DO WHILE ((i-1)%9)+1 == 9 .AND. INKEY() != 27
      * This loop does nothing but wait for Esc.
   ENDDO
NEXT
```

In this example, ASORT() is used to sort the entire array. You can also specify a starting element and the number of elements to sort. When you sort only a portion of the array elements, the other elements remain in place. The following example sorts only 10 elements in an existing array, beginning with element 5:

```
DECLARE names[30]
.
. <commands>
.
ASORT(names, 5, 10)
```

Note that if the array you are sorting contains mixed data types, the types are sorted in the following order: Character, logical, date, and numeric.

AT() Character Function

Syntax: AT(<C search>, <C target>)

Action: Evaluates the starting position of the search string in the target string.

Return: <expN> number that is the position of the character in <target> at which <search> begins, or zero if not found.

Detail: The following is a generalized procedure that uses AT() to process a character field containing a list separated by some character:

```
PROCEDURE Separate
PARAMETERS remainder, separator
* Continue until no more separators in string remainder.
DO WHILE separator $ remainder
   * Display first item in remainder of list.
   * LTRIM() eliminates leading blanks.
   ? LTRIM(LEFT(remainder, AT(separator, remainder)-1))
   * Update remainder by removing item to
   * the left of first separator.
   remainder = SUBSTR(remainder,;
                      AT(separator, remainder)+1)
ENDDO
* Handles the display of the last item in the list,
* a single item list with no commas, and an empty list.
IF "" # RTRIM(remainder)
   ? RTRIM(LTRIM(remainder))
ENDIF
```

To execute the procedure:

```
USE <dbf filename>
DO Separate WITH (<field>), "<separator>"
```

Also: $, SUBSTR(), RAT()

AVERAGE

Database Command

Syntax: AVERAGE [<scope>] [<expN list> TO <memory variable list>]

Action: Evaluates the arithmetic mean of each specified number in the active file.

Detail: To determine the average age and salary of your employees and save the results:

```
USE Employee
AVERAGE Age, Salary TO avg_age, avg_salary
```

Note that although it is syntactically correct to use AVERAGE with no parameters, such a command accomplishes nothing but a waste of time since it gives you no result.

Also: COUNT, SUM

BEGIN SEQUENCE

Program Command

Syntax: BEGIN SEQUENCE
<commands>
[BREAK]
<commands>
END

Action: Executes the commands in the control structure until the END is encountered.

Detail: The following example uses a BEGIN SEQUENCE...END construct to recover from a printer not ready error:

```
CLEAR
BEGIN SEQUENCE
   DO WHILE .NOT. ISPRINTER()
      @ 10, 0 SAY "Printer is not ready.  Retry? (Y/N)"
      IF CHR(INKEY(0)) $ "Nn"
         BREAK
      ENDIF
   ENDDO
   USE Mailing
   REPORT FORM Maillist TO PRINTER
   CLOSE DATABASES
END
```

Note that the BREAK statement can be issued from a subroutine and still break out of the structure in a higher level routine. For example:

```
PROCEDURE Main
sys_error = .F.              && initialize error flag
BEGIN SEQUENCE
   DO Sub1                   && might BREAK in subroutine
   .
   . <commands>
   .
END
* If Sub1 BREAKs, control is returned here,
* so test for the sys_error flag.
IF sys_error
   <commands>
ENDIF

PROCEDURE Sub1
.
. <commands>
.
IF <condition>
   sys_error = .T.  && set error flag
   BREAK  && returns control to Main after END command
ENDIF
```

BIN2I() Conversion Function

Syntax: BIN2I(<expC>)

Action: Converts character string representing a 16-bit signed integer to a number.

Return: <expN>

Detail: BIN2I() is used when reading information from file formats that have numbers stored as 16-bit signed integers (least significant byte first), so that those numbers can be manipulated in a program.

The following example opens a file and reads a portion of it to illustrate this function. The example assumes that there is a number in the third and fourth bytes of the file that you want to access:

```
handle = FOPEN("Invoice.TXT")
FSEEK(handle, 3)          && move pointer to 3rd position
readbuffer = SPACE(2)     && initialize buffer

* Read 2 bytes and convert to number.
number = BIN2I(FREAD(handle, @readbuffer, 2))
.
. <commands>
.
FCLOSE(handle)
```

Also: FREAD(), BIN2L(), BIN2W(), I2BIN(), L2BIN()

BIN2L() — Conversion Function

Syntax: BIN2L(<expC>)

Action: Converts a character string representing a 32-bit signed integer to a number.

Return: <expN>

Detail: BIN2L() is used when reading information from file formats that have numbers stored as 32-bit (long) integers (least significant byte first), so that those numbers can be manipulated in a program.

The following example opens a file and reads a portion of it to illustrate this function. The example assumes that there is a long integer in the four bytes 7 through 10 of the file that you want to access:

```
handle = FOPEN("Invoice.TXT")
FSEEK(handle, 7)          && move pointer to 7th position
readbuffer = SPACE(4)     && initialize buffer
```

```
* Read 4 bytes and convert to number.
number = BIN2L(FREAD(handle, @readbuffer, 4))
.
. <commands>
.
FCLOSE(handle)
```

Also: FREAD(), BIN2I(), BIN2W(), I2BIN(), L2BIN()

BIN2W() Conversion Function

Syntax: BIN2W(<expC>)

Action: Converts character string that is a 16-bit unsigned integer to a number.

Return: <expN>

Detail: BIN2W() is used when reading information from file formats that have numbers stored as 16-bit unsigned integers (least significant byte first), so that those numbers can be manipulated in a program.

The following example opens a file and reads a portion of it to illustrate this function. The example assumes that there is a such a number in bytes 5 and 6 of the file that you want to access:

```
handle = FOPEN("Invoice.TXT")
FSEEK(handle, 5)         && move pointer to 5th position
readbuffer = SPACE(2)    && initialize buffer

* Read 2 bytes and convert to number.
number = BIN2W(FREAD(handle, @readbuffer, 2))
.
. <commands>
.
FCLOSE(handle)
```

Also: FREAD(), BIN2I(), BIN2L(), I2BIN(), L2BIN()

BOF() **Database Function**

Syntax: BOF()

Action: Evaluates whether the record pointer is at the beginning of a database file.

Return: <expL> true if the record pointer is at the beginning of file, otherwise false.

Detail: BOF() is used most often in a program where you use SKIP with a negative parameter in order to move backwards in a database file. Checking the status of BOF() after skipping backwards prevents a run-time error. For example:

```
USE Mailing
GO BOTTOM
DO WHILE .NOT. BOF()  && process file backwards
   .
   . <commands>
   .
   SKIP -1
ENDDO
CLOSE DATABASES
```

To check the beginning of file condition for an unselected database file, use the alias name and pointer with the function. For example:

```
? Orders->(BOF())  && check BOF() status of Orders file
```

Also: EOF(), SKIP, ->

CALL

Extend Command

Syntax: CALL <module name> WITH <expression list>

Action: Executes a separately compiled or assembled routine.

Detail: The <expression list> can contain up to seven parameters. The following command executes a routine with a single parameter:

```
filename = "Output.txt"
CALL Redirect WITH filename
```

Note that the routine has been linked in and thus does not have to be LOADed.

Parameter Passing

All constants are passed by reference to value, and point to a copy rather than the original.

Character strings are passed by reference and are null terminated.

Numbers are passed by reference, but could be either two byte integers or eight byte floating point format.

To guarantee receiving numbers as integers, pass them with the WORD() function:

```
CALL Routine WITH WORD(number)
```

Dates are passed as pointers to long integers.

Logicals are passed as pointers to short integers.

As parameters are passed on the stack, normal C conventions and assembler offsets from SP will receive them.

In assembler, both the ES:BX and DX:BX registers also point to the first parameter. This is different from dBASE which uses DS:BX for this pointer.

C programs should look like this:

```
c_call(param1, param2)  /* declare function */
char *param1;           /* declare local variables */
int  param2;            /* use WORD() to pass integer */
{
    .
    .  <code goes here>
    .
}
```

Assembler programs should look like this:

```
PUBLIC asm_call                  ; make name available
_PROG  SEGMENT  BYTE  'CODE' ; declare code segment
ASSUME cs:_PROG
asm_call PROC FAR                ; declare far procedure
   push bp                       ; save base pointer
   mov  bp, sp                   ; get start of parameters
   push ss                 ; save registers that will change
   push si
   push ds
   push di
   push es
   .
   .  <code goes here>
   .
   pop  es                       ; restore saved registers
   pop  di
   pop  ds
```

```
    pop  si
    pop  ss
    pop  bp                    ; restore base pointer
asm_call ENDP                  ; declare procedure end
      _PROG  ENDS              ; declare segment end
      END                      ; declare program end
```

You will have more control if you change your CALL procedure to a function so that you can use the Extend system interface.

Also: WORD()

CANCEL

Program Command

Syntax: CANCEL

Action: Returns from program execution mode to the operating system.

Detail: The CANCEL command is identical in functionality to QUIT. The following example uses CANCEL as the action of a menu selection that is chosen when the user wishes to leave the program:

```
DO WHILE .T.
   .
   . <commands to display menu and get selection>
   .
   DO CASE
      CASE selection==0    && 0 is Cancel on the menu
         CANCEL
      CASE selection==1
         DO <program one>
      CASE selection==2
         DO <program two>
   ENDCASE
ENDDO
```

Also: RETURN, QUIT

CDOW() **Date Function**

Syntax: CDOW(<expD>)

Action: Evaluates the day of week (e.g., Tuesday) on which the specified date falls.

Return: <expC> string representing the day of the week.

Detail: The following, rather lengthy, character expression uses CDOW() along with several other date manipulation functions to format the current date. This expression can be used with @...SAY, ?, or any other command that allows the use of a character expression:

```
CDOW(DATE()) + ", " + CMONTH(        DATE())   +" " +;
                      LTRIM(STR( DAY(DATE()))) +", "+;
                      LTRIM(STR(YEAR(DATE())))
```

An example of the date format produced by this expression is:

```
Saturday, April 1, 1989
```

Use the CTOD() function with CDOW() to specify a particular date. For example, if I want to know the day on which I was born, I could use:

```
? CDOW(CTOD("12/10/41"))
```

Also: CMONTH(), CTOD(), DAY(), DOW(), DTOC(), MONTH(), YEAR(), DATE()

CHR() **Conversion Function**

Syntax: CHR(<expN>)

Action: Evaluates the ASCII character equivalent of the specified number.

Return: <expC> character.

Detail: Use CHR() to specify characters that you cannot type, or that might not work properly on your printer or in your editor:

```
@ 10,0, 15,79 BOX CHR(213)+CHR(205)+CHR(184)+CHR(179)+;
                  CHR(190)+CHR(205)+CHR(212)+CHR(179)+;
                  CHR(178)
```

Use CHR() to compare INKEY() values to a character string:

```
? "Are you sure? (Y/N)..."
IF CHR(INKEY(0)) $ "Yy"    && wait for user input
   QUIT
ENDIF
```

Use CHR() to send control characters to the printer. For example, to select the emphasized mode for the Epson FX-85:

```
* Turn on emphasized mode.
SET PRINTER ON
?? CHR(27) + "E"
SET PRINTER OFF
```

After these commands are issued, anything that you print (e.g., REPORT FORM TO PRINTER, SET DEVICE TO PRINTER followed by @...SAY commands, etc.) will be in emphasized mode. To turn it off:

```
SET PRINTER ON
?? CHR(27) + "F"
SET PRINTER OFF
```

Note that ?? is used to send control characters so as not to cause an unnecessary line feed on the printer.

CHR() and ASC() are inverse functions.

Also: ASC(), ??, SET PRINTER

CLEAR — Output Command

Syntax: CLEAR [SCREEN]

Action: Clears the entire screen and releases active GET variables from READ access.

Detail: To erase the entire screen, use:

```
CLEAR
```

To erase the screen without clearing the pending GET variables, use:

```
CLEAR SCREEN
```

Both forms of this command reset ROW() and COL() to zero.

Also: @...CLEAR, @...GET, CLEAR GETS, READ, SET STATUS

CLEAR ALL — Memory Command

Syntax: CLEAR ALL

Action: Closes database files, selects the first work area, and releases memvars.

Detail: CLEAR ALL is convenient if you are using several database files and PUBLIC memory variables because you can close all of the files and release the memory variables with a single command. For example:

```
DO WHILE .T.
   .
   . <menu display and selection commands>
   .
   DO CASE
      CASE response = "Q"
         CLEAR ALL
         RETURN
      .
      . <other menu CASE statements>
      .
   ENDCASE
ENDDO
```

Also: RELEASE, RELEASE ALL, PUBLIC

CLEAR GETS — Input Command

Syntax: CLEAR GETS

Action: Releases the active @...GET variables from READ access.

Detail: With CLEAR GETS, @...GET can be used to display a variable using the enhanced mode without allowing the variable to be edited. For example:

```
USE Parts
@ 10, 0 SAY "Part Number      " GET Part_No
CLEAR GETS     && don't allow Part_No to be edited
@ 13, 0 SAY "Price            " GET Price
@ 15, 0 SAY "Reorder point    " GET Reorder
READ           && activates GETs after last CLEAR GETS
```

CLEAR GETS is necessary if you use READ SAVE. For example this function allows you the choice of changing, saving, or undoing the GETs you are editing.

```
FUNCTION editor
* Syntax: editor()
* Return: True if saved, otherwise false.
* Action: Reads current GETs.
*       : User chooses save, change, undo
*
PRIVATE action, ret
DO WHILE .T.
   @ 1, 5 SAY "Editing current record.  "+;
              "Press PgDn to end, Esc to cancel."
   READ SAVE

   * Force Undo if Esc is pressed to exit READ.
   IF LASTKEY() == 27
      action = 3
      KEYBOARD CHR(13)
   ENDIF
```

```
    * Lightbar menu:    Change     Save     Undo
    @ 1,1 CLEAR TO 1,78
    @ 1, 5 PROMPT "Change" MESSAGE "Edit again."
    @ 1,16 PROMPT "Save"   MESSAGE "Save changes."
    @ 1,25 PROMPT "Undo"   MESSAGE "Discard changes."
    MENU TO action

    * Stay in loop to Change if action=1, otherwise exit.
    IF action != 1
       ret = (action==2)   && true if 2, otherwise false
       EXIT
    ENDIF
 ENDDO
 CLEAR GETS   && left by READ SAVE
 RETURN ret
```

To use the editor() function, query it after you do the GETs:

```
memvar = SPACE(10)
@ 2,3 GET memvar
IF editor()
   DO save_edit
ELSE
   RETURN
ENDIF
```

Also: @...GET, READ, CLEAR

CLEAR MEMORY — Memory Command

Syntax: CLEAR MEMORY

Action: Releases all memory variables, PUBLIC and PRIVATE.

Detail: It is necessary to use CLEAR MEMORY only in a routine that uses PUBLIC memory variables, since PRIVATE variables are released automatically. Code written for interpreters usually contains this command at the end of the main program to insure that no variables are left in memory that might interfere with other programs. The following program skeleton shows how CLEAR MEMORY typically is used:

```
DO WHILE .T.
   .
   . <menu display and selection commands>
   .
   DO CASE
      CASE response = "Q"
         CLEAR MEMORY
         RETURN
      .
      . <other menu CASE statements>
      .
   ENDCASE
ENDDO
```

Of course, if there are open database files in addition to PUBLIC memory variables, you may want to use CLEAR ALL to close the database files and release the memory variables all at once.

Also: PUBLIC, PRIVATE, RELEASE, STORE, CLEAR ALL, RELEASE ALL

CLEAR TYPEAHEAD **Environment Command**

Syntax: CLEAR TYPEAHEAD

Action: Removes all of the keystrokes from the typeahead buffer.

Detail: The following example clears the typeahead buffer to make sure that the user sees the message that is displayed on the screen. These commands could be included as part of an error processing routine:

```
? "Are you sure? (Y/N)..."
CLEAR TYPEAHEAD
IF CHR(INKEY(0)) $ "Yy"    && wait for user input
   CLEAR
   RETURN
ENDIF
```

The CLEAR TYPEAHEAD command prevents the next keystroke in the typeahead buffer from being accepted as the response to the WAIT command. Otherwise, the message would flash on the screen so quickly that the user might not see it.

Also: SET TYPEAHEAD TO, INKEY()

Clipper — Compile Info

Syntax: CLIPPER <prg filename> | @<clp filename>
[-l] [-m] [-o<directory name>] [-p] [-q] [-s]
[-t<drive letter>] [-v]

Action: Compiles the named program and all programs that it references.

Detail: The Clipper command line options are described below. These options must be specified as lowercase letters:

Option	Meaning
-l	No line numbers in object files (save 3 bytes per line)
-m	Compiles only the named file, not referenced files
-o	Creates object files in the named directory
-p	Loads the compiler and then pauses for a disk change
-q	Suppresses line number display (quiet)
-s	Syntax check only
-t	Creates temporary files on the specified drive
-v	Gives memory variables precedence over fields (good for generic "black-box" routines).

The following example compiles a program and the programs that it references. No command line options are specified:

```
CLIPPER Main
```

The next example compiles only the main program without compiling any program that it references. This requires the use of the -m option which is useful if you have to make a change to a single program and do not wish to recompile all programs in the application:

```
CLIPPER Main -m
```

In the next example, line numbers are suppressed in the object files to save disk space, temporary files are written to a RAM disk (D:) to save time, and object files are written to a separate directory:

```
CLIPPER Main -l -tD: -oC:\Object
```

The Clipper compiler has the ability to compile file names that are listed in a text file with a .CLP extension. Each file that you want to compile is listed in the file on a separate line and the result is a single object file with the same name as the .CLP file. To compile the programs listed in a .CLP file, you must precede the file name with an @ symbol. For example:

```
CLIPPER @Programs
```

The file, Programs.CLP, is a standard ASCII text file that might look something like the following:

```
Main
EditRecs
AddRecs
Reports
```

Also: EXTERNAL

CLOSE — Database Command

Syntax: CLOSE [ALL]

Action: Closes all open files of all types or only those in the current work area.

Detail: If you are working with one or more database files as well as a procedure or an alternate file, CLOSE ALL can be used instead of one of the other forms of the CLOSE command to close all of these files with a single command. For example:

```
USE Customer              && open database and index files
SELECT 2
USE Orders INDEX Ord_Num
SELECT 3
USE Parts INDEX Part_Num
SELECT Customer
SET ALTERNATE TO Output && open alternate file
SET ALTERNATE ON
SET PROCEDURE TO Orders && open procedure file
DO Ord_List               && output goes to alt file
SET ALTERNATE OFF
CLOSE ALL                 && all files are closed
```

Note that you must issue SET ALTERNATE OFF because closing the alternate file does not do this automatically.

CLOSE with no parameters closes only the files in the current work area.

Also: CLEAR ALL, SET PROCEDURE TO, SET ALTERNATE TO, USE

CLOSE ALTERNATE — Output Command

Syntax: CLOSE ALTERNATE

Action: Closes the alternate text file.

Detail: The following commands record the Last_Name and Phone field contents from the mailing list in a text file:

```
SET ALTERNATE TO Output
USE Mailing
SET ALTERNATE ON
LIST Last_Name, Phone
SET ALTERNATE OFF
CLOSE ALTERNATE
```

Note that the result of the @...SAY command is not recorded in the alternate file. In order to capture @...SAYs in a text file, you must use SET PRINTER TO <file> in conjunction with SET DEVICE TO PRINTER.

Also note that you must issue SET ALTERNATE OFF either before or after closing the alternate file, as this operation is not performed automatically.

Also: SET ALTERNATE, SET ALTERNATE TO, SET DEVICE TO

CLOSE DATABASES — Database Command

Syntax: CLOSE DATABASES

Action: Closes database and index files in all work areas and selects area 1.

Detail: Use CLOSE DATABASES to close one or more database files when you are finished with them. For example:

```
USE Orders
SELECT 2
USE Parts INDEX Part_No
SELECT Orders
SET RELATION TO Part_No INTO Parts
REPORT FORM Invoices
CLOSE DATABASES
```

Note that if a format file is open, CLOSE DATABASES does not close it.

Also: USE, SELECT

CLOSE FORMAT — Database Command

Syntax: CLOSE FORMAT

Action: Closes the format file in the active work area.

Detail: The following commands show how to use a format file and to close it:

```
USE Mailing
SET FORMAT TO EditRecs
APPEND BLANK
READ           && using EditRecs format file
CLOSE FORMAT
APPEND BLANK
READ           && using default format
```

Also: SET FORMAT TO

CLOSE INDEXES **Database Command**

Syntax: CLOSE INDEXES

Action: Closes all open index files in the current work area.

Detail: The following commands illustrate how to close the index files for the active database file in order to view it in its original order:

```
USE Parts INDEX Part_No
LIST Part_No, Price  && list in Part_No order
CLOSE INDEXES
LIST Part_No, Price  && list in natural order
```

SET ORDER TO 0 can be used to view the file in its natural, record number order without actually closing the index files.

Also: USE, SET INDEX TO, SET ORDER TO

CLOSE PROCEDURE **Program Command**

Syntax: CLOSE PROCEDURE

Action: This command is not operational.

Detail: In this program, once a procedure or user-defined function is compiled with SET PROCEDURE TO <prg filename>, that procedure or user-defined function is available. There is no need to close the procedure file.

Thus, CLOSE PROCEDURE is allowed in programs for compatibility with other dialects, but the command is not operational.

Also: SET PROCEDURE TO, DO, PROCEDURE, FUNCTION

CMONTH() — Date Function

Syntax: CMONTH(<expD>)

Action: Evaluates the character month (e.g., July) in which the specified date falls.

Return: <expC> string representing the month.

Detail: For example, to find out what month it is:

```
? CMONTH(DATE())
```

To display the birth months of the individuals in the Mailing list:

```
USE Mailing
LIST CMONTH(Birthday)
```

To format a particular date using a three letter month abbreviation followed by the day of the month and the year (e.g., Jan 23, 1987), use the following expression:

```
LEFT(CMONTH(<expD>), 3) + " " + LTRIM(STR(DAY(<expD>))+;
                         ", " + STR(YEAR(<expD>), 4)
```

Also: CDOW(), CTOD(), DAY(), DOW(), DTOC(), MONTH(), YEAR(), DATE()

COL() — Environment Function

Syntax: COL()

Action: Evaluates the current screen column position.

Return: <expN> representing the screen column position.

Detail: When SET DEVICE TO SCREEN is in effect, COL() is most often used to position information on the screen relative to the location of previously displayed information. For example, when you TRIM() a character variable, you don't know how long the result will be. The following commands display the first and last name fields side by side, regardless of how long the first name happens to be:

```
@ 3, 0       SAY TRIM(First_Name)
@ 3, COL()+1 SAY Last_Name
```

The CLEAR command resets COL() to zero.

Also: @...SAY, @...GET, ROW(), PCOL(), PROW(), CLEAR, SET DEVICE TO

COMMIT — Database Command

Syntax: COMMIT

Action: Writes the contents of all data buffers to the disk without closing files.

Detail: When you are adding data to a database file or making changes to existing data, the changes that you make are saved in a data buffer in memory instead of being written to the disk immediately. This feature is designed so that data entry and editing can be as fast as possible.

When a data buffer fills up or when you explicitly close the database file, all of the information in these buffers is written to disk. The COMMIT command allows you to control when the data buffers are written to disk. For example:

```
USE Orders INDEX Ord_Num
DO WHILE .T.
   key = SPACE(5)
   @ 10, 0 SAY "Enter the order number to change:";
           GET key
   READ
   @ 11, 0 SAY "          "  && clear Not found message
```

```
      IF EMPTY(key) .OR. LASTKEY()==27  && Esc key or blank
         EXIT
      ELSE
         SEEK key
         IF FOUND()
            @ 15, 0 SAY "Order number:" GET Ord_Num
            READ     && user makes changes
            COMMIT   && write changes to disk immediatly
         ELSE
            @ 11, 0 SAY "Not found"
         ENDIF
      ENDIF
   ENDDO
   CLOSE DATABASES
```

Note that if you are using DOS version 3.2 or lower, COMMIT only flushes Clipper's internal data buffers. Under DOS versions 3.3 and higher, COMMIT flushes the data buffers and performs a solid disk write to DOS.

Also: CLOSE DATABASES, CLEAR ALL, USE, QUIT

Config.sys — Configuration Info

Action: Defines the number of files and buffers allowed by the operating system.

Detail: The DOS configuration file, Config.SYS, is a standard ASCII text file that is read each time you boot your computer. It establishes the maximum number of open files allowed and the number of buffers that can be used. The format of the Config.SYS file is as follows:

```
FILES=<number of files>
BUFFERS=<number of buffers>
```

If you find that you need more files open, you will want to increase the FILES parameter. For the BUFFERS parameter, use the number recommended by your software. For example:

```
FILES=30
BUFFERS=8
```

Note that DOS uses five handles, leaving five less than you set for your application. To set files over 20, you must set the Clipper environmental variable at DOS. See the entry called Set Clipper.

To check if the number of file handles currently available are sufficient for your application, you can use this code:

```
* Validate number of file handles available.
handles = 10                    && number of file handles needed
DECLARE array[handles]
FOR i = 1 TO handles
   array[i] = FOPEN("NUL")  && open NUL device read only
   IF array[i] < 0
      EXIT
   ENDIF
NEXT
i = i-1
FOR j = 1 TO i
   FCLOSE(array[j])         && close handles opened
NEXT
* Quit if insuficient number of handles.
IF i < handles
   ? "Cannot open enough files.  Check CONFIG.SYS."
   QUIT
ENDIF
```

Also: FOPEN()

CONTINUE — Search Command

Syntax: CONTINUE

Action: Resumes the search initiated by the LOCATE command in the current work area.

Detail: CONTINUE can be used only after a LOCATE. LOCATE finds the first record that meets the condition, and CONTINUE finds subsequent records. For example:

```
USE Mailing
LOCATE FOR State = "CA"
DO WHILE FOUND()
   .
   . <commands>
   .
   CONTINUE
ENDDO
```

You can have a separate LOCATE/CONTINUE condition for each work area. CONTINUE automatically evaluates the correct LOCATE condition for the current work area.

Also: LOCATE, FOUND()

Conventions — TRHELP Info

Detail: This Book uses these conventions:

Text Conventions

::= Backus-Naur Form symbol meaning "is defined to be." Backus-Naur Form or "BNF" is a metalanguage used for syntactically describing programming languages. Metavariable <brackets> and the or bar (|) also come from BNF.

... Ellipsis means something was omitted.

Syntax Conventions

< >	Metavariable: something you must furnish
<exp?>	Expression of specific data-type where ? equals C for character, D for date, L for logical, N for numeric, or any type if omitted.
<? description>	Expression data-type where ? equals C for character, D for date, L for logical, N for numeric, or Literal (unquoted string) if omitted. <description> shows the purpose for which the expression is to be used.
[ ]	Optional syntax
[...]	Option may be repeated zero or more times
|	Or, a choice: ON | OFF, Numeric | Date

Code Conventions

Indentation	Three spaces
Uppercase	Reserved words
Lowercase	Procedure, memory variable, and array names
Initial Cap	File, Alias, and Field names
*	Begins a comment line
&&	Begins an in-line comment
;	Continues one line to the next

Metavariables

Metavariables are items enclosed in angle brackets that you must supply. These are commonly used metavariables:

<alias>	Another name for a database file which is assigned when you open the file. Alias names can be ten characters long. The first character must be a letter, and the rest can be any combination of letters, numbers, and underscores.
<array>	Name of an array. Array names can be ten characters long. The first character must be a letter, and the rest can be any combination of letters, numbers, and underscores.
<C...>	C preceding a description indicates that the item described must be represented as a character expression.
<D...>	D preceding a description indicates that the item described must be represented as a date expression.
<expression>	Expression of any data type. The entry named Expression gives details.
<expC>	Character expression
<expD>	Date expression
<expL>	Logical expression
<expN>	Numeric expression
<field>	Name of a field in a database file. Any field name can be prefixed by the alias symbol, ->, to indicate that the field is to be taken from the specified database file. Field names can be ten characters long. The first character must be a letter, and the rest can be any combination of letters, numbers, and underscores.

<filename>	Name of a disk file. The filename may include a drive specifier, path name, and extension. The default extension for a file name depends on the command or function, and is indicated in the syntax. All file names can be eight characters long. The first character must be a letter, and the rest can be any combination of letters, numbers, and underscores.
<L ...>	L preceding a description indicates that the item must be represented as a logical expression.
<... list>	Used where many items can be placed together in a list, like <field list> and <expression list>. Items in the list are separated from each other by a comma.
<memvar>	Name of a memory variable. Any memory variable name can be prefixed by the symbol, M->, to distinguish it from a field with the same name. Memory variable names can be up to ten characters long. The first character must be a letter, and the rest can be any combination of letters, numbers, and underscores. Memory variables may be referred to as "memvars."
<N ...>	N preceding a description indicates that the item must be represented as a numeric expression.
<scope>	Indicates that you can use scoping keywords to limit the command. The entry named Scope gives the syntax.

Also: Conventions Code, Expression, Scope

Conventions Code — TRHELP Info

Detail: These coding conventions are recommendations only. The importance is having consistant conventions that give useful information to anyone reading the program.

As a general rule, you should not use command, function, or keyword names for naming memory variables, arrays, fields, and files. And, you should avoid using the same name for two different objects such as a field and a memory variable.

Lowercase	Application function(), procedure, array, or memory variable name
Initial cap	Alias, Field, File, external Function(), or external Procedure name
Uppercase	COMMAND, FUNCTION(), or RESERVED WORD
///	Something unfinished
***	Code commented out
Strings	Delimited by double quotes like "string" unless the string itself contains double quotes, then the delimiters are square brackets: [st"ri"ng]
Indentation	Three spaces indent inside structures
Line width	Maximum 64 characters, excluding line numbers

Variable Naming

Mnemonics are conventions for naming variables:

a_<memvar>	Menu action memvar (user choice)
box_<memvar>	Prompt box memvar
f_<memvar>	File search/control memvar
i	Count memvar ("iteration")
is_<memvar>	Logical memvar
m_<memvar>	Field duplicate memvar
msg_<memvar>	Message memvar
p_<memvar>	Prompt memvar
prn_<memvar>	Printer code memvar
s_<memvar>	Screen attribute memvar
sc_<memvar>	Output scope memvar
scr_<memvar>	Screen buffer memvar
sys_<memvar>	Application system memvar
u_<memvar>	Control UDF for Clipper functions
<proc>_act	Specific menu action procedure
<proc>_ctrl	Program-logic control procedure
<proc>_scr	Screen procedure (@...SAY/GETs)
<proc>_setup	Preliminary set up procedure
<proc>_write	Save/delete procedure
act_<proc>	Generic menu action procedure
frm_<proc>	Single form procedure
get_<proc>	Parameter entry procedure
key_<proc>	SET KEY TO procedure

net_<proc>	Network procedure
prn_<proc>	Printer procedure
rpt_<proc>	Report procedure
u_<func>	UDF for ACHOICE(), DB/MEMOEDIT()
v_<func>	VALID expression function

Also: Conventions

COPY FILE — OS Command

Syntax: COPY FILE <filename> | (<C filename>)
TO <filename> | (<C filename>)

Action: Copies any disk file to another file.

Detail: COPY FILE is similar to the DOS Copy command except that it does not allow wildcard characters. It is used to make copies of files, one file at a time. In order to use COPY FILE, the file that you want to make a copy of must be closed, and you must specify the entire file name, including the extension.

Keep in mind that COPY FILE copies only a single file at a time. If you are making a copy of a database file that has one or more memo fields, you must also make a copy of the memo file in order to be able to use the copy. For example:

```
CLOSE DATABASES  && make sure file is closed
COPY FILE Mailing.DBF TO A:Mailing.DBF
COPY FILE Mailing.DBT TO A:Mailing.DBT
```

Either or both file names can be specified as character expressions by enclosing the expression in parentheses. For example:

```
file_one = "Mailing.DBF"
file_two = "A:Mailing.DBF"
COPY FILE (file_one) TO (file_two)
```

Also: COPY TO, RENAME, ERASE, DIR, CLOSE

COPY STRUCTURE **Database Command**

Syntax: COPY STRUCTURE [FIELDS <field list>]
TO <dbf filename> | (<C dbf filename>)

Action: Copies the structure of the active file to create an empty database file.

Detail: To copy the structure of a database file (i.e., its field definitions, but not its data), use COPY STRUCTURE. For example, if you want to start a new database file called Business to hold the names and addresses of your business associates, it would probably contain the same file structure as your Mailing list. Instead of creating the Business file structure from scratch, you could use:

```
USE Mailing
COPY STRUCTURE TO Business
```

If you only want to copy a subset of the fields, use a FIELDS clause:

```
COPY STRUCTURE TO Business;
               FIELDS Last_Name, First_Name, Address1,;
                      Address2, City, State, Zip, Phone
```

You can specify the file name as a character expression as long as you enclose the expression in parentheses. For example:

```
file_name = "Business"
COPY STRUCTURE TO (file_name)
```

Also: FIELDS

COPY STRUCTURE EXTENDED **Database Command**

Syntax: COPY STRUCTURE EXTENDED [FIELDS <field list>]
TO <dbf filename> | (<C dbf filename>)

Action: Creates a structure extended database file.

Detail: COPY STRUCTURE EXTENDED creates a database file whose records are the field defintions (i.e., field name, type, length, and number of decimals) of the active database file. Its main use is in conjunction with CREATE FROM so that you can design your own database file creation and modification routines. For example:

```
USE YourFile
COPY TO Backup      && back up data in YourFile
COPY STRUCTURE EXTENDED TO ExteFile
USE ExteFile
DO ModiStru  && a routine to edit ExteFile's contents
CREATE YourFile FROM ExteFile
USE YourFile
APPEND FROM Backup  && recover data from Backup
```

You can specify the file name as a character expression as long as you enclose the expression in parentheses. For example:

```
file_name = "ExteFile"
COPY STRUCTURE EXTENDED TO (file_name)
```

Note that although the use of a FIELDS clause with COPY STRUCTURE EXTENDED is syntactically correct, it has no effect on the outcome of the command. All fields are included in the structure extended file regardless of the presence of a FIELDS clause.

Also: CREATE FROM, CREATE, FIELDS

COPY TO

Database Command

Syntax: COPY TO <dbf filename> | (<C dbf filename>)
[FIELDS <field list>] [<scope>]

Action: Copies the active database file to another database file.

Detail: COPY is used to make copies of the active database file. The following example copies selected fields and records from the Customer file to create a file named OverDue:

```
USE Customer
* OverDue will contain the names and phone numbers of
* customers whose accounts are overdue.
COPY TO OverDue FOR Due_Date < DATE();
                FIELDS Last_Name, First_Name, Phone
USE OverDue
LIST
CLOSE DATABASES
```

The file name can be specified as a character expression as long as you enclose the expression in parentheses. For example:

```
file_name = "OverDue"
COPY TO (file_name)
```

Also: APPEND FROM, FIELDS

COPY TO (text) — Database Command

Syntax: COPY TO <txt filename> | (<C txt filename>)
[FIELDS <field list>] [<scope>]
SDF | DELIMITED [WITH BLANK | <delimiter> |
(<C delimiter>)]

Action: Copies the records from the active database file to a non-database text file.

Detail: The following example copies selected fields and records from the Orders and Parts files to a delimited text file:

```
USE Orders INDEX Cust_No
SELECT 2
USE Parts INDEX Part_No
SELECT 1
SET RELATION TO Part_No INTO Parts
SEEK "5135"
COPY TO Ord5135 DELIMITED WHILE Cust_No = "5135";
                FIELDS Cust_No, Part_No, Parts->Price
CLOSE DATABASES
```

To express the file name as a character expression rather than a literal value, simply enclose the expression in parentheses. For example:

```
txt_file = "Ord5135"
COPY TO (txt_file) DELIMITED WHILE Cust_No = "5135";
                   FIELDS Cust_No, Part_No, Parts->Price
```

File Types

SDF or "System Data Format" is a standard ASCII text (.TXT) file with fixed length fields/records, no field delimiters or separators, and records are separated by a carriage-return/line-feed pair.

DELIMITED [WITH BLANK | <delimiter> | (<C delimiter>)] is a standard ASCII text (.TXT) file with fields separated by commas and character fields enclosed in delimiters. The delimiter can be expressed either as a literal value or as a character expression. If a character expression is used, it must be enclosed in parentheses. DELIMITED WITH BLANK is a special format where each field is separated from the next by a blank space and no other field delimiters are used. In either case, the records are separated by a carriage-return/line-feed pair.

Also: FIELDS

COUNT — Database Command

Syntax: COUNT [<scope>] TO <memory variable>

Action: Counts the records in the active file.

Detail: To determine how many customers owe more than $1000.00 and save the result in a numeric memory variable:

```
USE Customer
COUNT FOR Amount > 1000 TO collect
```

If you want to count the records in a file just to determine the total number, it is easier and faster to use the RECCOUNT() function. This function quickly returns the total number of records in the active file. For example, instead of:

```
COUNT TO tot_count
```

you would use

```
STORE RECCOUNT() TO tot_count
```

For this reason, COUNT is seldom used without a scope.

Also: AVERAGE, SUM, RECCOUNT(), LASTREC()

CREATE **Database Command**

Syntax: CREATE <dbf filename> | (<C dbf filename>)

Action: Creates an empty structure extended database file.

Detail: CREATE is similar to COPY STRUCTURE EXTENDED in that it creates a file whose structure is designed to hold field definitions (i.e., field name, type, length, and number of decimals). The main difference is that CREATE does not require an existing database file and, thus, does not create a structure extended file with existing field definitions. Rather, it creates an empty structure extended file to which you add field definitions.

The main use of CREATE is in conjunction with CREATE FROM so that you can design your own database file creation routine. For example:

```
CREATE ExteFile
USE ExteFile
DO DBCreate   && a routine to add records to ExteFile
CREATE YourFile FROM ExteFile
USE YourFile
```

You can specify the file name as a character expression as long as you enclose the expression in parentheses. For example:

```
file_name = "ExteFile"
CREATE (file_name)
```

Also: CREATE FROM, COPY STRUCTURE EXTENDED

Create (interactive) — External Program

Syntax: Create <dbf filename>

Action: Allows you to create database files interactively.

Detail: Create.EXE prompts you through the creation of a database file.

Using the Create utility, you can create database files with up to 1,024 fields. Character fields can be up to 32,767 bytes long.

CREATE FROM — Database Command

Syntax: CREATE <dbf filename> | (<C dbf filename>)
FROM <dbf filename> | (<C dbf filename>)

Action: Creates a database file using a structure extended database file.

Detail: CREATE FROM uses a structure extended database file to create a regular database file structure. This command is used mainly in database file creation and modification routines. For example:

```
USE YourFile
COPY TO Backup      && back up data in YourFile
COPY STRUCTURE EXTENDED TO ExteFile
USE ExteFile
DO ModiStru         && a routine to edit ExteFile
CREATE YourFile FROM ExteFile
USE YourFile
APPEND FROM Backup  && recover data from Backup
```

Both or either of the database file names can be specified as a character expression by enclosing the expression in parentheses. For example:

```
from_file = "ExteFile"
new_file = "YourFile"
CREATE (new_file) FROM (from_file)
```

Also: COPY STRUCTURE EXTENDED, CREATE

CTOD() Conversion Function

Syntax: CTOD(<C date string>)

Action: Converts the specified character string to a date.

Return: <expD> date value of <date string>.

Detail: Since there is no direct representation for dates, CTOD() is used to create date constants. For example, to represent the date, October 25, 1989, you would use the expression:

```
CTOD("10/25/89")
```

To put that value in a date field in a database file, you would use:

```
REPLACE <date field> WITH CTOD("10/25/89")
```

To save the value in a memory variable:

```
date_var = CTOD("10/25/89")
```

Also: CDOW(), CMONTH(), DAY(), DOW(), DTOC(), MONTH(), YEAR()

CURDIR() Environment Function

Syntax: CURDIR([<C drive letter>])

Action: Evaluates the name of the current DOS directory for the specified drive.

Return: <expC> string representing the current directory, excluding the drive designation.

Detail: If no drive letter is specified, the currently logged DOS drive is assumed. The directory is returned using all uppercase letters. For example, if the current drive is C:

```
? CURDIR()       && queries drive C:
? CURDIR("A:")   && queries drive A: (colon is optional)
? CURDIR("D")    && queries drive D:
```

Note that SET DEFAULT TO has no effect on this function.

The root directory produces a null string result.

```
! cd \bin\tools
? CURDIR()       && returns BIN\TOOLS
! cd \
? CURDIR()       && returns null string
```

Also: SET PATH TO

DATE() **Environment Function**

Syntax: DATE()

Action: Evaluates the system date.

Return: <expD> system date.

Detail: The following routine uses the DATE() function to display the date at the bottom of each printed form:

```
USE Orders
SELECT 2
USE Parts INDEX Part_No
SELECT Orders
SET RELATION TO Part_No INTO Parts
SET DEVICE TO PRINTER
DO WHILE .NOT. EOF()
   @  3, 70 SAY Cust_No
   old_cust = Cust_No
   line = 5
   DO WHILE Cust_No = old_cust
      @ line,  0 SAY Quantity PICTURE "999"
      @ line,  5 SAY Part_No +" "+;
                     LEFT(Parts->Descrip, 50)
      @ line, 51 SAY Parts->Price PICTURE "9999999.99"
```

```
        @ line, 62 SAY Parts->Price*Quantity;
                   PICTURE "999999.99"
        line = line + 1
        SKIP
     ENDDO
     @ 60, 70 SAY DATE()
  ENDDO
  SET DEVICE TO SCREEN
  CLOSE DATABASES
```

Also: TIME(), SET DATE, DTOC(), DTOS()

DAY() Date Function

Syntax: DAY(<expD>)

Action: Evaluates the numeric day of the month for the specified date.

Return: <expN> representing the day of the month.

Detail: The DAY function is most often used to format date displays. Since it returns a numeric value, DAY() is often used with STR() which converts it to a character string. For example, the following expression formats a date value using a three letter month abbreviation followed by the day of the month and the year (e.g., Jun 12, 1989):

```
LEFT(CMONTH(<expD>), 3) + " " + LTRIM(STR(DAY(<expD>))+;
                         ", " + STR(YEAR(<expD>), 4)
```

Also: CDOW(), CMONTH(), CTOD(), DOW(), DTOC(), STR(), MONTH(), YEAR(), DATE()

DBEDIT() **Database Function**

Syntax: DBEDIT([<N top row> [,<N left col>
[,<N bottom row> [,<N right col>
[, <expression array> [, <C UDF name>
[, <picture array> [, <header array>
[, <separator array1> [, <separator array2>
[, <separator array3> [, <foot array>]]]]]]]]]]])

Action: Allows you to display and edit data in a tabular form, similar to a BROWSE in other dialects.

Return: <expL> true. Meaningless value since it is always true.

Detail: Note that any DBEDIT() parameter can be omitted by using a dummy parameter (i.e., a logical .F.) in its place. The display window defaults to the entire screen. The expression array defaults to all fields in the active file. All other arrays in the syntax can be a single character expression to be used for all columns.

The header array defaults to the names of the fields or columns as stored in the expression array. The first and third separator arrays refer to the horizontal separators between the column headers and footers, and the actual data. The second one refers to the vertical separator between columns.

The following example illustrates the use of DBEDIT() to edit the information in the Mailing list. This example illustrates every parameter of DBEDIT() except the final one that allows column footers:

```
CLEAR
USE Mailing
DECLARE names[9], lens[9], head[9], pic[9]

AFIELDS(names, .f., lens) && skip the field types
AINS(names, 1)      && insert element for delete status
names[1] = "DELETED()"
```

```
* Column headings.
head[1] = "Deleted?"
head[2] = "First Name"
head[3] = "Last Name"
head[4] = "Street Address"
head[5] = "Apt. #"
head[6] = "City"
head[7] = "State"
head[8] = "Zip Code"
head[9] = "Phone"

* Pictures for fields
pic[1] = "Y"
FOR i = 2 TO 6
   pic[i] = REPLICATE("X", lens[i])
NEXT
pic[7] = "@!A"
pic[8] = "99999"
pic[9] = "(999)999-9999"

* DBEDIT() displays fields.  Keys is a "user function"
* that allows you to actually edit the fields.
DBEDIT( 2, 2, 20, 78, names, "Keys", pic, head,;
        CHR(196), CHR(179), CHR(205) )

FUNCTION Keys
* Syntax: None, user function for DBEDIT().
* Action: Allows you to edit the contents of a field by
*         pressing Enter.  Pressing Del toggles record's
*         delete status.  Pressing Esc exits DBEDIT().
PARAMETERS db_mode, db_column
PRIVATE ret, key

key = LASTKEY()
ret = 1   && default unless changed

* All other db_mode values (besides 4) continue DBEDIT()
IF db_mode == 4     && db_mode of 4 is a key exception
```

```
        DO CASE
           CASE key == 13  && Enter to edit the field
              IF db_column > 1  && Can't edit delete status
                 SET CURSOR ON  && CURSOR is OFF in DBEDIT()
                 fld_name = names[db_column]
                 fld_pic  = pic[db_column]
                 @ ROW(), COL() GET &fld_name PICTURE fld_pic
                 READ
                 SET CURSOR OFF
              ENDIF
           CASE key = 27  && Esc exits DBEDIT()
              ret = 0
           CASE key = 7   && Toggles delete status on and off
              IF .NOT. DELETED()
                 DELETE
              ELSE
                 RECALL
              ENDIF
        ENDCASE
     ENDIF
     RETURN ret
```

The two parameters that are passed by DBEDIT() to the UDF user function are its mode and the current column number. The possible modes are listed below:

Mode	Meaning
0	DBEDIT() is idle
1	Attempt to cursor past BOF()
2	Attempt to cursor past EOF()
3	Active DBF is empty
4	Keystroke exception

A keystroke exception is any key that is not pre-defined to move the cursor. If no user function is specified with DBEDIT(), you cannot edit the data on the screen. You can only view the data and move from column-to-column and record-to-record. Pressing Esc or Enter exits DBEDIT(). Using a UDF, you can reprogram Esc and Enter as well as any other key that is not designed to move the cursor.

The value that is returned by the user function must be a number. DBEDIT() continues to perform based on its value as described below:

Return	Meaning
0	Exit DBEDIT()
1	Continue DBEDIT()
2	Repaint screen and continue DBEDIT()
3	Toggle append mode

DBFILTER() — Database Function

Syntax: DBFILTER()

Action: Evaluates the SET FILTER TO condition.

Return: <expC> string containing the filter condition. If no SET FILTER TO condition is in effect, DBFILTER() returns a null string.

Detail: The following example allows the user to edit the filter condition in the current work area:

```
FUNCTION EditFltr
condition = DBFILTER()
* Make condition at least 100 characters in length.
condition = condition + SPACE(100 - LEN(condition))
CLEAR
DO WHILE .T.
   @ 10, 0 SAY "Please edit the filter condition";
           GET condition
   READ
   IF TYPE(condition) == "L"
      SET FILTER TO &condition
      RETURN .T.
   ENDIF
ENDDO
RETURN .F.
```

Also: SET FILTER TO

DBRELATION() Database Function

Syntax: DBRELATION(<N relation order>)

Action: Evaluates the SET RELATION TO expression for the specified relation.

Return: <expC> string representing the specified relation expression for the active file.

Detail: The relation order referred to as the DBRELATION() parameter is the position of the relation in the SET RELATION TO list. For example:

```
USE Orders INDEX O_Cust
SELECT 2
USE Customer INDEX Cust_No
SELECT 3
USE Parts INDEX Part_No
SELECT Orders
SET RELATION TO Cust_No INTO Customer, TO Part_No ;
             INTO Parts
? DBRELATION(1)   && returns Cust_No
? DBRELATION(2)   && returns Part_No
```

Also: DBRSELECT(), SET RELATION TO

DBRSELECT() Database Function

Syntax: DBRSELECT(<N relation order>)

Action: Evaluates the SELECT work area number for the specified relation.

Return: <expN> representing the target work area for the relation.

Detail: The relation order referred to as the DBRSELECT() parameter is the position of the relation in the SET RELATION TO list. For example:

```
USE Orders INDEX O_Cust
SELECT 2
USE Customer INDEX Cust_No
SELECT 3
USE Parts INDEX Part_No
SELECT Orders
SET RELATION TO Cust_No INTO Customer, TO Part_No ;
             INTO Parts
? DBRSELECT(1)   && returns 2
? DBRSELECT(2)   && returns 3
```

Also: DBRELATION(), SELECT, SET RELATION TO

Dbu — External Program

Syntax: Dbu

Action: Creates or manipulates a database file through a menu-driven system.

Detail: Dbu, the database utility, is a utility program that allows you to interactively manipulate database files.

Before you can use Dbu, you must compile and link the programs that it comprises. For convenience, a batch file called MakeDbu.BAT is included with Clipper to do this. Once all of the programs are compiled and linked, you execute Dbu.EXE to access its menu-driven system.

DB_ERROR() — Error Function

Syntax: DB_ERROR(<C proc name>, <N file line>, <C error info>)

Action: Called by Clipper on database file operation error.

Return: <expL> true to retry the operation, or false to exit to DOS.

Detail: DB_ERROR() is called automatically by Clipper when a database file operation fails, such as with SKIP or REPLACE.

The error function below is part of the TRHELP high-level error system used to replace Clipper's default DB_ERROR() function. It uses the other high-level error functions documented under the ERRORSYS procedure.

Does not trap out of disk space error on APPEND BLANK or REPLACE a large string into a memo field. To prevent these errors, check DISKSPACE() before performing the operation.

```
* Syntax: None, called by Clipper on database operation
*         error
* Return: True to retry command that caused error,
*         false to exit to operating system.
* Action: Handle database operation errors.
*
PARAMETERS proc_name, file_line, error_info

* Sound warning and display error message on screen.
error_tone()
err_msg("Error in database command from: " + proc_name+;
        ".  File line: " + LTRIM(STR(file_line)) + ".",;
        "Press any key to continue...")

* Write error details to file; pause for user response.
err_write(PROCNAME(), proc_name, file_line, error_info)
CLEAR TYPEAHEAD
INKEY(0)
err_msg()  && clear error message

* Activate the debugger if sys_debug is true.
IF sys_debug
   err_msg("Set return value by making logical",;
           "variable 'ret_debug' true or false")
   ALTD()
   err_msg()
   IF TYPE("ret_debug") == "L"
      RETURN ret_debug
   ENDIF
ENDIF
```

```
* Without BEGIN/END SEQUENCE around operation that
* caused the error, BREAK behaves the same as RETURN .F.
BREAK
** DB_ERROR() ***************************************
```

Also: ERRORSYS, OPEN_ERROR(), MISC_ERROR(), EXPR_ERROR(), UNDEF_ERRO(), PRINT_ERRO()

DECLARE — Array Command

Syntax: DECLARE <array>[<N elements>] [, <array>[<N elements>]...]

Action: Creates one or more arrays with the specified number of elements.

Detail: Note that although square brackets normally indicate an optional item in the syntax, they are a literal part of the DECLARE command syntax that must surround the number of elements. For example, to create an array called Names that will hold 50 elements:

```
DECLARE Names[50]
Names[1] = "Debby"
Names[2] = "Tom"
Names[3] = "Leonard"
```

To create two or more arrays with a single DECLARE command, separate the array definitions using a comma. For example:

```
DECLARE Names[50], Numbers[10]
```

Array subscripts begin with 1. The number of arrays that can be created depends on the number of available memory variable slots and the amount of free memory. Each array uses a single memory variable slot and may have up to 4096 elements.

DECLARE creates PRIVATE arrays, and PRIVATE may be substituted:

```
PRIVATE Names[50], Numbers[10], memvar
```

To create PUBLIC arrays, DECLARE them in the first or top-level routine, or use the PUBLIC command:

```
PUBLIC Names[50], Numbers[10], memvar
```

Also: PRIVATE, PUBLIC, STORE

DELETE **Database Command**

Syntax: DELETE [<scope>]

Action: Marks records in the active database file for deletion.

Detail: The following program uses the DELETE command to remove all people from the Mailing list who live in California:

```
USE Mailing
COPY TO Local FOR State = "CA"      && create local list
DELETE FOR State = "CA"
LIST FOR DELETED()       && records indicated by asterisk
PACK               && permanently removes deleted records
CLOSE DATABASES
```

Also: PACK, RECALL, DELETED(), SET DELETED

DELETE FILE **OS Command**

Syntax: DELETE FILE <filename> | (<C filename>)

Action: Erases the named file from the disk.

Detail: The DELETE FILE command is similar to the DOS Erase command, except that it does not allow the use of wildcard characters. It is used to erase files from the disk, one at a time.

In order to use DELETE FILE, the file that you want to erase must be closed and you must specify the entire file name, including the extension. For example, to erase the backup of the mailing list file:

```
CLOSE DATABASES          && make sure file is closed
DELETE FILE Mailing.BAK  && erase database file backup
```

The file name can be specified as a character expression by enclosing the expression in parentheses. For example:

```
file_name = "Mailing.BAK"
DELETE FILE (file_name)
```

DELETE FILE is functionally equivalent to ERASE.

Also: ERASE, CLOSE

DELETED() — Database Function

Syntax: DELETED()

Action: Evaluates the delete status of the current record in a database file.

Return: <expL> true if the current record is marked for deletion, otherwise false.

Detail: To count all of the records in the Orders file that are marked for deletion:

```
USE Orders
COUNT FOR DELETED() TO marked
```

To check the delete status of a record in an unselected database file, use the alias name and pointer with the function:

```
* Check DELETED() status for Orders file.
? Orders->(DELETED())
```

Also: DELETE, RECALL, SET DELETED, ->

DESCEND() — Conversion Function

Syntax: DESCEND(<expression>)

Action: Evaluates a complemented form of the specified expression.

Return: Returns a complemented form that is the same data type as the parameter <expression>.

Detail: DESCEND() is used to create descending order index files and to find keys in those files. The following example illustrates:

```
USE Mailing
INDEX ON DESCEND(Last_Name) TO LastDesc
```

To SEEK keys in this index file, you must use DESCEND() as part of the SEEK expression. For example:

```
name = SPACE(20)
@ 10, 0 GET name
READ
SEEK DESCEND(name)
```

Also: INDEX, SEEK

DIR — OS Command

Syntax: DIR [<drive>:] [<skeleton>] | (<expC>)

Action: Displays a disk directory. By default, only .DBF files are shown.

Detail: If used with no parameters, DIR shows only the database files in the default disk directory. To show all files in the default directory:

```
DIR *.*
```

To show all format files in the active directory on the A: drive:

```
DIR A:*.FMT
```

To show the report form files in another directory on the D: drive:

```
skeleton = "D:\reports\*.FRM"
DIR (skeleton)
```

DISKSPACE() OS Function

Syntax: DISKSPACE([<N drive>])

Action: Evaluates the number of bytes available on the specified disk drive.

Return: <expN> amount of available disk space.

Detail: The numeric drive parameter uses 1 for drive A:, 2 for B:, 3 for C:, and so on. The following routine tells you whether there is more space available on drive C: or drive D:

```
d_space = DISKSPACE(4)
c_space = DISKSPACE(3)
? IF(c_space>d_space, "C: ", "D: ") + "has more space:"
```

If used with no parameter, DISKSPACE() refers to the DOS logged drive. It does not respect the current SET DEFAULT TO drive.

DISPLAY Output Command

Syntax: DISPLAY [[FIELDS] <expression list>] [<scope>] [OFF]
[TO PRINTER]
[TO FILE <txt filename> | (<C txt filename>)]

Action: By default, displays data from the current record in the active file.

Detail: The default scope of the DISPLAY command is the next record in the active file (i.e., NEXT 1). Use of the DISPLAY command requires an open database file in the current work area. Note that even though the expression list is optional, if you do not specify one, no information is displayed.

To suppress the record number and display all names:

```
USE Mailing
DISPLAY Last_Name, First_Name ALL OFF
```

To limit the fields that are displayed and to include calculations, constants or memory variables:

```
DISPLAY Last_Name, Phone, DATE() - Birthday, "Days old."
```

To display only selected records and write the result to a text file:

```
DISPLAY First_Name FOR Last_Name = "Jones" TO FILE Text
```

DISPLAY ALL and LIST are functionally identical commands.

Also: LIST, ?, TO PRINTER, USE

DO **Program Command**

Syntax: DO <prg filename> | <procedure name> [WITH <parameter list>]

Action: Executes the named program or procedure and, optionally, passes parameters.

Detail: To execute a procedure in a procedure file:

```
SET PROCEDURE TO Orders  && open Orders procedure file
DO Invoices              && execute PROCEDURE Invoices
```

To execute a program called Distance and pass three parameters:

```
result = 0
DO Distance WITH 53.64, 5.30, result

PROCEDURE distance
PARAMETERS rate, time, distance
* rate is 53.65, time is 5.30, distance is calculated
* and passed back to memvar, result, in calling program.
distance = rate * time
RETURN
```

Use PCOUNT() to determine the number of parameters passed to a Clipper procedure, and use TYPE() to determine the type of a passed parameter.

The file that you execute can also be written in C or assembly language. Parameters are passed by reference on the stack.

Also: SET PROCEDURE TO, PCOUNT(), PARAMETERS

DO CASE **Program Command**

Syntax: DO CASE
[CASE <L condition>
<commands> ...]
[OTHERWISE
<commands>]
END[CASE]

Action: Takes one of a number of paths based on the evaluation of a condition.

Detail: The following example uses DO CASE to determine which path to take based on a user's menu selection:

```
DO WHILE .T.
   * menuchoice() displays menu and returns user choice
   response = menuchoice()
   DO CASE
      CASE response == 0
         QUIT
      CASE response == 1
         DO AddRecs
      CASE response == 2
         DO EditRecs
      CASE response == 3
         DO Reports
      OTHERWISE
         @ 1, 5 SAY "Invalid choice, please reenter."
   ENDCASE
ENDDO
```

Note that END may be used as a short form of ENDCASE but can make your program harder to read and understand.

Also: IF

DO WHILE

Program Command

Syntax: DO WHILE <L condition>
<repeated commands>
[LOOP]
[EXIT]
END[DO]

Action: Performs a set of commands as long as the specified condition is true.

Detail: The DO WHILE loop is used to repeat a set of commands until a particular condition is no longer true. LOOP transfers control back to the beginning of the loop, and EXIT transfers control out of the loop to the command following the ENDDO. The following skeleton of a DO WHILE loop executes 100 times:

```
number = 1  && initialize counter
DO WHILE number <= 100  && perform loop 100 times
   .
   . <commands>
   .
   number = number + 1  && increment counter
ENDDO
```

The next example processes all records in the active file:

```
DO WHILE .NOT. EOF()
   .
   . <commands>
   .
   SKIP
ENDDO
```

Note that END may be used as a short form of ENDDO but can make your program harder to read and understand.

Also: FOR...NEXT

DOSERROR() **Debug Function**

Syntax: DOSERROR()

Action: Evaluates the error number of the last DOS error.

Return: <expN> representing the last DOS error that occurred.

Detail: DOSERROR() is used to trap errors that happen at the operating system level. The error numbers and their descriptions are listed below:

Error Number	DOS Error Message
1	Invalid function number
2	File not found
3	Path not found
4	Too many open files
5	Access denied
6	Invalid handle
7	Memory control blocks destroyed
8	Insufficient memory
9	Invalid memory block address
10	Invalid environment size specified
11	Invalid format file
12	Invalid access code
13	Invalid data
14	Reserved
15	Invalid drive specification
16	Cannot remove current directory
17	Not same device
18	No more files
19	Attempted write protect violation
20	Bad unit
21	Drive not ready error
22	Bad command
23	Data error
24	Bad request structure length
25	Seek
26	Unknown media type
27	Sector not found

28	No paper
29	Write fault
30	Read fault
31	General failure
32	Sharing violation
33	Lock violation
34	Invalid disk change
35	FCB unavailable
36	Sharing buffer overflow
37-49	Reserved
50	Network request not supported
51	Requested device not listening
52	Duplicate name on network
53	Network name not found
54	Network busy
55	Network device no longer exists
56	Network BIOS command limit exceeded
57	Network adapter hardware error
58	Incorrect response from netwrok
59	Unexpected network error
60	Incompatible remoter adapter
61	Print queue is full
62	Not enough space for print file
63	Print file deleted
64	Network name deleted
65	Network access denied
66	Network device type incorrect
67	Network name not found
68	Network name limit exceeded
69	Network BIOS session limit exceeded
70	Temporarily paused
71	Network request not accepted
72	Print or disk redirection paused
73-79	Reserved
80	Duplicate file name or file not found
81	Reserved
82	Cannot make directory entry
83	Fail on INT 24H
84	Too many redirections

85	Duplicate redirection
86	Invalid password
87	Invalid parameter
88	Network device fault

If no error occurs, DOSERROR() returns zero. You can check the function after each command that opens a file to determine if an error occurs and identify that error. The following example writes the error number to a text file:

```
SET ALTERNATE TO ErrorLog
USE Mailing
IF DOSERROR() > 0
   SET ALTERNATE ON
   ? DOSERROR(), "File open error on Mailing.DBF"
   SET ALTERNATE OFF
ENDIF
```

Also: FERROR()

DOW() — Date Function

Syntax: DOW(<expD>)

Action: Evaluates the numeric day of week (e.g., Sunday is 1) of the specified date.

Return: <expN> representing the day of the week.

Detail: The following example uses DOW() to create a backup file whose name depends on the day of the week. In this way, you can keep backups of a file for an entire week:

```
USE Orders

* today is the character string equivalent for DOW() to
* be used with macro substitution to create a unique
* file name for each day of the week.
today = STR(DOW(DATE()), 1)
```

```
* Orders2 is Monday's backup file, 3 is Tuesday's, etc.
COPY TO Orders&today

CLOSE DATABASES
```

Also: CDOW(), CMONTH(), CTOD(), DTOC(), MONTH(), DAY(), STR(), DATE(), YEAR()

DTOC() Conversion Function

Syntax: DTOC(<expD>)

Action: Converts the specified date to a character string.

Return: <expC> string equivalent of the specified date.

Detail: It is necessary to convert dates to character strings in order to include them in character expressions. For example, the following routine uses DTOC() to display a date value in the middle of some other text:

```
USE Customer
DO WHILE .NOT. EOF()
   IF Due_Date < DATE()
      ? "Customer "+ Cust_No +" : "+ DTOC(Due_Date) +"."
      ? LTRIM(STR(DATE() - Due_Date)) + " days overdue."
   ENDIF
   SKIP
ENDDO
CLOSE DATABASES
```

Also: CDOW(), CMONTH(), CTOD(), DTOC(), MONTH(), DAY(), STR(), DATE(), YEAR()

DTOS() Conversion Function

Syntax: DTOS(<expD>)

Action: Converts the specified date to a character string of the form CCYYMMDD.

Return: <expC> string equivalent of the specified date.

Detail: DTOS() is ideal for creating an index key expression that involves date and character fields. For example:

```
USE Mailing
INDEX ON Last_Name + DTOS(Birthday) TO LastBrth
```

DTOS() ignores the settings of SET DATE and SET CENTURY.

Also: INDEX, DTOC()

EJECT

Output Command

Syntax: EJECT

Action: Sends a form-feed, CHR(12), to the printer.

Detail: The following routine uses the EJECT command to eject the last form:

```
USE Orders
SELECT 2
USE Parts INDEX Part_No
SELECT Orders
SET RELATION TO Part_No INTO Parts
SET DEVICE TO PRINTER
DO WHILE .NOT. EOF()
   * Each customer starts on new form.
   @ 3, 70 SAY Cust_No
   old_cust = Cust_No
   line = 5
   DO WHILE Cust_No = old_cust
      @ line,  0 SAY Quantity PICTURE "999"
      @ line,  5 SAY Part_No + " " +;
                     LEFT(Parts->Descrip, 50)
      @ line, 51 SAY Parts->Price PICTURE "9999999.99"
```

```
        @ line, 62 SAY Parts->Price*Quantity ;
                   PICTURE "999999.99"
        line = line + 1
        SKIP
     ENDDO
  ENDDO
  EJECT                          && eject last form from printer
  SET DEVICE TO SCREEN
  CLOSE DATABASES
```

Also: SET DEVICE, SET PRINTER, CHR(), SETPRC()

EMPTY() — Comparison Function

Syntax: EMPTY(<expression>)

Action: Evaluates the expression and whether it is empty.

Return: <expL> true if the result of the expression is empty, otherwise false.

Detail: An EMPTY() expression is defined by its data type. The following table explains:

Type	EMPTY() Value
Character	"" null string or all blanks
Date	blank date
Logical	.F. false
Memo	No text
Numeric	0 zero

The following example uses EMPTY() to make sure the user enters something into an @...GET variable:

```
get_var = SPACE(5)
DO WHILE EMPTY(get_var)
   @ 10, 0 SAY "Enter a value" GET get_var
   READ
ENDDO
```

EOF() — Database Function

Syntax: EOF()

Action: Evaluates whether the record pointer is at the end of a database file.

Return: <expL> true if the record pointer is at the end of file, otherwise false.

Detail: The following program skeleton uses the EOF() function to process each record in the Orders database file:

```
USE Orders
DO WHILE .NOT. EOF()
   .
   . <commands>
   .
   SKIP
ENDDO
CLOSE DATABASES
```

To check the end of file condition for an unselected database file, use the alias name and pointer with the function. For example:

```
? Orders->(EOF())   && check EOF() status of Orders file
```

Also: BOF(), SKIP, DO WHILE, ->

ERASE — OS Command

Syntax: ERASE <filename> | (<C filename>)

Action: Erases the named file from the disk.

Detail: The ERASE command is similar to the DOS Erase command, except that it does not allow the use of wildcard characters. It is used to erase files from the disk, one at a time.

In order to use ERASE, the file that you want to erase must be closed and you must specify the entire file name, including the extension. For example, to erase the backup of the mailing list file:

```
CLOSE DATABASES         && make sure file is closed
ERASE Mailing.BAK       && erase database file backup
```

The file name can be specified as a character expression by enclosing the expression in parentheses. For example:

```
file_name = "Mailing.BAK"
ERASE (file_name)
```

ERASE is functionally equivalent to the DELETE FILE command.

Also: DELETE FILE, CLOSE

Error Codes — Error Info

Detail: Error code meanings from both DOS errors and Clipper internal errors.

Error Code	DOS Error
1	Invalid function number
2	File not found
3	Path not found
4	Too many open files
5	Access denied
6	Invalid handle
7	Memory control blocks destroyed
8	Insufficient memory
9	Invalid memory block address
10	Invalid environment size specified
11	Invalid format file
12	Invalid access code
13	Invalid data
14	Reserved
15	Invalid drive specification
16	Cannot remove current directory
17	Not same device
18	No more files
19	Attempted write protect violation
20	Bad unit
21	Drive not ready error

22	Bad command
23	Data error
24	Bad request structure length
25	Seek
26	Unknown media type
27	Sector not found
28	No paper
29	Write fault
30	Read fault
31	General failure
32	Sharing violation
33	Lock violation
34	Invalid disk change
35	FCB unavailable
36	Sharing buffer overflow
37-49	Reserved
50	Network request not supported
51	Requested device not listening
52	Duplicate name on network
53	Network name not found
54	Network busy
55	Network device no longer exists
56	Network BIOS command limit exceeded
57	Network adapter hardware error
58	Incorrect response from netwrok
59	Unexpected network error
60	Incompatible remoter adapter
61	Print queue is full
62	Not enough space for print file
63	Print file deleted
64	Network name deleted
65	Network access denied
66	Network device type incorrect
67	Network name not found
68	Network name limit exceeded
69	Network BIOS session limit exceeded
70	Temporarily paused
71	Network request not accepted
72	Print or disk redirection paused

73-79	Reserved
80	Duplicate file name or file not found
81	Reserved
82	Cannot make directory entry
83	Fail on INT 24H
84	Too many redirections
85	Duplicate redirection
86	Invalid password
87	Invalid parameter
88	Network device fault

Error Code	**Clipper Internal Error**
0	Error system integrity error
1	Evaluation stack underflow
2	Memory error
3	Memory error
4	Memory error
5	Memory error
6	Buffer error
7	Buffer error
8	Buffer error
9	Buffer error
10	Too many nested BEGIN SEQUENCEs
11	BEGIN/END SEQUENCE integrity error
12	Stack underflow after BEGIN/END SEQUENCE
14	SORT error
15	SORT error
16	Database not open
17	NTX file corrupted
18	NTX file corrupted
19	NTX file corrupted
20	NDX file key type error
21	NDX file key type error
22	NTX file key type error
92	SORT or INDEX error

Also: DOSERROR(), ERRORSYS, ERRORLEVEL(), FERROR()

ERRORLEVEL() — Program Function

Syntax: ERRORLEVEL([<expN>])

Action: Evaluates the current DOS error level and optionally resets its value.

Return: <expN> representing the current DOS error level.

Detail: The DOS error level provides a way for a program to terminate execution and pass a message to the next program to execute. Thus, ERRORLEVEL() is used almost exclusively with the Switch.EXE utility.

You set this function to tell Switch.EXE which program it is supposed to execute. The following example chains several programs together, assuming that only one can fit into memory at once:

```
* Menu.PRG
SET MESSAGE TO 24    && display menu messages on line 24

CLEAR
* Display menu prompts and messages.
@ 10,20 PROMPT "Exit";
       MESSAGE "Leave main menu."
@ 11,20 PROMPT "Add Records";
       MESSAGE "Append records to active database file."
@ 12,20 PROMPT "Edit Records";
       MESSAGE "Edit records in active database file."
@ 13,20 PROMPT "Print Labels";
       MESSAGE "Print mailing labels."
@ 14,20 PROMPT "Print Reports";
       MESSAGE "Print reports for active database file."
* Activate menu.
MENU TO choice

* Set ERRORLEVEL based on menu choice.
ERRORLEVEL(choice - 1)

* Quit back to Switch.
RETURN
```

Once Menu.PRG, Add.PRG, Edit.PRG, Labels.PRG, and Reports.PRG are compiled and linked as separate programs, you would issue at the DOS prompt to begin the application:

```
C> SWITCH Menu Add Edit Labels Reports
```

Each subprogram would use the function ERRORLEVEL(0) to recall the main menu program. The main menu would use ERRORLEVEL(0) to return to DOS.

Also: DOSERROR()

ERRORSYS — Error Procedure

Action: Called by Clipper on start-up.

Detail: If you want to substitute your own error function for any of Clipper's, you must also include your own ERRORSYS procedure.

All error system functions are contained in Clipper.lib. To override them, make an Error.prg containing this procedure and the error functions you want to use. Naming Error.obj in your link command will cause the linker to take the routines in it before those of the same name in Clipper.lib. If using overlays, Error.obj must link into the EXE file.

The error functions provided with Clipper are primitives. They allow you to design a high-level error system customized specifically for your application.

These are the Clipper functions that were rewritten for this error system presented in TRHELP. The source code is in the detail screen of each separate keyword.

```
FUNCTION  DB_ERROR    Handle database operation errors
PROCEDURE ERRORSYS    Called by Clipper on startup
FUNCTION  EXPR_ERROR  Handle expression errors
FUNCTION  MISC_ERROR  Handle miscellaneous errors
FUNCTION  OPEN_ERROR  Handle file-opening errors
FUNCTION  PRINT_ERRO  Handle printing errors
FUNCTION  UNDEF_ERRO  Handle undefined variable errors
```

These are the additional functions needed to complete the system. The source code for each additional function is presented below.

```
FUNCTION  err_msg     Display error message on screen
FUNCTION  err_write   Write error details to text file
FUNCTION  error_tone  Sound a tone to warn of error
FUNCTION  ret_debug   Sets ret_debug variable
```

Source Code

```
PROCEDURE ERRORSYS
* Syntax: None
* Action: Called by Clipper on startup.
* Note  : Executes once before the main program.
*

* Buffer in which to save and restore message windows.
PUBLIC msg_window   && used by err_msg() below

* Global message window coordinates are set in err_msg().
PUBLIC msg_top, msg_left, msg_bottom, msg_right

* Set system printer flag true when output is to printer.
PUBLIC sys_print    && used by err_msg() below

* Set system debug flag true to change error function
* return values interactively from the debugger.
PUBLIC sys_debug    && used by all error functions

* Comment out to prevent debugger activation on start-up.
ALTD()

RETURN
** ERRORSYS ************************************************


FUNCTION err_msg
* Syntax: err_msg( [<C message1> [, <C message2>]] )
* Action: Displays error message(s) on one or two lines in
*         window.  No parameters clear previous message.
```

```
* Return: Null string.
* Notes : Expects global variable 'sys_print' initialized
*            and set true when output is to the printer.
*         Expects global variable 'msg_window' in which to
*            save and restore message windows.
*         Expects global variables 'msg_top', 'msg_left',
*            'msg_bottom', 'msg_right' window coordinates.
*         All global variables are made PUBLIC in ERRORSYS
*            procedure.
*
*         Automatically adjusts to size and number of
*            messages.
*
*         Window coordinates are hard coded.  Change to
*            meet your application's display requirements.
*            Or, you could set this up to take msg_top and
*            and msg_left as the first two parameters.
*
PARAMETERS message1, message2
PRIVATE p_count, box_double
p_count = PCOUNT()      && count parameters

* Hard coded window coordinates, and double box frame.
msg_top    =  5
msg_left   = 15
box_double = CHR(201) + CHR(205) + CHR(187) + CHR(186) +;
             CHR(188) + CHR(205) + CHR(200) + CHR(186)

* Clear previous message, if any.
IF !EMPTY(msg_window)
  RESTSCREEN(msg_top, msg_left, msg_bottom, msg_right,;
             msg_window)
  msg_window = ""  && empty the buffer after clearing
ENDIF

* Exit after clearing message if no parameters are passed.
IF p_count==0
  RETURN ""
ENDIF
```

```
* Variable window coordinates set by length of message(s).
IF p_count==2
  msg_bottom = msg_t+3
  msg_right  = msg_l+3+ MAX( LEN(message1), LEN(message2) )
ELSEIF p_count==1
  msg_bottom = msg_t+2
  msg_right  = msg_l+3+ LEN(message1)
ENDIF

* sys_print is expected true when output is to the printer.
IF sys_print
   SET DEVICE TO SCREEN   && alternate may be SET PRINT OFF
ENDIF

* Display message.
msg_window = SAVESCREEN(msg_top, msg_left,;
                        msg_bottom, msg_right)
@ msg_top, msg_left CLEAR TO msg_bottom, msg_right
@ msg_top, msg_left, msg_bottom, msg_right BOX box_double
@ msg_t+1, msg_l+2 SAY message1
IF params==2
   @ msg_t+2, msg_l+2 SAY message2
ENDIF

IF sys_print
   SET DEVICE TO PRINT     && alternate may be SET PRINT ON
ENDIF
RETURN ""
** err_msg() ***********************************************


FUNCTION err_write
* Syntax: err_write(<C calling proc>,
*                   <C proc causing error>,
*                   <N line number>
*                   [,<C error info>
*                     [,<C attempted operation>
*                       [,<C/D/L/N operation parameter>]]])
* Return: Nothing.
```

```
* Action: Write error details to text file 'Errors.dbe'.
* Notes : Called from all *_error() functions to write
        :   details of error to the 'Errors.dbe' text file.
*       : This is lowest level file in the error system.
*       : Displays details on screen if cannot open file.
*
PARAMETERS error_proc, proc_name, file_line, error_info,;
           operation, info1, info2, info3, info4

PRIVATE p_count, m_info, crlf, j, k, filehandle,
        stringsize, writesize, error_file, err_string,
        data_type, retry

* Initialize local variables.
p_count    = PCOUNT()
error_file = "Errors.dbe"     && .dbe will copy with "*.db?"
crlf       = CHR(13)+CHR(10) && carriage-return + line-feed

* Build string of error details.
err_string = "Date/Time: " + DTOC( DATE() ) + "  " +;
                             TIME() + crlf +;
           "Procedure: " + proc_name + crlf +;
           "File Line: " + LTRIM(STR(file_line)) + crlf +;
           "ErrorProc: " + error_proc + crlf
IF p_count > 3
   err_string = err_string +"Error    : "+ error_info +crlf
ENDIF
IF p_count > 4
   IF ! EMPTY(operation)
      err_string = err_string +"Operation: "+operation+crlf
   ENDIF
ENDIF

* Add all the _<n> parameters to the string.
IF error_proc == "OPEN_ERROR"
   m_info = "File Name: "
ELSEIF error_proc == "UNDEF_ERRO"
   m_info = "Var Name : "
ELSE
```

```
      m_info = "Operand  : "
   ENDIF
   FOR j = 1 TO p_count - 5
      k = LTRIM(STR(j))            && string for macro
      data_type = TYPE("info&k")   && parameter data type
      err_string = err_string + m_info + "_&k <exp" +;
                   data_type + ">: "

      IF data_type == "D"      && date
         err_string = err_string + DTOC(info&k) + crlf
      ELSEIF data_type == "L"  && logical
         err_string = err_string + IF(info&k,".T.",".F.")+crlf
      ELSEIF data_type == "N"  && numeric
         err_string = err_string + LTRIM(STR(info&k)) + crlf
      ELSEIF data_type == "M"  && memo
         err_string = err_string + "memo" + crlf
      ELSEIF data_type == "A"  && array
         err_string = err_string + "array" + crlf
      ELSE                     && character
         err_string = err_string + info&k + crlf
      ENDIF
   NEXT

   * Add the DOS error if there is one.
   IF DOSERROR() != 0
      err_string = err_string + "DOS Error: " +;
                                 LTRIM(STR(DOSERROR())) + crlf
   ENDIF
   err_string = err_string + crlf   && record separator

   BEGIN SEQUENCE    && in case cannot open, create, or write
      * Test available disk space before writing.
      IF DISKSPACE() < LEN(err_string)+64
         error_tone()
         err_msg("ERROR: " +;
                 "Insufficient disk space for error file.",;
                 "Press any key to view details on screen...")
         CLEAR TYPEAHEAD
         INKEY(0)
```

```
      CLEAR
      ? err_string
      WAIT "Press any key to continue..."
      BREAK  && branches past END SEQUENCE below to return
   ENDIF

   * Open the error text file, or create one if not found.
   IF FILE(error_file)
      * Open error file in read-write mode.
      filehandle = FOPEN( error_file, 2 )
      IF FERROR() != 0     && could not open
         * Close database files and retry.
         CLOSE DATABASES
         filehandle = FOPEN( error_file, 2 )
         * Retry for two seconds in case of network delay.
         retry = 0
         DO WHILE FERROR() != 0 .AND. retry < 10
            INKEY(.2)
            filehandle = FOPEN( error_file, 2 )
            retry = retry + 1
         ENDDO
         * Still cannot open, probably not due to network.
         IF FERROR() != 0
            error_tone()
            err_msg("ERROR: " + LTRIM(STR(FERROR())) +;
                    " opening error file.",;
                    "Press any key to display error"+;
                    " details on screen...")
            CLEAR TYPEAHEAD
            INKEY(0)
            CLEAR
            ? err_string
            WAIT "Press any key to continue..."
            BREAK  && branches past END SEQUENCE below
         ENDIF
      ENDIF
      * Position to end of existing text in error file.
      FSEEK( filehandle, 0, 2 )          && end of file
```

```
ELSE
   * Create new error file.
   filehandle = FCREATE( error_file, 0 )
   IF filehandle == -1     && could not create
      * Close database files and retry.
      CLOSE DATABASES
      filehandle = FCREATE( error_file, 0 )
      * Still unable to create.
      IF filehandle == -1
         error_tone()
         err_msg("ERROR: " + LTRIM(STR(FERROR())) +;
                 " creating error file.",;
                 "Press any key to display error"+;
                 " details on screen...")
         CLEAR TYPEAHEAD
         INKEY(0)
         CLEAR
         ? err_string
         WAIT "Press any key to continue..."
         BREAK  && branches past END SEQUENCE below
      ENDIF
   ENDIF
ENDIF

* Write string to text file, and close it.
stringsize = LEN(err_string)
writesize = FWRITE( filehandle, err_string, stringsize )
FCLOSE( filehandle )

* Check for error in writing to or closing text file.
IF writesize != stringsize .OR. FERROR() != 0
   error_tone()
   err_msg("ERROR: " + LTRIM(STR(FERROR())) +;
           " writing error file.",;
           "Press any key to display error details"+;
           " on screen...")
   CLEAR TYPEAHEAD
   INKEY(0)
   CLEAR
```

```
      ? err_string
      WAIT "Press any key to continue..."
   ENDIF
END sequence
** err_write() ****************************************


FUNCTION error_tone
* Syntax: error_tone()
* Return: Nothing
* Action: Sound a siren-like tone to warn of error.
PRIVATE i
FOR i = 1 TO 3
   TONE(1650-(18*i), 3)
   TONE( 650-( 5*i), 3)
NEXT
** error_tone *****************************************


FUNCTION ret_debug
* Syntax: ret_debug( [<expL>] )
* Return: <expL> same as parameter,
*              or true if no parameter is passed.
* Action: Sets the ret_debug variable by entering an
*              expression.
* Notes : ret_debug() can be used by the E expression
*              evaluator in Clipper's debugger to set the
*              ret_debug memvar.
*           All error functions check the ret_debug memvar
*              to determine their return value.  By setting
*              ret_debug from the debugger, you can change
*              the function's return value interactively.
*
PARAMETERS true_false
IF PCOUNT() == 1
   ret_debug = true_false
ELSE
   ret_debug = .T.  && default true if no parameters passed
ENDIF
```

```
RETURN ret_debug
** ret_debug() ********************************************
```

Also: OPEN_ERROR(), DB_ERROR(), MISC_ERROR(), EXPR_ERROR(), UNDEF_ERRO(), PRINT_ERRO()

EXP() Numeric Function

Syntax: EXP(<expN>)

Action: Evaluates *e* raised to the power represented by the numeric expression.

Return: <expN>

Detail: The exponential function is used mostly in statistical and financial calculations. For example, to compute interest compounded continuously at a rate of r, you could use the following formula to find the return on each dollar:

```
EXP(r)
```

For example, if you invested $10,000.00 at an interest rate of 7% which is compounded continuously, the total amount of the investment (i.e., principal plus interest) at the end of the first period (e.g., a year) would be:

```
10000 * EXP(.07)
```

To query this expression:

```
? 10000 * EXP(.07)
```

Also: **, ^, LOG()

Expression **Language Info**

Detail: An expression is made up of data, operators, and functions which are all evaluated together to result in a value of a single data type.

An expression is referred to as <exp?>, or <? description>, where the question mark is an uppercase letter indicating the data type of the evaluated expression.

Error Code	Meaning
<expC>	"Hello, world" or "A string"
<D date>	DATE() or CTOD("07/04/88")
<N number>	123 or 4.567

You cannot mix different data types in a single expression without using functions to convert everything to a single data type.

```
string  =  "String" + STR(number) + DTOC(DATE())
date    =  DATE() - number
number  =  123 + VAL(string)
```

Some commands can take an expression list. Lists comprise two or more individual expressions separated or "delimited" by commas.

```
? string, number, date
```

Some commands require a literal or "constant" parameter and do not accept an expression. These are usually file or other names and must be given literally, i.e., without quote marks.

```
USE Filename
```

If the literal name is stored in a memory variable, that variable contains a character expression.

```
file_name = "Filename"
```

To use the stored expression where a literal is required, put the memvar name in parentheses to use the fast extended expression, or use the slower macro to retain compatibility with products lacking extended expressions.

```
USE &file_name          && macro expansion (slow)
USE (file_name)         && extended expression (fast)
```

Note that Clipper allows character strings up to 64K in length.

Also: Precedence, (), &, User-Defined Function

EXPR_ERROR() Error Function

Syntax: EXPR_ERROR(<C proc name>, <N file line>,
<C error info>, <parameter list>)

Action: Called by Clipper on expression error.

Return: Expression expected by the code that caused the error.

Detail: EXPR_ERROR() is called automatically by Clipper when an expression fails due to data type mismatch, zero divide, or array subscript range error.

The error function below is part of the TRHELP high-level error system used to replace Clipper's default EXPR_ERROR() function. It uses the other high-level error functions documented under the ERRORSYS procedure.

The <parameter list> contains a list of data items (operands) that caused the error. The number of operands varies depending upon the operation performed. E.g., MIN(2, "1") will pass two operands, 2 and "1".

```
FUNCTION EXPR_ERROR
* Syntax: <none>, called by Clipper on expression error.
* Return: <exp>, to replace result of failed expression.
* Action: Handle expression errors.
*
PARAMETERS proc_name, file_line, error_info, operation,;
           op_1, op_2, op_3, op_4, op_5

* Sound warning and display error message on screen.
error_tone()
err_msg("Error in expression from: " + proc_name +;
    ".  File line: " + LTRIM(STR(file_line)) + ".",;
    "Press any key to continue...")
```

```
* Write error details to file; pause for user response.
IF TYPE("op_5") != "U"
   err_write( PROCNAME(), proc_name, file_line,;
              error_info, operation, op_1, op_2, op_3,;
              op_4, op_5 )
ELSEIF TYPE("op_4") != "U"
   err_write( PROCNAME(), proc_name, file_line,;
              error_info, operation, op_1, op_2, op_3,;
              op_4,
ELSEIF TYPE("op_3") != "U"
   err_write( PROCNAME(), proc_name, file_line,;
              error_info, operation, op_1, op_2, op_3
ELSEIF TYPE("op_2") != "U"
   err_write( PROCNAME(), proc_name, file_line,;
              error_info, operation, op_1, op_2
ELSEIF TYPE("op_1") != "U"
   err_write( PROCNAME(), proc_name, file_line,;
              error_info, operation, op_1
ENDIF
CLEAR TYPEAHEAD
INKEY(0)
err_msg()  && clear error message

* Activate the debugger if sys_debug is true.
IF sys_debug
   err_msg("Change operands op_1 thru op_5 and set",;
           "variable 'ret_debug' true to retry.")
   ALTD()
   err_msg()
   IF TYPE("ret_debug") == "L"
      IF ret_debug
         RETURN &operation
      ENDIF
   ENDIF
ENDIF
** EXPR_ERROR() ****************************************
```

Also: ERRORSYS, OPEN_ERROR(), DB_ERROR(), MISC_ERROR(), UNDEF_ERRO(), PRINT_ERRO()

EXTERNAL **Extend Command**

Syntax: EXTERNAL <procedure list>

Action: Declares a list of symbols for the linker.

Detail: When you compile a program, all explicit references to functions and procedures are automatically compiled. However, some references cannot be recognized by the compiler because they do not come up until execution time.

For example, you may use a more obscure function, such as MEMOTRAN(), in a REPORT FORM definition but nowhere else in your application. Another example is if you call a procedure using macro substitution to form the procedure name. In cases like these, you must declare the function or procedure name as EXTERNAL in order for the linker to include them.

An example is:

```
EXTERNAL MEMOTRAN, MYFUNC, YOURFUNC
```

Also: &

FCLOSE() File Function

Syntax: FCLOSE(<N file handle>)

Action: Closes the file identified by the specified file handle.

Return: <expL> true if the file close was successful, otherwise false.

Detail: The following example illustrates how to do low level file input and output. FCLOSE() is demonstrated along with other file operations:

```
read_file = FOPEN("Names.TXT")   && open file to read
IF FERROR() # 0
   ? "File open unsuccessful. Error number is", FERROR()
   RETURN
ENDIF

write_file = FCREATE("New.TXT")  && create file to write
IF FERROR() # 0
   ? "File creation unsuccessful. Error number is",;
                                                 FERROR()
   RETURN
ENDIF

* Allocate a buffer into which to read the file.
buf_size = 2000
buffer   = SPACE(buf_size)
```

```
* Read buf_size bytes of file.
readbytes = FREAD(read_file, @buffer, buf_size)
IF FERROR() # 0
   ? "File read unsuccessful. Error number is", FERROR()
   RETURN
ENDIF

* Check number of bytes actually read.
IF readbytes < buf_size
   ? "File read less than " + LTRIM(STR(buf_size)) +;
     " bytes.  Continue? (Y/N)..."
   IF ! CHR(INKEY(0)) $ "Yy"
      RETURN
   ENDIF
ENDIF

MEMOEDIT(buffer)   && change file contents

* Write changed contents to new file.
FWRITE(write_file, buffer, buf_size)
IF FERROR() # 0
   ? "File write unsuccessful. Error number is",;
                                                FERROR()
   RETURN
ENDIF

FCLOSE(read_file)       && close old file
IF FERROR() # 0
   ? "File close unsuccessful. Error number is",;
                                                FERROR()
   RETURN
ENDIF

FCLOSE(write_file)      && close new file
IF FERROR() # 0
   ? "File close unsuccessful. Error number is",;
                                                FERROR()
ENDIF
RETURN
```

Also: FOPEN()

FCOUNT() Database Function

Syntax: FCOUNT()

Action: Evaluates the number of fields in a database file.

Return: <expN> representing the number of fields in the file structure.

Detail: The following example uses FCOUNT() to determine when to stop displaying the field names in the active database file:

```
FOR i = 1 TO FCOUNT()
   ? FIELDNAME(i)
NEXT
```

To check the field count in an unselected database file, use the alias name and pointer with the function. For example:

```
? Orders->(FCOUNT())  && Check FCOUNT() for Orders
```

Also: FIELDNAME(), ->

FCREATE() File Function

Syntax: FCREATE(<C filename> [, <N attribute>])

Action: Creates the named file and assigns a file attribute.

Return: <expN> representing the DOS file handle number of the new file.

Detail: The file attribute parameter is described in the table below:

Parameter	Attribute
0	Read/Write (default)
1	Read Only
2	Hidden
4	System

Caution: FCREATE() will overwrite an existing file without warning. For this reason, you might want to test for the existence of a file with FILE() before creating it.

FCREATE() ignores the status of SET DEFAULT TO.

The following example illustrates how to do low level file input and output. FCREATE() is demonstrated along with other file operations:

```
read_file  = FOPEN("Names.TXT")   && open file to read
IF FERROR() # 0
   ? "File open unsuccessful. Error number is", FERROR()
   RETURN
ENDIF

write_file = FCREATE("New.TXT")  && create file to write
IF FERROR() # 0
   ? "File creation unsuccessful. Error number is",;
                                                  FERROR()
   RETURN
ENDIF

* Allocate a buffer into which to read the file.
buf_size = 2000
buffer   = SPACE(buf_size)

* Read buf_size bytes of file.
readbytes = FREAD(read_file, @buffer, buf_size)
IF FERROR() # 0
   ? "File read unsuccessful. Error number is", FERROR()
   RETURN
ENDIF
```

```
* Check number of bytes actually read.
IF readbytes < buf_size
   ? "File read less than " + LTRIM(STR(buf_size)) +;
     " bytes.  Continue? (Y/N)..."
   IF ! CHR(INKEY(0)) $ "Yy"
      RETURN
   ENDIF
ENDIF

* Change file contents.
MEMOEDIT(buffer)

* Write changed contents to new file.
FWRITE(write_file, buffer, buf_size)
IF FERROR() # 0
   ? "File write unsuccessful. Error number is",;
                                               FERROR()
   RETURN
ENDIF

FCLOSE(read_file)       && close old file
IF FERROR() # 0
   ? "File close unsuccessful. Error number is",;
                                               FERROR()
   RETURN
ENDIF

FCLOSE(write_file)      && close new file
IF FERROR() # 0
   ? "File close unsuccessful. Error number is",;
                                               FERROR()
   RETURN
ENDIF
RETURN
```

Also: FOPEN(), FCLOSE(), FILE(), FWRITE()

FERROR() File Function

Syntax: FERROR()

Action: Evaluates whether the last File operation caused a DOS error.

Return: <expN> representing the DOS error from the last file operation.

Detail: FERROR() returns a value of zero if no file error occurs. The following example illustrates how to do low level file input and output. FERROR() is demonstrated along with other file operations:

```
read_file  = FOPEN("Names.TXT")   && open file to read
IF FERROR() # 0
   ? "File open unsuccessful. Error number is", FERROR()
   RETURN
ENDIF

write_file = FCREATE("New.TXT")  && create file to write
IF FERROR() # 0
   ? "File creation unsuccessful. Error number is",;
                                                  FERROR()
   RETURN
ENDIF

* Allocate a buffer into which to read the file.
buf_size = 2000
buffer   = SPACE(buf_size)

* Read buf_size bytes of file.
readbytes = FREAD(read_file, @buffer, buf_size)
IF FERROR() # 0
   ? "File read unsuccessful. Error number is", FERROR()
   RETURN
ENDIF
```

```
* Check number of bytes actually read.
IF readbytes < buf_size
   ? "File read less than " + LTRIM(STR(buf_size)) +;
     " bytes.  Continue? (Y/N)..."
   IF ! CHR(INKEY(0)) $ "Yy"
      RETURN
   ENDIF
ENDIF

* Change file contents.
MEMOEDIT(buffer)

* Write changed contents to new file.
FWRITE(write_file, buffer, buf_size)
IF FERROR() # 0
   ? "File write unsuccessful. Error number is",;
                                                FERROR()
   RETURN
ENDIF

FCLOSE(read_file)        && close old file
IF FERROR() # 0
   ? "File close unsuccessful. Error number is",;
                                                FERROR()
   RETURN
ENDIF

FCLOSE(write_file)       && close new file
IF FERROR() # 0
   ? "File close unsuccessful. Error number is",;
                                                FERROR()
ENDIF
RETURN
```

Also: DOSERROR(), Error codes

FIELDNAME() Database Function

Syntax: FIELD[NAME](<expN>)

Action: Evaluates the name corresponding to the field number in a database file structure.

Return: <expC> string representing the field name.

Detail: The following procedure lists all fields in the active database file:

```
PROCEDURE ListStru
FOR i = 1 TO FCOUNT()
   ? FIELDNAME(i)
NEXT
RETURN
```

To check the field name in an unselected database file, use the alias name and pointer with the function. For example:

```
? Orders->(FIELDNAME(1))  && check Orders field number 1
```

Also: FCOUNT(), TYPE(), LEN(), AFIELDS(), ->

FIELDS Database Keyword

Syntax: <command> FIELDS <field list>

Action: Limits the fields that a command processes.

Detail: Several commands in the language allow a FIELDS phrase to limit the fields that are processed by the command. These commands require an open database file and all fields in that file are processed unless a FIELDS phrase is specified. Two examples of the FIELDS phrase follow:

```
USE Orders
* Copy only two fields to new database file.
COPY TO Temp FIELDS Cust_No, Part_No

SET INDEX TO Part_No
```

```
* Totaled file contains only two fields.
TOTAL ON Part_No TO OrdTotal FIELDS Part_No, Quantity
```

Commands that allow a FIELDS phrase usually also allow a scope to limit the records that are processed. See Scope for more information.

Also: Scope

FILE() OS Function

Syntax: FILE(<C filename>)

Action: Evaluates whether the named file exists.

Return: <expL> true if the file is found, otherwise false.

Detail: The FILE() function is most often used to check for the existence of a file before attempting to open it. This is done to prevent an error and to provide a more tightly controlled environment when a file that you need cannot be found.

The following example prompts the user for a database file name and then checks for its existence before attempting to USE the file.

```
CLEAR
yourfile = SPACE(8)
* Continue prompting while the file name does not exist.
DO WHILE .T.
   @ 10, 10 SAY "Enter file name that you want to use:";
            GET yourfile   && does not include extension
   READ
   IF .NOT. FILE(TRIM(yourfile)+".DBF") && add extension
      @ 12, 0 SAY "File not found.  Please reenter."
   ELSE
      EXIT
   ENDIF
ENDDO
USE (yourfile)
```

The <C filename> parameter may contain wildcard characters "?" and "*". FILE() will return true if a single match is found.

Note that the FILE() function will search the directories defined by SET PATH TO if the named file cannot be found in the default directory. FILE() will return false only after searching all directories in the path.

Also: SET PATH TO

FIND — Search Command

Syntax: FIND <key value> | (<C key value>)

Action: Locates the first record in an indexed file whose key matches the value.

Detail: The following example uses FIND to locate the record belonging to someone with the Last_Name of Smith:

```
USE Mailing INDEX Last
FIND Smith
```

FIND can be used with a character expression if you enclose the expression in parentheses or use the macro operator:

```
name = "Smith"
Smith
FIND (name)   && is better than FIND &name
```

FIND can also be used with a numeric key. For example:

```
USE Mailing INDEX Age
FIND 33
```

If FIND does not find a match, the record pointer will be at EOF() unless SOFTSEEK is SET ON.

FIND originated in the language with interpreters where it was inconvenient to type quotes around character expressions. In programs, expressions are commonly used instead of literal values, making the SEEK command preferable to FIND.

Also: FOUND(), SEEK, SET EXACT, SET SOFTSEEK, SET INDEX TO, USE, INDEX, SET ORDER TO

FLOCK() Network Function

Syntax: FLOCK()

Action: Attempts to lock the active file, and returns the result of that attempt.

Return: <expL> true if the file lock was successful, otherwise false.

Detail: The following program demonstrates how to obtain a file lock:

```
SET EXCLUSIVE OFF && locking unnecessary if ON (default)
USE Orders
* This loop tries to lock the file 200 times,
* then prompts the user.
times = 0
DO WHILE times < 200 .AND. (!FLOCK())
   times = times + 1
   IF times = 200
      WAIT "Try file lock again? (Y/N) " TO response
      IF UPPER(response) = "Y"
         times = 0
      ELSE
         SET EXCLUSIVE ON
         CLOSE DATABASES
         RETURN  && cannot continue without file lock
      ENDIF
   ENDIF
ENDDO
SET FORMAT TO EditRecs
DO WHILE Part_No = "B235"  && lock was successful
   READ
   SKIP
ENDDO
SET EXCLUSIVE ON
CLOSE DATABASES  && releases file lock
```

Also: Networking, LOCK(), RLOCK(), UNLOCK

FOPEN() File Function

Syntax: FOPEN(<C filename> [, <N mode>])

Action: Opens the named file using the specified file attribute.

Return: <expN> representing the DOS file handle number of the file.

Detail: The mode parameter is described in the table below:

Parameter	Attribute
0	Read Only (default)
1	Write Only
2	Read/Write

The following example uses FOPEN() to open the NUL device in order to check how many file handles are available. It is useful to put in the start-up portion of an application to determine if all the necessary files can be opened.

```
* Validate number of file handles available.
handles = 10              && number of file handles needed
DECLARE array[handles]
FOR i = 1 TO handles
   array[i] = FOPEN("NUL")  && open NUL device read only
   IF array[i] < 0
      EXIT
   ENDIF
NEXT
i = i-1
FOR j = 1 TO i
   FCLOSE(array[j])         && close handles opened
NEXT
```

```
* Quit if insuficient number of handles.
IF i < handles
   ? "Not enough files can be opened. Check CONFIG.SYS."
   QUIT
ENDIF
.
. <application code>
.
```

See FREAD() for a description of how to do low-level file input/output.

Also: FCLOSE(), FREAD(), FWRITE()

FOR...NEXT — Program Command

Syntax: FOR <memvar> = <N begin> TO <N end> [STEP <N increment>]
<repeated commands>
[LOOP]
[EXIT]
NEXT

Action: Performs a set of commands a specified number of times.

Detail: The FOR...NEXT loop is used in a program when you need to repeat a set of commands a particular number of times. LOOP transfers control back to the FOR, the same as NEXT does. EXIT transfers control out of the loop to the command following the NEXT. The following skeleton of a FOR...NEXT loop executes 100 times:

```
FOR i = 1 TO 100  && perform loop 100 times
   .
   . <commands>
   .
NEXT
```

With this specialized loop, the loop counter is automatically initialized and incremented by 1 each time through the loop. The STEP option changes the increment value. For example:

```
even_sum = 0
* This loop adds together even numbers from 2 to 1000.
FOR i = 2 TO 1000 STEP 2   && counter increment set to 2
   even_sum = even_sum + i
NEXT
```

A particularly useful application for the FOR...NEXT loops is in processing arrays. The following example fills an array with database file names and displays them on the screen:

```
CLEAR
dbf_count = ADIR("*.dbf")
DECLARE dbf[dbf_count]
ADIR("*.dbf", dbf)
ASORT(dbf)
@ 0, 8 TO 10, 23 DOUBLE
@ 12, 5 SAY "Press Esc for more files"
FOR i = 1 TO dbf_count
   @ ((i-1)%9)+1, 10 SAY SPACE(12-LEN(dbf[i])) + dbf[i]

   * When the box is filled with file names, wait for
   * the user to press Esc.
   DO WHILE ((i-1) % 9) + 1 == 9 .AND. INKEY() != 27
      * This loop does nothing but wait for Esc keypress
   ENDDO
NEXT
```

Also: DO WHILE

FOUND() — Search Function

Syntax: FOUND()

Action: Evaluates whether or not the most recent Search command was successful.

Return: <expL> true if the Search command was successful, otherwise false.

Detail: The Search commands are FIND, SEEK, LOCATE, and CONTINUE. The following program skeleton illustrates the use of FOUND() with LOCATE/CONTINUE to process all records that meet a specific condition:

```
.
. <commands>
.
LOCATE FOR <field> == <expression>
DO WHILE FOUND()
   .
   . <commands>
   .
   CONTINUE
ENDDO
.
. <commands>
.
```

Also: LOCATE, CONTINUE, FIND, SEEK

FREAD() — File Function

Syntax: FREAD(<N file handle>, @<memory variable>, <N bytes>)

Action: Reads the specified number of bytes from a file into a memory variable.

Return: <expN> representing the number of bytes read.

Detail: The following example illustrates how to do low level file input and output. FREAD() is demonstrated along with other file operations:

```
read_file  = FOPEN("Names.TXT")   && open file to read
IF FERROR() # 0
   ? "File open unsuccessful. Error number is", FERROR()
   RETURN
ENDIF
```

```
write_file = FCREATE("New.TXT")  && create file to write
IF FERROR() # 0
   ? "File creation unsuccessful. Error number is",;
                                                           FERROR()
   RETURN
ENDIF

* Allocate a buffer into which to read the file.
buf_size = 2000
buffer   = SPACE(buf_size)

* Read buf_size bytes of file.
readbytes = FREAD(read_file, @buffer, buf_size)
IF FERROR() # 0
   ? "File read unsuccessful. Error number is", FERROR()
   RETURN
ENDIF

* Check number of bytes actually read.
IF readbytes < buf_size
   ? "File read less than " + LTRIM(STR(buf_size)) +;
     " bytes.  Continue? (Y/N)..."
   IF ! CHR(INKEY(0)) $ "Yy"
      RETURN
   ENDIF
ENDIF

* Change file contents.
MEMOEDIT(buffer)

* Write changed contents to new file.
FWRITE(write_file, buffer, buf_size)
IF FERROR() # 0
   ? "File write unsuccessful. Error number is",;
                                                           FERROR()
   RETURN
ENDIF
```

```
FCLOSE(read_file)       && close old file
IF FERROR() # 0
   ? "File close unsuccessful. Error number is",;
                                                FERROR()
   RETURN
ENDIF

FCLOSE(write_file)      && close new file
IF FERROR() # 0
   ? "File close unsuccessful. Error number is",;
                                                FERROR()
ENDIF
RETURN
```

Also: FOPEN(), FWRITE()

FREADSTR() File Function

Syntax: FREADSTR(<N file handle>, <N bytes>)

Action: Reads the specified number of characters from the specified file.

Return: <expC> string of the data read.

Detail: FREADSTR() returns a string, unlike FREAD() that places binary data into a preinitialized buffer. If the string being read by FREADSTR() contains a null character CHR(0), FREADSTR() will read the number of bytes told, but return only the characters before the null.

The following example illustrates FREADSTR() to read a single byte from a file:

```
handle = FOPEN("Invoice.FRM")
FSEEK(handle, 3)   && position file pointer to 3rd byte
```

```
* Read 1 character and convert it to a number.
number = BIN2I(FREADSTR(handle, 1))
.
. <commands>
.
FCLOSE(handle)
```

Also: FREAD(), FWRITE(), FCLOSE()

FSEEK() File Function

Syntax: FSEEK(<N file handle>, <N bytes> [, <N start>])

Action: Repositions the file pointer in the specified file.

Return: <expN> representing the new file position as number of bytes from the file beginning.

Detail: The start parameter is described in the table below:

Parameter	Meaning
0	Beginning of file
1	Current file position
2	End of file

When FSEEKing from a position, the sign of the <N bytes> parameter determines whether FSEEK() moves forward or backward. Positive numbers move from beginning toward end of file, and negative numbers move from end toward beginning of file.

Caution: it is possible to FSEEK() past the file end or before the file start!

The following example illustrates how to do low level file input and output. FSEEK() is demonstrated along with other file operations:

```
read_file  = FOPEN("Names.TXT")   && open file to read
IF FERROR() # 0
   ? "File open unsuccessful. Error number is", FERROR()
   RETURN
ENDIF

write_file = FCREATE("New.TXT")  && create file to write
IF FERROR() # 0
   ? "File creation unsuccessful. Error number is",;
                                               FERROR()
   RETURN
ENDIF

* Allocate a buffer into which to read the file.
buf_size = 2000
buffer   = SPACE(buf_size)

* Read buf_size bytes of file.
readbytes = FREAD(read_file, @buffer, buf_size)
IF FERROR() # 0
   ? "File read unsuccessful. Error number is", FERROR()
   RETURN
ENDIF

* Check number of bytes actually read.
IF readbytes < buf_size
   ? "File read less than " + LTRIM(STR(buf_size)) +;
     " bytes.  Continue? (Y/N)..."
   IF ! CHR(INKEY(0)) $ "Yy"
      RETURN
   ENDIF
ENDIF

* Change file contents.
MEMOEDIT(buffer)
```

```
* Write changed contents to new file.
FWRITE(write_file, buffer, buf_size)
IF FERROR() # 0
   ? "File write unsuccessful. Error number is",;
                                                FERROR()
   RETURN
ENDIF

FCLOSE(read_file)        && close old file
IF FERROR() # 0
   ? "File close unsuccessful. Error number is",;
                                                FERROR()
   RETURN
ENDIF

FCLOSE(write_file)       && close new file
IF FERROR() # 0
   ? "File close unsuccessful. Error number is",;
                                                FERROR()
ENDIF
RETURN
```

Also: FOPEN(), FREAD(), FWRITE()

FUNCTION — Program Command

Syntax: FUNCTION <function name>

Action: Names a user-defined function and marks its beginning.

Detail: The following program has an internal user-defined function that illustrates the use of RETURN with a value:

```
CLEAR
name = SPACE(50)
@ 10, 0 SAY "Enter your first name" GET name
READ
? capital(name)
```

```
FUNCTION capital
* Syntax: capital(<C name>)
* Action: Capitalizes the first letter of parameter and
*         converts remaining characters to lowercase.
PARAMETERS first_name
RETURN UPPER(SUBSTR(first_name, 1, 1)) + ;
       LOWER(SUBSTR(first_name, 2))
```

By default, parameters are passed to user-defined functions by value. There are, however, two exceptions to this rule. If the parameter is an array reference, the entire array is passed by reference, and if the parameter is a string, it is passed by reference.

To force a user-defined function parameter by reference, precede the parameter with the at (@) symbol. For example:

```
number = 123
change_it(@number)
? number              && returns 456

FUNCTION change_it
PARAMETERS num
num = 456
RETURN 0
```

Note that even though the function's return value has no meaning, it is still required in the RETURN command of a FUNCTION.

User-defined functions are particularly powerful when used in connection with the VALID clause of the @...GET command because they let you easily handle all the data validation tasks.

```
variable = SPACE(8)
@ 5, 5 GET variable VALID v_noblank()
READ

FUNCTION v_noblank
* Action: Does not allow blank entries in GET variable.
PRIVATE ret
ret = ! EMPTY(memvar)
IF ret
   @ 1,5 CLEAR TO 1,38
```

```
ELSE
   @ 1,5 SAY "Entry required, no blanks allowed."
ENDIF
RETURN ret
```

Also: PARAMETERS, User-Defined Function, VALID, PROCEDURE

FWRITE() File Function

Syntax: FWRITE(<N file handle>, <memory variable>, [, <N bytes>])

Action: Writes the specified number of bytes from a memory variable into a file.

Return: <expN> representing the number of bytes written.

Detail: The following example illustrates how to do low level file input and output. FWRITE() is demonstrated along with other file operations:

```
read_file  = FOPEN("Names.TXT")   && open file to read
IF FERROR() # 0
   ? "File open unsuccessful. Error number is", FERROR()
   RETURN
ENDIF

write_file = FCREATE("New.TXT")  && create file to write
IF FERROR() # 0
   ? "File creation unsuccessful. Error number is",;
                                                   FERROR()
   RETURN
ENDIF

* Allocate a buffer into which to read the file.
buf_size = 2000
buffer   = SPACE(buf_size)

* Read buf_size bytes of file.
readbytes = FREAD(read_file, @buffer, buf_size)
IF FERROR() # 0
```

```
      ? "File read unsuccessful. Error number is", FERROR()
      RETURN
   ENDIF

   * Check number of bytes actually read.
   IF readbytes < buf_size
      ? "File read less than " + LTRIM(STR(buf_size)) +;
        " bytes.  Continue? (Y/N)..."
      IF ! CHR(INKEY(0)) $ "Yy"
         RETURN
      ENDIF
   ENDIF

   * Change file contents.
   MEMOEDIT(buffer)

   * Write changed contents to new file.
   FWRITE(write_file, buffer, buf_size)
   IF FERROR() # 0
      ? "File write unsuccessful. Error number is",;
                                                  FERROR()
      RETURN
   ENDIF

   FCLOSE(read_file)       && close old file
   IF FERROR() # 0
      ? "File close unsuccessful. Error number is",;
                                                  FERROR()
      RETURN
   ENDIF

   FCLOSE(write_file)      && close new file
   IF FERROR() # 0
      ? "File close unsuccessful. Error number is",;
                                                  FERROR()
   ENDIF
   RETURN
```

Also: FCREATE(), FOPEN()

GETE() OS Function

Syntax: GETE(<expC>)

Action: Evaluates the specified operating system environmental variable.

Return: <expC> string contained in the environmental variable, or null string if there is no environment setting for the specified string.

Detail: To make the path setting the same as the one in DOS:

```
set_path = GETE("Path")
SET PATH TO &set_path
```

The following code fragment searches the DOS path for a file and prefixes the file name with the correct path name:

```
filename = "Required.TRM"
IF !FILE(filename)      && check current directory first
   dospath = GETE("path")
   DO WHILE !EMPTY(dospath)
      filepath = IF(";" $ dospath,;
                    SUBSTR(dospath,1,AT(";",dospath)-1),;
                    dospath)
      IF SUBSTR(filepath,-1)!="\"
         filepath = filepath+"\"
      ENDIF
```

```
            IF FILE(filepath+filename)
               filename = filepath+filename
               is_found = true
               EXIT
            ENDIF
            dospath = SUBSTR(dospath, AT(";",dospath)+1)
         ENDDO
         IF !is_found
            ? "File REQUIRED.TRM not found."
            QUIT
         ENDIF
      ENDIF
```

Examples of other DOS settings that you can access with GETE() are Comspec and Prompt.

GETE() is not case-sensitive to its parameter. Also, the function does not return error messages for settings that it does not understand because the DOS Set command can be used to assign arbitrary string names as environmental variables.

Also: SET PATH TO

GO **Database Command**

Syntax: GO[TO] <N record number> | BOTTOM | TOP

Action: Moves the record pointer directly to the specified record.

Detail: The GO command with a numeric expression is not used very often in application programs because you rarely can identify the record that you want by its record number. Instead, you usually access a record based on its index key value or some other location criteria (SEEK or LOCATE), or you access a record based on its position in the file relative to the current record with SKIP.

However, GO TOP and GO BOTTOM are quite often used as quick ways to move to the first and last record in a file. For example, GO TOP is almost always used after a SET FILTER TO command to make sure that the record pointer is positioned correctly. For example:

```
USE Mailing
SET FILTER TO State = "CA"
GO TOP
DO WHILE .NOT. EOF()
    .
    . <commands>
    .
ENDDO
CLOSE DATABASES
```

GO TOP and GO BOTTOM refer to the position in the index file if one is in use.

When specifying a <record number>, the command verb GO may be omitted, although the code is more readable by using it. Each line in the next example does exactly the same thing:

```
* These all move the record pointer to record number 96.
96
GO 96
GOTO 96
```

Also: SKIP, RECNO()

HARDCR()

Output Function

Syntax: HARDCR(<expC> | <memo field>)

Action: Replaces all soft carriage-returns in a string with hard carriage returns.

Return: <expC> string with no soft carriage-returns.

Detail: The primary purpose of HARDCR() is to display memo fields without soft carriage returns, which would normally be visible.

```
USE Mailing
SET DEVICE TO PRINTER
DO WHILE .NOT. EOF()
   ? HARDCR(Notes)       && Notes is a memo field
   SKIP
ENDDO
SET DEVICE TO SCREEN
CLOSE DATABASES
```

Soft carriage returns are defined as CHR(141) and hard carriage returns as CHR(13).

Also: MEMOEDIT(), STRTRAN()

HEADER() **Database Function**

Syntax: HEADER()

Action: Evaluates the length of the header record for a database file.

Return: <expN> representing the header size of the active file.

Detail: HEADER() is used to calculate the complete size of a database file before copying it. The following formula gives the size of the active database file:

```
(RECCOUNT() * RECSIZE()) + HEADER() + 1
```

Before copying a file to drive A:, you could first check to see if there is enough free disk space with the following routine:

```
USE File
IF DISKSPACE(1) >= (RECCOUNT()*RECSIZE()) + HEADER() + 1
   COPY TO A:Backup
ELSE
   ? "Not enough free diskette space for backup copy."
ENDIF
CLOSE DATABASES
```

To check the size of the header record for an unselected database file, use the alias name and pointer with the function:

```
? Orders->(HEADER())  && check HEADER() for Orders
```

Also: DISKSPACE(), RECCOUNT(), RECSIZE(), ->

I2BIN() — Conversion Function

Syntax: I2BIN(<N integer>)

Action: Converts numeric value to a string representing a 16-bit unsigned integer.

Return: <expC> two-byte string formatted as binary integer.

Detail: I2BIN() is used when writing information to file formats that have numbers stored as 16-bit integers, least significant byte first.

The following example opens a file, reads a binary number, changes it, and writes the new number back to the file. The example assumes that there is an integer in bytes 3 and 4 of the file that you want to access:

```
handle = FOPEN("Invoice.TXT", 2)     && read/write mode
FSEEK(handle, 3)     && move file pointer to 3rd position
readbuffer = SPACE(2)                 && initialize buffer
* Read 2 bytes and convert to number.
number = BIN2I(FREAD(handle, @readbuffer, 2))
@ 5, 5 SAY "Enter a new number" GET number
READ
FSEEK(handle, 3)     && move file pointer to 3rd position
* Convert changed number to binary format; write 2 bytes
FWRITE(handle, I2BIN(number), 2)
FCLOSE(handle)
```

Also: FREAD(), BIN2L(), BIN2W(), BIN2I(), L2BIN()

IF — Program Command

Syntax: IF <L condition>
    <commands>
[ELSEIF <L condition>
    <commands> ...]
[ELSE
    <commands>]
END[IF]

Action: Takes one of several paths based on the evaluation of a condition.

Detail: The following example uses the IF programming construct to count the number of males and females in the mailing list:

```
USE Mailing
STORE 0 TO males, females
DO WHILE .NOT. EOF()
   IF Sex = "M"
      males = males + 1
   ELSE
      females = females + 1
   ENDIF
   SKIP
ENDDO
? "Males:", males
? "Females:", females
CLOSE DATABASES
```

The next example illustrates the ELSEIF option. An IF construct that includes ELSEIF statements is identical in functionality to a DO CASE construct.

```
DO WHILE .T.
   response = MenuDisp()   && display menu, get response
   IF response = 0
      QUIT
   ELSEIF response = 1
      DO AddRecs
   ELSEIF response = 2
      DO EditRecs
   ELSEIF response = 3
      DO Reports
   ELSEIF response = 4
      DO Labels
   ENDIF
ENDDO
```

Note that END may be used as a short form of ENDIF but can make your program harder to read and understand.

Also: DO CASE, IF()

IF() — Program Function

Syntax: IF(<L condition>, <true expression>, <false expression>)

Action: Returns the value of the second or third parameter based on the condition.

Return: Expression of same data type as the returned parameter.

Detail: This function can shorten the code and execution time for certain simple IF constructs. For example:

```
IF Married
   ? "Not available"
ELSE
   ? First_Name + " " + Phone
ENDIF
```

could be replaced by:

```
? IF(Married, "Not available", First_Name + " " + Phone)
```

This is very useful in REPORT FORMs and other places where the structured IF...ENDIF command is not allowed.

IF() is identical in functionality to IIF().

Also: DO CASE, IF, IIF()

IIF() Program Function

Syntax: IIF(<L condition>, <true expression>, <false expression>)

Action: Returns the value of the second or third parameter based on the condition.

Return: Expression of same data type as the returned parameter.

Detail: The IIF() function can shorten the code and execution time for certain simple IF constructs. For example:

```
IF Married
   ? "Not available"
ELSE
   ? First_Name + " " + Phone
ENDIF
```

could be replaced by:

```
? IIF(Married, "Not available", First_Name +" "+ Phone)
```

This is very useful in REPORT FORMs and other places where the structured IF...ENDIF command is not allowed.

IIF() is identical in functionality to IF().

Also: DO CASE, IF, IF()

INDEX — Index Command

Syntax: INDEX ON <expression> TO <index filename> | (<C index filename>)

Action: Creates an index for the active file using the expression as the key.

Detail: To create an index for the Parts file based on the part number field:

```
USE Parts
INDEX ON Part_No TO Part_No
CLOSE DATABASES
```

To open the file for later use:

```
USE Parts INDEX Part_No
```

To create a more complex index for the Orders file based on the part number and customer number:

```
USE Orders
INDEX ON Cust_No + Part_No TO CustPart
CLOSE DATABASES
```

Note that by default, index files are created with a .NTX extension. However, if you have linked Ndx.OBJ the default changes to .NDX.

Use SET UNIQUE to create unique indexes.

Caution: INDEX expressions must evaluate to the same length for every record. Thus, you cannot use TRIM(Field) because the length would vary.

Also: SET INDEX TO, USE, REINDEX, FIND, SEEK, SET ORDER TO, SET UNIQUE, SORT, DESCEND(), DTOS()

Index — External Program

Syntax: Index <dbf filename>

Action: Creates an index file.

Detail: Index.PRG must be compiled and linked in order for you to use it. This utility is included with Clipper so that you can create the necessary index files for your applications. When you execute Index.EXE by typing

```
INDEX <database filename>
```

from DOS, you are prompted to enter the index file name and key expression.

Also: INDEX

INDEXEXT() — Index Function

Syntax: INDEXEXT()

Action: Evaluates what kind of index files are currently being used.

Return: <expC> string representing the index extension, either Clipper's "NTX" or the dBASE III compatible "NDX".

Detail: By default, Clipper programs use .NTX index files. If an application is linked with Ndx.OBJ, the program will use .NDX files. INDEXEXT() allows you to determine which type of index file is being used by the current application by returning either "NTX" or "NDX".

The following example attaches the appropriate extension onto an index file name so that the FILE() function can be used to test for its existence:

```
USE Mailing
name = "Last." + INDEXEXT()
IF .NOT. FILE(name)
   INDEX ON Last_Name TO Last
ELSE
   SET INDEX TO Last
ENDIF
```

Also: FILE()

INDEXKEY() — Index Function

Syntax: INDEXKEY(<N order>)

Action: Evaluates the index key expression of the specified index file.

Return: <expC> string containing the specified index's expression, or a null string if there is no index file corresponding to the specified order.

Detail: The parameter for INDEXKEY() corresponds to the order number of the index file (i.e., its position in the INDEX file list). An parameter of zero refers the function to the controlling index file regardless of its position.

The following function shows the index key expression for all open index files for the active database file, and allows you to select which one you want to use as the controlling index:

```
FUNCTION Ndxswitch
CLEAR
i = 1
DO WHILE .NOT. EMPTY(INDEXKEY(i))
   @ i, 1 SAY STR(i, 1) + ". " + NDX(i)
   i = i + 1
ENDDO

* If there is at least one open index file, choose one.
IF i > 1
   choice = 1
   @ i+1, 1 SAY "Which index do you want to use?";
            GET choice PICTURE "9" RANGE 1, i-1
   READ
   SET ORDER TO choice
ENDIF
RETURN .T.
```

Also: USE, SET INDEX TO, SET ORDER TO, INDEXORD()

INDEXORD() — Index Function

Syntax: INDEXORD()

Action: Evaluates which of the open index files is the controlling index.

Return: <expN> representing the current index order.

Detail: The following function shows the index key expression for all open index files for the active database file, and allows you to select which one you want to use as the controlling index. INDEXORD() is used to determine if the user's selection changes the order or not.

```
FUNCTION Ndxswitch
CLEAR
original = INDEXORD()
i = 1
DO WHILE .NOT. EMPTY(INDEXKEY(i))
   @ i, 1 SAY STR(i, 1) + ". " + NDX(i)
   i = i + 1
ENDDO

* If there is at least one open index file, choose one.
IF i > 1
   choice = 1
   @ i+1, 1 SAY "Which index do you want to use?";
            GET choice PICTURE "9" RANGE 1, i-1
   READ
   SET ORDER TO choice
   IF INDEXORD() != original
      RETURN .T.
   ENDIF
ENDIF
RETURN .F.
```

Also: SET ORDER TO, USE, SET INDEX TO, INDEXKEY()

INKEY() **Program Function**

Syntax: INKEY([<expN>])

Action: Evaluates a numeric equivalent for a key pressed.

Return: <expN> ASCII value if the key has one, otherwise the value listed below, or zero if there is no keypress.

Detail: The numeric parameter for INKEY() is used to specify the number of seconds that INKEY() waits for a response. Specifying a parameter of zero stops the program until a key is pressed. INKEY() does not pause when not passed a parameter.

The following example illustrates the use of the INKEY() function to test for a particular keypress. The routine displays the date and time on the screen until the user presses Q or q:

```
CLEAR
@ 24, 0 SAY "Type Q to stop clock display."
DO WHILE .T.
   @ 0, 60 SAY DTOC(DATE()) + "  " + TIME()
   x = INKEY(1)      && updates clock every second
   IF CHR(x) $ "Qq"
      EXIT
   ENDIF
ENDDO
```

Non-Printable Keys

For the values returned by the non-printable keys, use the following table:

Key	INKEY()	Key	INKEY()	Key	INKEY()
Alt F10	-39	(no keypress)	0	Alt Q	272
Alt F9	-38	Home	1	Alt W	273
Alt F8	-37	^Right Arrow	2	Alt E	274
Alt F7	-36	PgDn	3	Alt R	275
Alt F6	-35	Right Arrow	4	Alt T	276
Alt F5	-34	Up Arrow	5	Alt Y	277
Alt F4	-33	End	6	Alt U	278
Alt F3	-32	Del	7	Alt I	279
Alt F2	-31	Backspace	8	Alt O	280
Alt F1	-30	Tab	9	Alt P	281
Ctrl F10	-29	^J	10	Alt A	286
Ctrl F9	-28	^K	11	Alt S	287
Ctrl F8	-27	^L	12	Alt D	288
Ctrl F7	-26	Enter	13	Alt F	289
Ctrl F6	-25	^N	14	Alt G	290
Ctrl F5	-24	^O	15	Alt H	291
Ctrl F4	-23	^P	16	Alt J	292
Ctrl F3	-22	^Q	17	Alt K	293
Ctrl F2	-21	PgUp	18	Alt L	294
Ctrl F1	-20	Left Arrow	19	Alt Z	300
Shift F10	-19	^T	20	Alt X	301
Shift F9	-18	^U	21	Alt C	302
Shift F8	-17	Ins	22	Alt V	303
Shift F7	-16	^End	23	Alt B	304
Shift F6	-15	Down Arrow	24	Alt N	305
Shift F5	-14	^Y	25	Alt M	306
Shift F4	-13	^Left Arrow	26	Alt 1	376
Shift F3	-12	Esc	27	Alt 2	377
Shift F2	-11	F1	28	Alt 3	378
Shift F1	-10	^Home	29	Alt 4	379
F10	-9	^PgDn	30	Alt 5	380
F9	-8	^PgUp	31	Alt 6	381
F8	-7	^Backspace	127	Alt 7	382
F7	-6	^2	259	Alt 8	383
F6	-5	Backtab	271	Alt 9	384
F5	-4			Alt 0	385
F4	-3			Alt –	386
F3	-2			Alt =	387
F2	-1				

Note that INKEY() returns the numeric ASCII equivalent for the control and printable keys so you can use CHR() to convert the INKEY() value to the ASCII character for comparison:

```
? "Are you sure? (Y/N)..."
IF CHR(INKEY(0)) $ "Yy"    && wait for user input
   QUIT
ENDIF
```

Test Program

This program is useful for finding the INKEY() value for any particular key:

```
x = 0
DO WHILE x != 27  && Esc key exits
   x = INKEY(0)
   ? x
ENDDO
```

If you run this program and press the key you are interested in, its INKEY() value is displayed on the screen. Press Esc to stop the program at any time.

Also: SET TYPEAHEAD TO, CLEAR TYPEAHEAD, SET KEY, ASC(), CHR(), LASTKEY(), NEXTKEY()

INPUT — Input Command

Syntax: INPUT [<C prompt>] TO <memory variable>

Action: Waits for keyboard input and saves it in a memvar that it creates.

Detail: Although INPUT is most commonly used to create a numeric memory variable, it can be used to create a memory variable of any type. The variable type depends on the user's typed response. In fact, the response to INPUT can be any valid expression, so that a user can type a field name, a function, or a more complicated expression. For example, if in response to:

```
INPUT "Enter your age " TO m_age
```

a user typed the following:

```
CTOD("12/20/59")
```

m_age would be a date-type memory variable containing the date.

You can use TYPE() to make sure the user enters a particular data type. For example:

```
DO WHILE .T.
   INPUT "Enter your age: " TO m_age
   IF TYPE("m_age")=="N" .OR. TYPE("m_age")=="U"
      EXIT
   ELSE
      ? "Invalid entry, number required."
   ENDIF
ENDDO
```

If the user responds to the INPUT command by pressing Enter without typing anything else, the INPUT command is terminated without creating the memory variable.

Also: ACCEPT, WAIT, @...GET, TYPE()

INT() — Numeric Function

Syntax: INT(<expN>)

Action: Evaluates the integer portion of the specified number.

Return: <expN> representing the integer portion of the number.

Detail: The following example calculates the approximate age of individuals in the Mailing list using the INT() function to display the age in years:

```
USE Mailing
LIST INT((DATE() - Birthday) / 365.00)
```

Note that INT() truncates rather than rounds.

Also: ROUND()

ISALPHA() Character Function

Syntax: ISALPHA(<expC>)

Action: Evaluates whether the first character in the specified string is an alphabetic letter.

Return: <expL> true if the first character is a letter from A-Z or a-z, otherwise false.

Detail: You can use ISALPHA() anytime you want to test a character string to make sure the first character is a letter. The applications of this function are not very widespread, but it can be useful in testing data appended from foreign file types. Also, it is common for various key fields to begin with a letter. Whatever your application for this function, it is illustrated below to show its result with various strings:

```
ISALPHA("124ABC")     && returns .F.
ISALPHA("A124")       && returns .T.
ISALPHA("c876")       && returns .T.
ISALPHA("#AZDO")      && returns .F.
```

ISALPHA() is not case-sensitive. It returns true for any string that begins with a letter, uppercase or lowercase.

Also: ISUPPER(), ISLOWER(), TYPE()

ISCOLOR() Environment Function

Syntax: ISCOLOR() | ISCOLOUR()

Action: Evaluates whether you are operating in a color or monochrome environment.

Return: <expL> true if your monitor is being driven by a color card, otherwise false.

Detail: The following section of code tests the ISCOLOR() function before using SET COLOR TO. Using this code in the setup portion of an application, you can use the application on either a monochrome or a color system:

```
* Program: Main.PRG
* Syntax : Main [MONO]
* Action : Application start-up.
* Note   : Optional MONO parameter forces monochrome
*        : attributes on color systems.  This is useful
*        : on systems with color cards and monochrome
*        : monitors, or anywhere color attributes fail.
*
PARAMETERS param1
sys_mono = IF(PCOUNT()==1, UPPER(param1)=="MONO", .F.)

IF ISCOLOR() .AND. (!sys_mono)
   s_standard = "W+/B"            && standard SAY
   s_enhanced = "W+/G"            && enhanced GET
   s_backgr   = "B"               && background
   s_border   = "G"               && border
   s_unselect = "W+/BG"           && active unselected GET
   s_noprompt = "W/B"             && inaccessible prompts
   s_warning  = "W+/R*"           && warning message
   s_blank    = "G/G"             && blank, for password
ELSE           && monochrome
   s_standard = "W+"              && standard SAY
   s_enhanced = "I"               && enhanced GET
   s_backgr   = "N"               && background
   s_border   = "N"               && border
   s_unselect = "I"               && active unselected GET
   s_noprompt = "W"               && inaccessible prompts
   s_warning  = "W+*"             && warning message
   s_blank    = "X"               && blank, for password
ENDIF
```

```
* Save user's screen attributes and set ours.
user_row = ROW()
SAVE SCREEN TO scr_user
SET COLOR TO (s_standard +","+ s_enhanced +","+;
              s_backgr   +","+ s_border   +","+;
              s_unselect)

* Begin application.
DO main_menu && application's top level until user quits

* Quit to the operating system.
RESTORE SCREEN FROM scr_user
@ user_row-1, 0 SAY ""         && reposition cursor
QUIT
```

Also: SET COLOR TO

ISLOWER() — Character Function

Syntax: ISLOWER(<expC>)

Action: Evaluates whether the first character in the string is a lowercase letter.

Return: <expL> true if the first character is a lowercase letter, otherwise false.

Detail: ISLOWER() is a special case of the ISALPHA() function that can be used when you must test for a lowercase letter. The function is illustrated below to show its result with various strings:

```
ISLOWER("1abcde")   && returns .F.
ISLOWER("A124")     && returns .F.
ISLOWER("a8B6")     && returns .T.
ISLOWER("#A876")    && returns .F.
```

Also: ISUPPER(), ISALPHA(), LOWER()

ISPRINTER() Environment Function

Syntax: ISPRINTER()

Action: Evaluates whether or not the print device is ready to print.

Return: <expL> true if the current print device is on line and ready, otherwise false.

Detail: ISPRINTER() is used to avoid errors that involve printing when the printer is not ready (e.g., turned off, off line, out of paper). The following example illustrates:

```
CLEAR
DO WHILE ! ISPRINTER()
   @ 10, 0 SAY "Printer is not ready.  Continue? (Y/N)"
   response = INKEY(0)
   IF CHR(response) $ "Nn"
      RETURN
   ELSEIF CHR(response) $ "Yy"
      EXIT
   ENDIF
ENDDO
USE Mailing
REPORT FORM MailList TO PRINTER
CLOSE DATABASES
```

Also: SET DEVICE TO

ISUPPER() Character Function

Syntax: ISUPPER(<expC>)

Action: Evaluates whether the first character in the string is an uppercase letter.

Return: <expL> true if the first character is an uppercase letter, otherwise false.

Detail: ISUPPER() is a special case of the ISALPHA() function that can be used when you must test for an uppercase letter. The function is illustrated below to show its result with various strings:

```
ISUPPER("124ABC")   && returns .F.
ISUPPER("Axbc")     && returns .T.
ISUPPER("a8B6")     && returns .F.
ISUPPER("#AZTF")    && returns .F.
```

Also: ISLOWER(), ISALPHA(), UPPER()

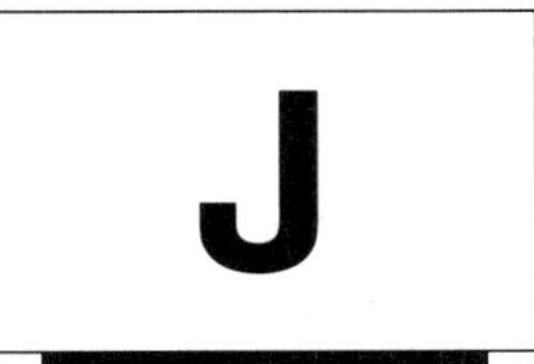

JOIN

Database Command

Syntax: JOIN WITH <alias> | (<C alias>)
TO <new dbf filename> | (<C new dbf filename>)
FOR <L condition>
[FIELDS <field list>]

Action: Performs a join operation between two database files to produce a new file.

Detail: JOIN scans all records in the WITH file for each record in the current file and writes a new record to the TO file every time the FOR condition is true. This can produce a very large file as the maximum possibility is the number of records in one file times the number of records in the other.

The following example uses the JOIN command to produce a file of customers and their orders. All fields are included in the joint file except those with duplicate names:

```
USE Customer
SELECT 2
USE Orders
SELECT Customer
JOIN WITH Orders TO Cust_Ord;
                 FOR Cust_No = Orders->Cust_No
CLOSE DATABASES
```

```
USE Cust_Ord   && open joint file and list contents
LIST
```

Note that both the WITH alias name and the TO file name can be represented as character expressions by enclosing the expressions in parentheses. For example:

```
alias_name = "Orders"
to_name    = "Cust_Ord"
JOIN WITH (alias_name) TO (to_name);
     FOR Cust_No = Orders->Cust_No
```

Also: SET RELATION TO, TOTAL, SORT, FIELDS

KEYBOARD — Input Command

Syntax: KEYBOARD <expC>

Action: Stuffs the typeahead buffer with the specified character string.

Detail: The following example illustrates how to use KEYBOARD to make a self-running program. Note that a carriage return and other non-printable keys are simulated using the CHR() function with the INKEY() value of the key:

```
CLEAR TYPEAHEAD    && clear stray characters from buffer
KEYBOARD "Mailing"+CHR(13) && input used in next command
ACCEPT "Enter the name of file to use: " TO file_name
USE &file_name
CLEAR
CLEAR TYPEAHEAD
KEYBOARD "Tom" +CHR(13)+ "Rettig" +CHR(13)+;
   "9300 Wilshire Bl." +CHR(13)+ "Suite 470" +CHR(13)+;
   "Beverly Hills" +CHR(13)+ "CA" + "90212" + ;
   "(213)272-3784" + "122059" + " 28" +CHR(30)+;
   "This sentence goes in Memo field." +CHR(31)+CHR(23)
SET FORMAT TO Mailing
APPEND BLANK
READ             && record is stuffed with KEYBOARD string
```

Note that if CLEAR TYPEAHEAD is issued after a KEYBOARD command, the KEYBOARD characters will be cleared from the typeahead buffer along with any pre-typed characters. On the other hand, if you do not issue CLEAR TYPEAHEAD before each KEYBOARD command, you cannot be sure that there are no stray characters in the typeahead buffer because there is nothing to prevent the user from typing on the keyboard. KEYBOARD "" (null string) is functionally the same as CLEAR TYPEAHEAD.

```
KEYBOARD ""        && same as CLEAR TYPEAHEAD
```

SET TYPEAHEAD TO 0 renders the KEYBOARD command useless since no character can be saved to the typeahead buffer.

To use KEYBOARD effectively, place the command as close as possible before the statement for which you want it to serve as input. This can be any command or function that accepts keyboard input.

Non-Printable Keys

Non-printable keys can be KEYBOARDed using CHR(), as long as they have an ASCII value between zero and 127 inclusive.

Key	ASCII	Key	ASCII	Key	ASCII
(no keypress)	0	^K	11	Ins	22
Home	1	^L	12	^End	23
^Right Arrow	2	Enter	13	Down Arrow	24
PgDn	3	^N	14	^Y	25
Right Arrow	4	^O	15	^Left Arrow	26
Up Arrow	5	^P	16	Esc	27
End	6	^Q	17	F1	28
Del	7	PgUp	18	^Home	29
Backspace	8	Left Arrow	19	^PgDn	30
Tab	9	^T	20	^PgUp	31
^J	10	^U	21	^Backspace	127

Also: SET TYPEAHEAD TO, CLEAR TYPEAHEAD, INKEY(), CHR()

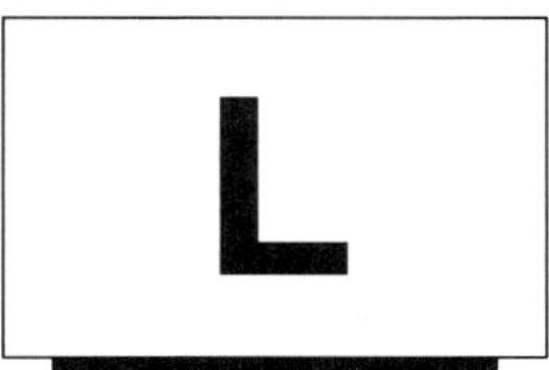

L2BIN() — Conversion Function

Syntax: L2BIN(<N long integer>)

Action: Converts a number to a string representing a 32-bit signed integer.

Return: <expC> four-byte string formatted as binary integer.

Detail: L2BIN() is used when writing information to file formats that have numbers stored as 32-bit (long) integers, least significant byte first.

The following example opens a file, reads a binary number, changes it, and writes the new number back to the file. The example assumes that there is a long integer in bytes 7 through 10 of the file that you want to access:

```
handle = FOPEN("Invoice.TXT", 2)      && read/write mode
FSEEK(handle, 7)    && move file pointer to 7th position
readbuffer = SPACE(4)                && initialize buffer

* Read 4 bytes and convert to number.
number = BIN2L(FREAD(handle, @readbuffer, 4))
@ 5, 5 SAY "Enter a new number" GET number
READ
FSEEK(handle, 7)    && move file pointer to 7th position
```

```
* Convert changed number to binary and write 4 bytes.
FWRITE(handle, L2BIN(number), 4)
FCLOSE(handle)
```

Also: FREAD(), BIN2I(), BIN2W(), I2BIN(), BIN2L()

LABEL FORM — Output Command

Syntax: LABEL FORM <lbl filename> | (<C lbl filename>)
[SAMPLE] [<scope>]
[TO PRINTER]
[TO FILE <txt filename> | (<C txt filename>)]

Action: Displays labels for the active file using the definition in the label file.

Detail: To print sample labels for the Mailing list and make sure the labels are aligned correctly in the printer:

```
USE Mailing
LABEL FORM Party SAMPLE TO PRINTER
```

To display labels on the screen without printing them:

```
LABEL FORM Party
```

To write them to a text file for later use:

```
LABEL FORM Party TO FILE Mail
```

Both the label file name and the text file name can be specified as character expressions by enclosing the expression in parentheses. For example:

```
lbl_file = "Party"
txt_file = "Mail"
LABEL FORM (lbl_file) TO FILE (txt_file)
```

Also: TO PRINTER, RL

LASTKEY() Input Function

Syntax: LASTKEY()

Action: Evaluates the last key pressed from a wait state.

Return: <expN> INKEY() value representing the last key pressed.

Detail: A wait state is produced by executing any command or function that waits for or traps user input. Specifically, these commands and functions are: ACCEPT, ACHOICE(), DBEDIT(), INKEY(), INPUT, MENU TO, MEMOEDIT(), READ, and WAIT.

The following example uses LASTKEY() in the user function Save_It to determine what key was pressed in an ACHOICE() menu:

```
USE Mailing
num_fields = FCOUNT()
* choices[] and i are used by the UDF for ACHOICE().
DECLARE fields[num_fields], choices[num_fields]
i = 0
* Fill the fields[] array with Mailing list field names.
AFIELDS(fields)
SET COLOR TO W+/N,,,,W/N
CLEAR

@ 24, 0 SAY "Press Enter to select fields, Esc to list."
userchoice = ACHOICE(1,10,23,35, fields, .T., "Save_It")

* Display fields that user selected.
CLEAR
DO WHILE .NOT. EOF()
   FOR x = 1 TO i
       temp = choices[x]
       ?? &temp
   NEXT
   ?
   SKIP
ENDDO
RETURN
```

```
FUNCTION Save_It
PARAMETERS mode, element, row_num
key = LASTKEY()
DO CASE
   * If Enter pressed, field name is marked and saved.
   CASE key = 13
      i = i + 1
      choices[i] = fields[element]
      @ row_num + 1, 9 SAY CHR(175)
      RETURN 2
   CASE key = 27
      RETURN 0
   OTHERWISE
      RETURN 2
ENDCASE
```

Also: INKEY(), NEXTKEY(), KEYBOARD

LASTREC() — Database Function

Syntax: LASTREC()

Action: Evaluates the number of records in a database file.

Return: Returns a numeric value representing the number of records in the file.

Detail: LASTREC() is the functional equivalent of RECCOUNT(). It is a quick way of telling how many records are in the active database file. The function is sometimes used to calculate the size of a database file before copying it. The following formula gives the size of a resulting SDF text file:

```
LASTREC() * RECSIZE()
```

Before copying an SDF file to drive A:, you could first check to see if there is enough free disk space with the following routine:

```
USE <database file>
IF DISKSPACE(1) >= LASTREC() * RECSIZE()
   COPY TO A:<text file> SDF
ELSE
   ? "Not enough free disk space for copy."
ENDIF
CLOSE DATABASES
```

Note that the return value of LASTREC() is not affected by any filter condition that might be in effect. This function returns the actual number of physical records in the database file.

To check the record count for an unselected database file, use the alias name and pointer with the function. For example:

```
? Orders->(LASTREC())  && check LASTREC() for Orders
```

LASTREC() and RECCOUNT() are functionally identical.

Also: RECNO(), RECSIZE(), COUNT, RECCOUNT(), ->, HEADER()

LEFT() — Character Function

Syntax: LEFT(<expC>, <N length>)

Action: Extracts a substring of designated length starting with the first character.

Return: <expC> substring.

Detail: To extract the first word from the character field Notes that is known to contain a list of words separated by commas:

```
USE Mailing
? LEFT(Notes, AT(",", Notes) - 1)
```

The AT() function locates the position of the first comma in Notes. Subtracting one from this location insures that the comma does not appear in the LEFT() substring.

Also: SUBSTR(), RIGHT()

LEN() Character Function

Syntax: LEN(<expC> | <array>)

Action: Evaluates the length of a string or the number of elements in an array.

Return: <expN> representing the string length or number of array elements.

Detail: When trying to find the length of a string in a character field, make sure you use the TRIM() function. Otherwise, LEN() returns the full length of the field as defined in the file structure. For example:

```
USE Mailing
? LEN(Last_Name)            && returns 20
? LEN(TRIM(Last_Name))      && returns 5
```

If a field is known to have leading blanks, you may also want to use LTRIM() to avoid counting those in the length.

If the LEN() parameter is the name of an array, LEN() returns the number of array elements. For example:

```
DECLARE names[20]
? LEN(names)            && returns 20
```

Also: TYPE(), TRIM(), LTRIM(), RECSIZE()

Line External Program

Syntax: Line <filename> [line number]

Action: Lists the named program adding line numbers.

You must specify the file name extension when you use the Line utility. If you do not include the optional line number parameter, the entire program is listed with line numbers. For example:

```
Line Main.PRG
```

The line number parameter causes the Line utility to list only specified lines in the file. The five lines before and ten lines after the specified line number are listed. For example, to display lines 2 through 17:

```
Line Main.PRG 7
```

To print the file, redirect the output to the printer using DOS redirection:

```
Line Main.PRG > PRN
```

To create a new file with line numbers, redirect the output to a specified file using DOS redirection:

```
Line Main.PRG > Newfile.txt
```

Link

Link Info

Syntax: LINK <obj filename list> [, <exe filename>
[, <map filename>
[, <lib filename list>
[/<option>]]]]

Action: Links the named object files using the Microsoft Linker.

Detail: This is the Microsoft linker, version 3.51 or higher. Common Link command line options are described below. Link is not case sensitive to these options:

Option	**Meaning**
/he	Help. Lists all link options.
/se:<number>	Number of segments. Use to increase the 128 default if you get "too many segments" error.
/noe	Ignore duplicate symbols. Use only if you get an error telling you to do so.

The object and library file name lists are lists in which the file names are separated by a single space or a plus (+) sign. By default, the .EXE file that is generated has the same name as the first object file in the list, and no .MAP file is generated. Thus, in order to generate a .MAP file, you must specify the map file name parameter. Any of the optional filename parameters can be omitted using a comma instead of the parameter.

The following example links the file Main.OBJ that is known to reference functions in both Clipper.LIB and Extend.LIB:

```
LINK Main,,,Clipper Extend
```

The next example links several object files using an additional library file called TR.LIB. A map file is generated, and segments are increased to 256:

```
LINK Main AddRecs EditRecs,,Map_Out,CLIPPER TR /se:256
```

The LINK parameters can be taken from one or more ASCII text files called response files by preceding the file name with an @ symbol. No file extension is assumed for response files. When you use a response file, each parameter must be on a separate line; however, you can continue a line using a plus sign the same as you do with the semicolon in Clipper. For example, the response file, Resp1, listed below

```
Main + AddRecs +
EditRecs
Exe_Out
Map_Out
Clipper Tr Extend
```

could be used with LINK as follows:

```
LINK @Resp1 /se:512
```

Also: Make

LIST **Output Command**

Syntax: LIST [[FIELDS] <expression list>] [<scope>] [OFF]
[TO PRINTER]
[TO FILE <txt filename> | (<C txt filename>)]

Action: By default, lists data from all records in the active file.

Detail: Use of the LIST command requires an open database file in the current work area. Note that even though the expression list is optional, if you do not specify one, no information is displayed.

The default scope of the LIST command is all records in the active file (i.e., ALL).

To suppress the record number and print the display:

```
USE Mailing
LIST Last_Name, First_Name OFF TO PRINTER
```

To limit the fields that are displayed and to include calculations, constants, or memory variables:

```
LIST Last_Name, Phone, DATE() - Birthday, "Days old."
```

To display only selected records and write the result to a text file:

```
LIST First_Name FOR Last_Name = "Jones" TO FILE Text
```

DISPLAY ALL and LIST are functionally identical commands.

Also: DISPLAY, ?, @...SAY, TO PRINTER, USE

LOCATE — Search Command

Syntax: LOCATE [<scope>]

Action: Locates a record in the active file using conditions that you specify.

Detail: You can have a separate LOCATE/CONTINUE condition for each of the 255 database file work areas. CONTINUE is designed to evaluate the correct condition for the current work area. For example:

```
USE Orders
SELECT 2
USE Parts
SELECT Orders
LOCATE FOR Cust_No == "5135"
```

```
DO WHILE FOUND()
   m_part = Part_No
   SELECT Parts
   LOCATE FOR Part_No = m_part
   SELECT Orders
   ? Cust_No, Part_No, Parts->Price
   * Even though the most recently issued LOCATE was for
   * the Parts work area, this CONTINUE resumes the
   * search for "5135" because Orders is SELECTed.
   CONTINUE
ENDDO
CLOSE DATABASES
```

Also: CONTINUE, FOUND(), SEEK, FIND

LOCK() — Network Function

Syntax: LOCK()

Action: Attempts a record lock, and returns the result of that attempt.

Return: <expL> true if the record lock was successful, otherwise false.

Detail: LOCK() and RLOCK() are identical functions. The following example illustrates the use of LOCK() to obtain a record lock before editing a record with an @...GET/READ sequence of commands:

```
SET EXCLUSIVE OFF  && locking unnecessary if ON
USE Mailing
LOCATE FOR First_Name = "Gloria"
IF FOUND()
   * This loop tries to lock the record 200 times,
   * then prompts you.
   times = 0
   DO WHILE times < 200 .AND. (!LOCK())
      times = times + 1
```

```
            IF times = 200
               WAIT "Try record lock again? (Y/N)" TO response
               IF UPPER(response) = "Y"
                  times = 0
               ELSE
                  RETURN  && to try a different record
               ENDIF
            ENDIF
         ENDDO
         @ 10, 5 SAY "First Name " GET First_Name
         @ 17, 5 SAY "Phone      " GET Phone
         READ
      ENDIF
      UNLOCK  && releases record lock and program continues...
```

Also: Networking, RLOCK(), FLOCK(), UNLOCK, SET EXCLUSIVE, USE

LOG() — Numeric Function

Syntax: LOG(<expN>)

Action: Evaluates the natural logarithm (base *e*) of the specified number.

Return: <expN> representing the natural logarithm of the number.

Detail: A base 10 logarithm function is not provided but, using the natural logarithm function, you can calculate it. For example, to find the base 10 logarithm of any postive number x, use the following formula:

```
LOG(x) / LOG(10)
```

Change the denominator to any base logarithm you want. For example, to find the base 2 logarithm of x:

```
LOG(x) / LOG(2)
```

Also: EXP()

LOWER() — Character Function

Syntax: LOWER(<expC>)

Action: Converts the specified character string to all lowercase letters.

Return: <expC> string consisting of all lowercase letters.

Detail: The following example uses LOWER() and UPPER() to format the display of the first and last names in the mailing list so that the names appear with an initial capital letter and the rest in lowercase:

```
USE Mailing
LIST UPPER(LEFT( First_Name,  1)) +;
     LOWER(RIGHT(First_Name, 19)),;
     UPPER(LEFT( Last_Name,   1)) +;
     LOWER(RIGHT(Last_Name,  19))
CLOSE DATABASES
```

Characters other than alphabetic letters are not affected.

Also: UPPER(), ISLOWER()

LTRIM() — Character Function

Syntax: LTRIM(<expC>)

Action: Removes leading blanks from the specified character string.

Return: <expC> string with no leading blank spaces.

Detail: The following example uses the LTRIM() and RTRIM() functions to make sure that there are no leading and trailing blank spaces in the first and last name fields:

```
USE Mailing
? LTRIM(RTRIM(First_Name)), LTRIM(RTRIM(Last_Name))
CLOSE DATABASES
```

LTRIM() is used frequently with the STR() function because converting a number to a string often results in leading blanks.

Also: RTRIM(), TRIM(), STR()

LUPDATE() Database Function

Syntax: LUPDATE()

Action: Evaluates the date on which a database file was last updated.

Return: <expD> representing the date of last update for the active file.

Detail: The following program skeleton uses LUPDATE() to determine whether the Orders file has been updated today:

```
USE Orders
IF LUPDATE()==DATE()  && file has been changed today
   @ 10, 0 SAY "File has already been updated.  "+;
               "Continue? (Y/N)"
   IF ! CHR(INKEY(0)) $ "yY"
      CLOSE DATABASES
      RETURN
   ENDIF
ENDIF
.
. <commands to update file>
.
```

Updating a file includes adding new records and changing existing ones.

To check the date of last update for an unselected database file, use the alias name and pointer with the function in parentheses. For example:

```
? Orders->(LUPATE())
```

Also: ->

Make

External Program

Syntax: Make [/N] <description filename>

Action: Allows you to compile and link only the changed programs in a group.

Detail: In order to use the Make utility, you must create a description file that describes how to compile and link the programs in your application. Once this is done, Make is able to keep track of which individual programs in the completed application have been changed and need to be recompiled.

The description file is a standard ASCII text file that contains rules telling what files are dependent on one another as well as the necessary compile and link commands. The rules must take on the following format:

```
<filename>: <dependent filename list>
```

The dependent file name list is separated by spaces. Rules and other commands in the description file can be continued using the forward slash character "/" at the end of a line. Avoid blank spaces at end of line.

The /N option tells Make to display the commands that would be executed without actually executing them.

The following example illustrates the simplest type of make description file:

```
#  MAIN.MAK

# ASM files
AS.OBJ: AS.ASM
  masm AS;

# C files
MS_C.OBJ: MS_C.C
  cl /AL /c /FPa /Gs /Oalt /Zl MS_C.C

TURBO_C.OBJ: TURBO_C.C
  tcc -c -f- -G -ml -O -Z TURBO_C.C

# PRG files
MAIN.OBJ: MAIN.PRG
  clipper MAIN -m

FILE1.OBJ: FILE1.PRG
  clipper FILE1 -m

# Linking (assumes use of Main.lnk file).
MAIN.EXE: MAIN.OBJ FILE1.OBJ AS.OBJ MS_C.OBJ TURBO_C.OBJ
   PLINK86 @main
```

MAX() Comparison Function

Syntax: MAX(<expN1>, <expN2>) | MAX(<expD1>, <expD2>)

Action: Evaluates the maximum of the two specified numbers or dates.

Return: <expN | D> depending on the data type of the parameters passed.

Detail: The following example uses the MAX() function to raise the salary of each employee with a particular job code to a minimum of $50,000. After this REPLACE command is executed, no person with a job code of P will earn less than $50,000; however, the salary for those people who were already earning at least that much will not change:

```
USE Employee
REPLACE Salary WITH MAX(50000, Salary) FOR Job_Code="P"
CLOSE DATABASES
```

MAX() can be applied to date values to determine which one is chronologically greater than the other. For example:

```
? MAX(DATE(), CTOD("03/11/89"))
```

Also: MIN()

MEMOEDIT() Input Function

Syntax: MEMOEDIT([<memo field> | <expC>
[,<N top row> [,<N left col>
[,<N bottom row> [,<N right col>
[,<L edit> [,<C UDF name>
[, <N line length> [, <N tab size>
[, <N start row> [, <N start col>
[, <N relative row> [, <N relative col>]]]]]]]]]]]])

Action: Displays and optionally allows editing of a memo field or character string.

Return: <expC> edited string.

Detail: Note that MEMOEDIT(), although designed to edit memo fields, can also be used to edit long character strings.

Any MEMOEDIT() parameter can be omitted by using a dummy parameter (i.e., a logical .F.) in its place; however, omitting the memo field name does not make any sense. If you replace the UDF with a dummy parameter in order to use subsequent parameters, you cannot edit the memo field.

The display window defaults to the entire screen. The edit flag defaults to .T. so that you can edit the memo field rather than simply displaying it. The UDF (user function) has no default. The line length defaults to the window width, the tab size to four, and the starting row and column to zero. The final two parameters are useful if the entire memo field does not fit inside the edit window because you can have MEMOEDIT()

begin editing on line five, column one, and have this positioned in the first line (line zero) of the edit window.

The following example allows you to edit the Letter memo field in the Mailing list in a window. The UDF is very simple. It performs the default action for all keys except Alt-W which is used for the word wrapping toggle:

```
CLEAR
USE Mailing
@ 1, 1 TO 10, 31
DO WHILE .NOT. EOF()
   @ 3, 3 CLEAR TO 8, 29
   new = MEMOEDIT(Letter, 3, 3, 8, 29, .T., "u_keys")
   IF LASTKEY() = 23
      REPLACE Letter WITH new
   ENDIF
   SKIP
ENDDO
CLOSE DATABASES

FUNCTION u_keys
key = LASTKEY()
ret = 0
IF key == 273  && Alt-W
   ret = 34
ENDIF
RETURN ret
```

Even without a user function to process keystrokes, MEMOEDIT() provides a reasonably full-featured range of navigation and editing keys that are standard and cannot be changed:

Fixed Key	**Action**
UpArrow, Ctrl-E	Move up one line
DownArrow, Ctrl-X	Move down one line
LeftArrow, Ctrl-S	Move left one character
RightArrow, Ctrl-D	Move right one character
Ctrl-LeftArrow, Ctrl-A	Move left one word
Ctrl-RightArrow, Ctrl-F	Move right one word
Home	Beginning of line
End	End of line
Ctrl-Home	Beginning of current window
Ctrl-End	End of current window
PgUp	Previous window
PgDn	Next window
Ctrl-PgUp	Beginning of text
Ctrl-PgDn	End of text
Enter	Move to beginning of next line
Del	Delete character at cursor
Backspace	Delete character left of cursor
Tab	Insert tab character or spaces
Printable characters	Insert character

These keys are also provided by MEMOEDIT() and can be changed:

Configurable Key	**Action**
Ctrl-Y	Delete current line
Ctrl-T	Delete word right
Ctrl-B	Format paragraph
Ctrl-V, Ins	Toggle insert mode
Ctrl-W	Save and exit
Esc	Cancel and exit, return unchanged

Three numeric parameters are automatically passed by MEMOEDIT() to the user function. These are its mode, current row number, and current column number.

```
FUNCTION u_keys
PARAMETERS mode, cur_row, cur_col
```

The possible modes are listed below:

Mode	Meaning
0	MEMOEDIT() is idle
1	Keystroke exception, data unchanged
2	Keystroke exception, data changed
3	MEMOEDIT() has just been invoked

A keystroke exception is any key that is pressed, other than the Fixed Keys listed above.

MEMOEDIT() calls the user function with a mode of 3 immediately upon start-up. In this mode, you can RETURN requests to configure word-wrap, scroll, or insert. MEMOEDIT() calls the user function repeatedly, remaining in the start-up mode until the UDF returns a zero. If word-wrap is on when the start-up mode completes, the entire memo is formatted to the current line length.

MEMOEDIT() calls the user function once, with a mode of zero, when there is no pending key to process. In this mode, you can update any screen displays you wish.

MEMOEDIT() calls the user function whenever a key exception occurs. You can configure these keys to operate as you wish by returning a number to MEMOEDIT() that tell it what to do.

Return	Action
0	Perform default action for keystroke
1 – 31	Perform action corresponding to key value. For example, 4 is the value for Right Arrow, and the default action for this key value is to move the cursor one character to the right.
32	Ignore keystroke
33	Use keystroke as data
34	Toggle automatic word wrapping
35	Toggle scrolling within window
100	Move cursor to next word
101	Move cursor to end of window

You can also use KEYBOARD from the user function to stuff strings or other keystrokes into MEMOEDIT().

```
FUNCTION u_memoedit
* Syntax: <none>, called by MEMOEDIT().
* Action: UDF for MEMOEDIT() editing.
* Note  : Enables these keystrokes:
*            F5 = start of current line
*            F6 = end of current line
*            F9 = delete current line
*         Alt-I = insert blank line above current line
*         Alt-X = exit (with save)
*
PARAMETERS mode, line, column
PRIVATE keypress, ret
ret = zero   && default is to return the actual keypress
keypress = LASTKEY()     && get the last keypress
IF mode==1 .OR. mode==2  && enable alternate keys
   DO CASE
      CASE keypress ==  -4   && F5, beginning of line
         ret = 1   && Home
      CASE keypress ==  -5   && F6, end of line
         ret = 6   && End
      CASE keypress ==  -8   && F9, delete line
         * Does not work if a macro is assigned to F9.
         ret = 25  && Ctrl-Y
      CASE keypress == 279   && Alt-I, insert blank line
         KEYBOARD IF(READINSERT(),;
                     REPLICATE(CHR(19),COL()) +CHR(13)+;
                         CHR(5),;
                     REPLICATE(CHR(19),COL()) +CHR(22)+;
                         CHR(13) + CHR(22) + CHR(5))
      CASE keypress == 301   && Alt-X, exit
         ret = 23  && Ctrl-W
   ENDCASE
ENDIF
RETURN ret
```

Note that paragraph formatting and word-wrap insert soft carriage-returns, CHR(141), which can cause display problems. These can be replaced with hard carriage-returns, CHR(13), with the HARDCR() function.

Also: MEMOLINE(), MEMOREAD(), MEMOTRAN(), MEMOWRIT(), MLPOS(), MLCOUNT(), HARDCR()

MEMOLINE() Output Function

Syntax: MEMOLINE(<memo field> | <expC>
[, <N line width> [, <N line number>
[, <N tab size> [, <L word wrap>]]]])

Action: Extracts a single line of text from the specified memo field or string.

Return: <expC> string representing one line of text at a given width.

Detail: The following example uses MEMOLINE() to print the contents of a memo field at a line width of 65:

```
SET MARGIN TO 8
SET PRINTER ON
USE Mailing
DO WHILE .NOT. EOF()
   ? "Dear " + First_Name
   ?
   num_lines = MLCOUNT(Letter, 65)
   FOR x = 1 TO num_lines
      ? MEMOLINE(Letter, 65, x)
   NEXT
   EJECT
   SKIP
ENDDO
CLOSE DATABASES
SET PRINTER OFF
SET MARGIN TO       && reset margin setting to default
```

Also: MEMOEDIT(), MEMOREAD(), MEMOTRAN(), MEMOWRIT(), MLPOS(), MLCOUNT(), HARDCR()

MEMOREAD() — Input Function

Syntax: MEMOREAD(<C filename>)

Action: Reads the named text file and saves its contents as a character string.

Return: <expC> contents of the text file.

Detail: The following example replaces a memo field with the contents of a text file.

```
USE Mailing
REPLACE Letter WITH MEMOREAD("Letter.TXT")
```

Note that you must specify the file extension if there is one.

Also: MEMOEDIT(), MEMOLINE(), MEMOTRAN(), MEMOWRIT(), MLPOS(), MLCOUNT(), HARDCR()

MEMORY() — Environment Function

Syntax: MEMORY(<expN>)

Action: Evaluates the amount of available memory.

Return: <expN> representing the amount of free memory in kilobytes.

Detail: The numeric parameter for MEMORY() must evaluate to zero. All other values cause the function to return zero. To query this function, use:

```
? MEMORY(0)
```

Use MEMORY(0) to test if there is enough available memory for a particular operation:

```
* Multiply by 1024 converts MEMORY's kilobytes to bytes.
IF MEMORY(0)*1024 > 100000
   RUN <external program>
ELSE
   ? "Insufficient memory."
ENDIF
```

MEMOTRAN() Output Function

Syntax: MEMOTRAN(<memo field> | <expC>
[, <C hard return replacement>
[, <C soft return replacement>]])

Action: Replaces carriage return/line feed pairs.

Return: <expC> string with the replacements.

Detail: MEMOTRAN() is designed to replace carriage returns in a memo field. By default, hard carriage returns, CHR(13), are replaced with semicolons and soft carriage returns, CHR(141), with blank spaces. This default is designed to make the resulting string compatible for printing with REPORT FORM, but you can replace the formatting characters to suit your own needs.

The following example replaces hard returns with soft returns, while leaving the soft carriage returns intact:

```
USE Mailing
new_form = MEMOTRAN(Letter, CHR(141), CHR(141))
```

To actually replace the memo field, you would use:

```
REPLACE Letter WITH MEMOTRAN(Letter, CHR(141), CHR(141))
```

Also: MEMOEDIT(), MEMOREAD(), MEMOLINE(), MEMOWRIT(), MLPOS(), MLCOUNT(), HARDCR()

MEMOWRIT() — Output Function

Syntax: MEMOWRIT(<C filename>, <memo field> | <expC>)

Action: Writes the contents of the memo field or character string to the named file.

Return: <true> if the file write was successful, otherwise false.

Detail: To write the contents of a memo field to a text file for some other use, as with another program, you would use MEMOWRIT(). The following example writes the Letter from a record in the Mailing list to a text file called Letter.TXT:

```
USE Mailing
is_okay = MEMOWRIT("Letter.TXT", Letter)
IF ! is_okay
   ? "File write error."
ENDIF
CLOSE DATABASES
```

Note that you must specify a file name extension if you want the resulting file to have one.

Also: MEMOEDIT(), MEMOREAD(), MEMOTRAN(), MEMOWRIT(), MLPOS(), MLCOUNT(), HARDCR()

MENU TO — Menu Command

Syntax: MENU TO <memory variable>

Action: Activates the menu defined by previously issued @...PROMPT commands.

Detail: The following example illustrates the use of @...PROMPT and MENU TO in constructing and activating a "lightbar" menu:

```
* Menu messages are displayed on line 2.
SET MESSAGE TO 2  && turn on messages

* Allow left/right arrow keys to wrap around.
SET WRAP ON

DO WHILE .T.  && infinite loop for menu display
   CLEAR
   @ box_home, 0, 3, 79 BOX box_double
   @ 1, 5 PROMPT "Customer" MESSAGE;
          "Add/search/edit customers and transactions."
   @ 1,17 PROMPT "Invoice"  MESSAGE;
          "Print invoices from customer transactions."
   @ 1,28 PROMPT "Label"    MESSAGE;
          "Print labels from customers or transactions."
   @ 1,37 PROMPT "Report"   MESSAGE;
          "Print reports."
   @ 1,47 PROMPT "Shipping" MESSAGE;
          "Browse ship-to names and companies."
   @ 1,59 PROMPT "Maintain" MESSAGE;
          "File and system maintenance utilities."
   @ 1,71 PROMPT "Quit"     MESSAGE;
          "Quit to the operating system."

   MENU TO action

   DO CASE    && make decision based on option selected.
      CASE action == 1
         DO Customer
      CASE action == 2
         DO Report WITH "INVOICES"
      CASE action == 3
         DO Report WITH "LABELS"
      CASE action == 4
         DO Report
      CASE action == 5
         DO Shipping
      CASE action == 6
         DO Maintain
```

```
        CASE action == 7
           SET MESSAGE TO    && turn off messages
           SET WRAP OFF      && turn off menu wrap
           RETURN
     ENDCASE
  ENDDO
```

Also: @...PROMPT, SET MESSAGE TO, SET WRAP, READVAR()

Microsoft C — Compile Info

Syntax: cl /AL /c /FPa /Gs /Oalt /Zl <filename>.c

Action: Compiles the named C program with Microsoft's C compiler.

Detail: The Microsoft C command line options are described below. These options must be specified when preparing C programs for use with Clipper.

Option	Meaning
/AL	Large memory model
/c	Compile only (no automatic link)
/FPa	Use alternate floating-point routines, if any
/Gs	Disable stack checking
/Oalt	Optimize alias checking, loops, execution speed
/Zl	Disable default library searching

The following example compiles a C program called Foo.c:

```
cl /AL /c /FPa /Gs /Oalt /Zl Foo.c
```

You must use the Microsoft C compiler, version 5.0 or higher, if your C program contains any double or floating point numbers. Otherwise, you may use the Turbo C compiler from Borland.

Also: Make, Turbo C

MIN() Comparison Function

Syntax: MIN(<expN1>, <expN2>) | MIN(<expD1>, <expD2>)

Action: Evaluates the minimum of the two specified numbers or dates.

Return: <expN | D> depending on the data type of the parameters passed.

Detail: Use the MIN() function whenever you need to place a limit on how big a particular number can get. For example, if you want to give a company-wide 10% bonus not to exceed $3,000, you could use the following expression with the Employee database file in a LIST command or as one of the columns in a REPORT FORM.

```
MIN(Salary * .10, 3000)
```

MIN() can be used with date values to determine which of two dates is chronologically smaller. For example:

```
? MIN(DATE(), CTOD("03/11/89")
```

Also: MAX()

MISC_ERROR() Error Function

Syntax: MISC_ERROR(<C proc name>, <N file line>, <C error info>, <C operation> [,<operand>])

Action: Called by Clipper on type mismatch or RUN error.

Return: <expL> true to retry the operation, or false to exit to DOS.

Detail: MISC_ERROR() is called automatically by Clipper when a RUN operation fails, or when a data type mismatch occurs.

The error function below is part of the TRHELP high-level error system used to replace Clipper's default MISC_ERROR() function. It uses the other high-level error functions documented under the ERRORSYS procedure.

```
FUNCTION MISC_ERROR
* Syntax: <none>, called by Clipper on miscellaneous
            error.
* Return: True to retry command that caused error,
*         false to exit to the operating system.
* Action: Handle errors from RUN or type mismatch.
*
PARAMETERS proc_name, file_line, error_info, operation,
           op_1

* Sound warning and display error message on screen.
error_tone()
err_msg("Error in: "+ operation+".  From: "+ proc_name+;
    ".  File line: " + LTRIM(STR(file_line)) + ".",;
    "Press any key to continue...")

* Write error details to file; pause for user response.
IF TYPE("op_1") != "U"
   err_write( PROCNAME(), proc_name, file_line,;
              error_info, operation, op_1 )
ELSE
   err_write( PROCNAME(), proc_name, file_line,;
              error_info, operation )
ENDIF
CLEAR TYPEAHEAD
INKEY(0)
err_msg()  && clear error message

* Activate the debugger if sys_debug is true.
IF sys_debug
   err_msg("Set return value by making logical",;
           "variable 'ret_debug' true or false")
   ALTD()
   err_msg()
   IF TYPE("ret_debug") == "L"
      RETURN ret_debug
   ENDIF
ENDIF
```

```
* Without BEGIN/END SEQUENCE around operation that
* caused the error, BREAK behaves the same as RETURN .F.
BREAK
```

Also: ERRORSYS, OPEN_ERROR(), DB_ERROR(), EXPR_ERROR(), UNDEF_ERRO(), PRINT_ERRO()

MLCOUNT() Output Function

Syntax: MLCOUNT(<memo field> | <expC>
[, <N line width> [, <N tab size> [, <L word wrap>]]])

Action: Counts the number of lines in the specified memo field or character string.

Return: <expN> number of lines at given width.

Detail: The following example uses MLCOUNT to count the number of lines in a memo field at a line width of 65:

```
SET MARGIN TO 8
SET PRINTER ON
USE Mailing
DO WHILE .NOT. EOF()
   ? "Dear " + First_Name
   ?
   num_lines = MLCOUNT(Letter, 65)
   FOR x = 1 TO num_lines
      ? MEMOLINE(Letter, 65, x)
   NEXT
   EJECT
   SKIP
ENDDO
CLOSE DATABASES
SET PRINTER OFF
SET MARGIN TO        && reset margin setting to default
```

Also: MEMOEDIT(), MEMOREAD(), MEMOTRAN(), MEMOWRIT(), MEMOLINE(), MLPOS(), HARDCR()

MLPOS() Character Function

Syntax: MLPOS(<memo field> | <expC>, <N line length>, <N line number>)

Action: Evaluates the position of a line number in a memo field at a given line length.

Return: <expN> representing the starting position of a line number.

Detail: To find the position in the Letter memo field of the fifth line, given a line length of 25, you would use:

```
MLPOS(Letter, 25, 5)
```

To output the entire letter:

```
letter_len = MLCOUNT(Letter, 25)
FOR i = 1 TO letter_len
   ? SUBSTR(Letter, MLPOS(Letter, 25, i), 25)
NEXT
```

Also: MEMOEDIT(), MEMOREAD(), MEMOTRAN(), MEMOWRIT(), MLCOUNT(), MEMOLINE(), HARDCR(), SUBSTR()

MONTH() Date Function

Syntax: MONTH(<expD>)

Action: Evaluates the numeric month (e.g., January is 1) of the specified date.

Return: <expN> representing the month number.

Detail: The following example uses the MONTH() function to show all individuals in the mailing list who have a birthday this month:

```
USE Mailing
LIST First_Name, Last_Name, Address, City, State, Zip ;
     FOR MONTH(Birthday) == MONTH(DATE())
CLOSE DATABASES
```

Also: CDOW(), CMONTH(), CTOD(), DAY(), DOW(), DTOC(), YEAR(), DATE()

NETERR() **Network Function**

Syntax: NETERR()

Action: Evaluates if certain commands fail in a network environment.

Return: <expL> true if the command fails, otherwise false.

Detail: NETERR() applies to the USE and APPEND BLANK commands only. If either of these commands fails for any reason, the function returns true. For example:

```
CLEAR
USE Mailing EXCLUSIVE
IF NETERR()
   ? "Another user has exclusive use of mailing list."
   ? "Try again later."
ENDIF
RETURN
```

Also: Networking, USE, APPEND BLANK

NETNAME() Network Function

Syntax: NETNAME()

Action: Evaluates the name of the current workstation in a network environment.

Return: <expC> workstation name, or a null string if used in a single-user environment or if the workstation identification has never been set.

Detail: To query the workstation identification, use:

```
? NETNAME()
```

Also: Networking

Networking Network Info

Action: High level network functions.

Detail: The network functions provided with Clipper are primitives. They allow you to design a high-level network system customized specifically for your application.

These functions demonstrate an application-specific networking system that uses Clipper's primitive functions. Failed lock requests notify the user, and keep attempting to lock until the user cancels. All network requests should call these functions instead of calling Clipper's primitives.

```
PROCEDURE key_lock    Simulate locks for runtime testing
FUNCTION  net_appe    Add blank record or notify user
FUNCTION  net_flock   Lock current file or notify user
FUNCTION  net_rlock   Lock current record or notify user
FUNCTION  net_use     Open file or notify user if unable
```

These functions expect the existence of a global variable called sys_lock that should be initialized false in your application's main, or first, procedure. When sys_lock is true, these functions behave as though another user's lock already exists, allowing you to test the result on a single-user system. You set sys_lock true with the Alt-L key and false with the Alt-U key.

```
PROCEDURE key_lock
* Syntax: SET KEY 294 TO key_lock  && Alt-L
*         SET KEY 278 TO key_lock  && Alt-U
* Action: Simulate network locks at runtime for testing.
* Notes : Alt-L locks everything, Alt-U unlocks
*           everything.  The two SET KEY commands
*           activate these Alt keys.
*
sys_lock = ( LASTKEY() == 294 )
RETURN
** key_lock ********************************************


FUNCTION net_appe
* Syntax: net_appe()
* Action: Add a blank record or notify user if unable.
* Return: True if successful, otherwise false.
*
PRIVATE keypress
keypress = 0
BEGIN SEQUENCE    && BREAK occurs in db_error()
   DO WHILE keypress == 0
      APPEND BLANK
      IF NETERR() .OR. sys_lock
         ? "Waiting for busy network, " +;
           "press any key to cancel."
         * Delay eases network traffic.
         keypress = INKEY(1)
      ELSE
         RETURN .T.
      ENDIF
   ENDDO
END SEQUENCE
RETURN .F.
** net_appe() *****************************************
```

```
FUNCTION net_flock
* Syntax: net_flock()
* Action: Lock the selected file; notify user if unable.
* Return: True if successful, otherwise false.
*
PRIVATE keypress
keypress = 0
DO WHILE keypress == 0
   IF FLOCK() .AND. !sys_lock
      RETURN .T.
   ELSE
      ? "Waiting for busy network, " +;
        "press any key to cancel."
      * Delay eases network traffic.
      keypress = INKEY(1)
   ENDIF
ENDDO
RETURN .F.
** net_flock() ****************************************

FUNCTION net_rlock
* Syntax: net_rlock()
* Action: Lock currently selected record or notify user.
* Return: True if successful, otherwise false.
*
PRIVATE keypress
keypress = 0
DO WHILE keypress == 0
   IF RLOCK() .AND. !sys_lock
      RETURN .T.
   ELSE
      ? "Waiting for busy network, " +;
        "press any key to cancel."
      * Delay eases network traffic.
      keypress = INKEY(1)
   ENDIF
ENDDO
RETURN .F.
** net_rlock() ****************************************
```

```
FUNCTION net_use
* Syntax: net_use( <C dbf file>, <L is exclusive> )
* Action: Open file in current work area or notify user.
* Return: True if successful, otherwise false.
*
PARAMETERS filename, is_excl
PRIVATE keypress, ret
keypress = 0
ret = .F.
BEGIN SEQUENCE    && BREAK occurs in open_error()
   DO WHILE keypress == 0
      IF is_excl
         USE (filename) EXCLUSIVE
      ELSE
         USE (filename)
      ENDIF
      IF NETERR() .OR. sys_lock
         ? "Waiting for busy network, " +;
           "press any key to cancel."
         * Delay eases network traffic.
         keypress = INKEY(1)
      ELSE
         ret = .T.
         EXIT
      ENDIF
   ENDDO
END SEQUENCE
RETURN ret
** net_use() ******************************************
```

Also: FLOCK(), LOCK(), NETERR(), RLOCK(), UNLOCK

NEXTKEY() — Input Function

Syntax: NEXTKEY()

Action: Evaluates the value of the next keystroke in the typeahead buffer.

Return: <expN> representing the INKEY() value of the pending keystroke.

Detail: Unlike INKEY(), NEXTKEY() does not remove the keystroke from the typeahead buffer. The following example displays the time until the user presses the letter Q - uppercase or lowercase:

```
CLEAR
@ 24, 0 SAY "Type Q to stop clock display."
DO WHILE .T.
   @ 0, 60 SAY DTOC(DATE()) + "  " + TIME()
   IF INKEY() == ASC("Q") .OR. NEXTKEY() == ASC("q")
      EXIT
   ENDIF
ENDDO
```

Note that the IF statement that tests for the keypress is evaluated from right to left. For this reason, NEXTKEY() is used after the .OR. to examine the next key in the typeahead buffer without removing the keystroke. Then, INKEY() is used to test the key again and remove it from the typeahead buffer.

See INKEY() for a complete table of return values for this function.

Also: INKEY(), LASTKEY(), KEYBOARD

NOTE — Program Command

Syntax: NOTE [<text>]

Action: Used to comment programs. The text is ignored.

Detail: NOTE is identical to * (comment). Which one you use is a matter of personal preference, but * is used more often because the comments are more readable without NOTE on every line.

The following example uses NOTE to illustrate the command:

```
NOTE Open files.
USE Orders INDEX Part_No
NOTE Process records.
DO WHILE .NOT. EOF()
   .
   . <commands>
   .
   SKIP
ENDDO
NOTE Close files.
CLOSE DATABASES
```

As you can see from this example, it is difficult to separate the comments from the actual commands when reading the code. Replacing NOTE with * makes it much easier to read.

```
* Open files.
USE Orders INDEX Part_No
* Process records.
DO WHILE .NOT. EOF()
   .
   . <commands>
   .
   SKIP
ENDDO
* Close files.
CLOSE DATABASES
```

Also: * (comment), &&

OPEN_ERROR() — Error Function

Syntax: OPEN_ERROR(<C proc name>, <N file line>, <C error info>, <C operation>, <C file name>)

Action: Called by Clipper on file opening error.

Return: <expL> true to retry the operation, or false to cancel and continue.

Detail: OPEN_ERROR() is called automatically by Clipper when a file opening error occurs, other than with FCREATE() and FOPEN().

The error function below is part of the TRHELP high-level error system used to replace Clipper's default OPEN_ERROR() function. It uses the other high-level error functions documented under the ERRORSYS procedure.

```
FUNCTION OPEN_ERROR
* Syntax: <none>, called by Clipper on file-opening
*            error.
* Return: True to retry command that caused error,
*         false to continue command execution.
* Note  : Does not handle FCREATE() or FOPEN().
*

PARAMETERS proc_name, file_line, error_info, operation,;
           filename
```

```
* Sound warning and display error message on screen.
error_tone()
err_msg("Error opening file: " + filename + " from: " +;
        proc_name +". File line: "+;
        LTRIM(STR(file_line)) +;
        ".", "Press any key to continue...")

* Write error details to file; pause for user response.
err_write( PROCNAME(), proc_name, file_line,;
           error_info, operation, filename )
CLEAR TYPEAHEAD
INKEY(0)
err_msg()  && clear error message

* Activate the debugger if sys_debug is true.
IF sys_debug
   err_msg("Set return value by making logical",;
           "variable 'ret_debug' true or false")
   ALTD()
   err_msg()
   IF TYPE("ret_debug") == "L"
      RETURN ret_debug
   ENDIF
ENDIF

* Without BEGIN/END SEQUENCE around operation that
* caused the error, BREAK returns to DOS.
BREAK
```

Also: ERRORSYS, DB_ERROR(), MISC_ERROR(), EXPR_ERROR(), UNDEF_ERRO(), PRINT_ERRO()

PACK

Database Command

Syntax: PACK

Action: Physically removes records that are marked for deletion from the active database file.

Detail: The following example removes the orders that have been filled from the Orders file. Open index files are automatically reindexed by the PACK command:

```
USE Orders INDEX Part_No, Cust_No

* Make back-up copy before permanently removing records.
COPY TO Filled FOR Filled

* Mark records for deletion.
DELETE FOR Filled

* Permanently remove records.
PACK

CLOSE DATABASES
```

Once you use PACK, you will not be able to recover the deleted records unless you have a backup of the database file before the command was issued.

A better method for applications keeps a self-maintaining database and never requires PACK. When the user deletes a record, simply REPLACE all fields with empty values (e.g., character with space, date with blank date, logical with false, and numeric with zero). Before adding a record, seek on an empty key expression to reuse deleted records:

```
SEEK SPACE(10)
IF .NOT. FOUND()
   APPEND BLANK
ENDIF
.
. <commands that use new record>
.
```

In applications where there is more than one key field and either may be blank, use a special character in one key field (character type) to denote a blank record:

```
del_char = CHR(250)

* On deletion:
REPLACE <primary key field> WITH del_char,;
        <all other fields> WITH <blank value>

* To search:
SET ORDER TO <primary key>
SEEK del_char
IF .NOT. FOUND()
   APPEND BLANK
ENDIF
SET ORDER TO <wanted key>
.
. <commands that use new record>
.
```

Also: DELETE, DELETED(), RECALL, ZAP, SET DELETED

PARAMETERS — Program Command

Syntax: PARAMETERS <memory variable list>

Action: Defines the parameters passed to a procedure or user-defined function.

Detail: Variables named in the PARAMETERS list are PRIVATE to the subroutine.

The following example is a general purpose routine to convert a number expressed in inches to yards, feet, and inches:

```
PROCEDURE Convert
PARAMETERS length, yards, feet, inches
yards  = INT(length / 36)
feet   = INT((length % 36) / 12)
inches = length % 12
RETURN
```

To convert the 1578 inches and display the result:

```
STORE 0 TO yds, ft, in
DO Convert WITH 1578, yds, ft, in
? yds, "Yards", ft, "Feet", in, "Inches"
```

Note that the number of parameters that are actually passed to a procedure or UDF does not have to match the number of parameters in the PARAMETERS statement. This allows you to create routines that take a variable number of parameters. PARAMETERS variables that do not receive a passed parameter remain uninitialized.

Normally, parameters are passed to user-defined functions by value. This means that the UDF gets its own private copy of the passed parameter, so any changes made to the PARAMETERS variable in the UDF are not passed back to the calling routine's variable. Preceding a memory variable function parameter with an @ sign passes that parameter by reference, so that changes made will be passed back to the caller's variable.

```
foo = 123
? udf(foo)     && passed by value, foo still equals 123
? udf(@foo)    && passed by reference, foo now equals 456
```

```
FUNCTION udf
PARAMETERS number
number = 456
RETURN number
```

Normally, parameters are passed to procedures by reference with these exceptions: array elements, fields, expressions, and constants are passed by value. To pass a memory variable parameter to a procedure by value, you can enclose it in parentheses. Note that fields cannot be passed by reference, so you must enclose them in parentheses or precede them with an alias-> in order to pass them as a parameter.

```
DO udp WITH 120+3      && pass by value, cannot change

foo = 123
DO udp WITH foo        && pass by reference, foo now 456
DO udp WITH (foo)      && pass by value, remains unchanged

DECLARE array[1]
array[1] = 123
DO udp WITH array[1] && pass by value, remains unchanged

USE File
DO udp WITH Field      && run-time error
DO udp WITH (Field)   && pass by value, remains unchanged
DO udp WITH File->Field   && by value, remains unchanged

PROCEDURE udp
PARAMETERS number
number = 456
RETURN
```

Also: DO, FUNCTION, PCOUNT(), PRIVATE

PCOL() — Environment Function

Syntax: PCOL()

Action: Evaluates the current printer column position.

Return: <expN> representing the printer column position.

Detail: PCOL() is most often used with the @...SAY command when SET DEVICE TO PRINTER is in effect. The function is used to position information on the printer relative to the location of previously printed information.

For example, when you TRIM() a character variable, you don't know how long the result will be. The following commands print the first and last name fields side by side, regardless of how long the first name happens to be:

```
SET DEVICE TO PRINTER
@ 3, 0        SAY TRIM(First_Name)
@ 3, PCOL()+1 SAY Last_Name
SET DEVICE TO SCREEN
```

The EJECT command resets PCOL() to zero.

The SETPRC() function allows you to reset PCOL() to any value.

Also: PROW(), COL(), ROW(), @...SAY, SET DEVICE TO, SETPRC(), EJECT

PCOUNT() — Program Function

Syntax: PCOUNT()

Action: Counts the parameters passed to a procedure or user-defined function.

Return: <expN> representing the number of parameters passed.

Detail: PCOUNT() is useful because neither procedures nor user-defined functions require that the number of parameters passed match the number of variables in the PARAMETERS statement. Thus, certain parameters might be undefined when the procedure or function is executed. For example:

```
FUNCTION File_Open
PARAMETERS dbf_file, ndx_list
p_count = PCOUNT()
IF p_count == 1
   USE (dbf_file)
   ret = .T.
ELSEIF p_count == 2
   USE (dbf_file) INDEX (ndx_list)
   ret = .T.
ELSE
   ret = .F.
ENDIF
RETURN ret
```

You can use PCOUNT() in a loop when all parameters are the same data type, like those passed to the main program on start-up. The following example allows variable parameters to be passed in any order:

```
* Program: Main.prg
* Syntax : Main [MONO] [NOBAK] [DEBUG] [DRIVE]
PARAMETERS sys_par1, sys_par2, sys_par3, sys_par4
no_params = PCOUNT()
FOR i = 1 TO no_params
   j = STR(i,1)
   sys_par&j = UPPER(sys_par&j)
   IF sys_par&j = "MONO"
      sys_mono = true       && mono mode on color monitor
   ELSEIF sys_par&j = "NOBAK"
      sys_bak = false       && no backup files
   ELSEIF sys_par&j = "DEBUG"
      SETCANCEL(true)          && Alt-C stops program
   ELSEIF sys_par&j = "DRIVE"
      sys_drive = SUBSTR(sys_par&j,6,1)+":"     && drive
   ENDIF
NEXT
```

Also: PARAMETERS, DO, FUNCTION

PICTURE **Output Keyword**

Syntax: @...SAY...PICTURE <C template> |
@...GET...PICTURE <C template>

Action: Controls data display and data entry using specific symbols.

Detail: The PICTURE template symbols affect only a single character in the GET variable or SAY expression, so that you normally use a string of template symbols for a single expression or variable. For example "999999.99" or "!AAAAAAAAAA". The template symbols are explained in the table below:

Template	Effect
!	Forces letters (input and display) to uppercase
$	Displays a floating dollar sign in front of a number
*	Displays leading zeros in a number as asterisks
.	Displays a decimal point
,	Displays a comma
#	Allows input of numbers, signs and blanks only
9	Allows input of numbers and signs only
A	Allows input of letters only
L	Allows input of logical values (Y, N, T, and F) only
N	Allows input of letters and numbers only
X	Allows input of any character
Y	Allows input of a Y or an N only

Function Symbols

The PICTURE function symbols affect the entire GET variable or SAY expression, and must be preceded by the @ symbol to distinguish them from template symbols. Functions can be combined with one another to create more complex functions, and can be used with template symbols for greater control. For example "@!A" or "@(999,999,999.99".

Function	Effect
!	Forces letters (input and display) to uppercase
(	Displays negative numbers surrounded by parentheses with leading spaces
)	Displays negative numbers surrounded by parentheses without leading spaces
A	Allows input of letters only
B	Left justifies the display of numeric type data
C	Displays positive numbers followed by CR, for credit
D	Displays dates in the SET DATE format
E	Displays dates in European date format, DD/MM/YY
K	Clears current GET variable if the first key is not a cursor movement key
R	Causes non-template symbols in PICTURE template to be inserted in the display, but does not save them as part of the variable
S<n>	Data is scrolled in the specified width, <n>, where n is an integer
X	Displays negative numbers followed by DB, for debit
Z	Displays zeros as blanks

Also: @...SAY, @...GET, @...SAY...GET, RANGE, TRANSFORM()

Plink86 — Link Info

Syntax: PLINK86 FILE <obj filename list>
[OUTPUT = <exe filename>]
[MAP = <map filename> [<option list>]]
[LIBRARY <lib filename list>]
[<option list>]

Action: Links the named object files using the PLINK86-Plus overlay linker.

Detail: The options listed in the syntax are the most commonly used and are described below:

Option	Meaning
FILE	Names the object files to link. If more than one file is specified, the file names must be separated by commas. Abbreviation: FI.
LIBRARY	Names the library files to include. By default, Clipper.LIB is included, and Overlay.LIB is included if overlays are used. Abbreviation: LIB.
MAP	Generates memory map file. MAP options are: A - All segments are included G - Global (public) symbols are included M - Module names and addresses are included S - Program sections are included Any combination of the MAP options can be used. By default, A is assumed.
OUTPUT	Identifies the name of the .EXE output file.

The object and library file name lists are lists in which the file names are separated by a comma. By default, the .EXE file that is generated has the same root name as the first object file in the list. No map file is generated unless you specify the MAP option.

The following example links the file Main.OBJ that is known to reference functions in both Clipper.LIB and Extend.LIB. No map file is generated:

```
PLINK86 FI Main LIB Clipper, Extend
```

The next example links several object files and generates a .MAP file:

```
PLINK86 FI Main, AddRecs, EditRecs MAP = Map_Out G, S
```

Other Options

The Plink86 command line options that are not specifically listed in the syntax are described below. All of these options may be abbreviated to the first two letters:

Option	**Meaning**
BATCH	Terminates the linker if an object or library file cannot be found
BEGINAREA	Marks the beginning of an overlay area Abbreviation: BEGIN
DEBUG	Displays debugging information on the screen
ENDAREA	Marks the end of an overlay area Abbreviation: END
HEIGHT	Defines the number of lines per page of memory map (default is 64). HEIGHT = <page height> is the complete syntax for this option.
LOWERCASE	Converts identifiers and symbols to lowercase
NOBELL	Suppresses the bell when PLINK86 displays a message
SEARCH	Names the library files to include, and causes multiple passes through the library files in an attempt to resolve any undefined symbols. The syntax is: SEARCH <lib filename list>.
SECTION	Names the object files to be contained in an internal overlay file. The syntax is: SECTION FILE <obj filename list>.
SECTION INTO	Names the object files to be contained in an external overlay file. The syntax is: SECTION INTO <overlay file> FILE <obj file list>.
UPPERCASE	Converts identifiers and symbols to uppercase
VERBOSE	Displays the current operation of the linker on the screen
WIDTH	Defines the page width of the memory map (default is 80). The syntax is: WIDTH = <page width>.
WORKFILE	Redirects temporary work file to another directory. The syntax is: WORKFILE = <filename>.

PLINK86 parameters can be taken from one or more ASCII text files by preceding the file names with an @ symbol. The text files are assumed to have a .LNK extension. For example, the file, Link1.LNK, listed below:

```
# Link1.lnk
FILE Main
OUTPUT = Exe_Out
MAP = Map_Out
LIBRARY Clipper, Tr, Extend
BEGINAREA
   SECTION                FILE AddRecs   #internal overlay
   SECTION INTO EditRecs FILE EditRecs #external overlay
ENDAREA
```

To use a LNK file with PLINK86, precede the file name with the @ symbol:

```
PLINK86 @Link1
```

Also: Make

Precedence

Language Info

Action: Natural order of evaluation.

Detail: Numeric operators evaluate first in this order of precedence:

Operator	Action
^ and **	Exponentiation
* and / and %	Multiplication, division, and modulus
+ and -	Addition and subtraction

Relational operators evaluate next, all with equal precedence.

Logical operators evaluate last in this order of precedence:

Operator	Action
.NOT. and !	Complement (negation)
.AND.	Conjunction
.OR.	Disjunction

Use parentheses to force evaluation in a different order.

```
 4 + 2 * 3      && 2 times 3 is 6, 6 plus 4 is 10
(4 + 2) * 3     && 4 plus 2 is 6, 6 times 3 is 18
```

Expressions within innermost nested parentheses evaluate first.

Also: (), Expression, .NOT., .AND., .OR., <, <=, >, >=, <>, #, = (compare), ==, !=, ! (logical), **, ^, /, %, $, ()

PRINT_ERRO() — Error Function

Syntax: PRINT_ERRO(<C proc name>, <N file line>, <C error info>)

Action: Called by Clipper on printing error.

Return: Return logical true to retry operation, or false to cancel and continue.

Detail: PRINT_ERRO() is called automatically by Clipper when a printer error occurs.

This error function is part of the high-level error system used to replace Clipper's default PRINT_ERRO() function. It uses the other high-level error functions documented under the ERRORSYS procedure.

Although documented by Nantucket as print_error(), Clipper keeps track of only ten characters, thus the PROCNAME() function will return "PRINT_ERRO" when queried.

The third parameter always contains "Printer error" and therefore is not necessary to capture.

```
FUNCTION PRINT_ERRO
* Syntax: <none>, called by Clipper on printing error.
* Return: True to retry command that caused error,
*         false to continue with following command.
* Action: Handle printing errors.
* Note  : Do not specify "P" in the DOS MODE command for
*         a serial printer.
*
PARAMETERS proc_name, file_line
PRIVATE cursor_row, cursor_col, ret
```

```
* Turn off output to the printer.
SET DEVICE TO SCREEN
SET PRINT OFF

* Save current screen cursor position.
cursor_row = ROW()
cursor_col = COL()

* Sound warning and display error message on screen.
error_tone()
err_msg("Error printing from: " + proc_name +;
        ".  File line: " + LTRIM(STR(file_line)) + ".",;
        "Press any key to continue...")

* Write error details to file; pause for user response.
err_write( PROCNAME(), proc_name, file_line,;
           "Printing error" )
CLEAR TYPEAHEAD
INKEY(0)

* Offer retry (no need to activate debugger here).
err_msg("Fix the printer and press <P> to continue,",;
        "or press any other key to cancel...")

* Act on user choice.
IF CHR(INKEY(0)) $ "pP"  && retry printer operation
   * Use SET DEVICE or SET PRINT depending on which one
   * your printer output routine uses.
   SET DEVICE TO PRINTER
   ret = true
ELSE
   ret = false
ENDIF

* Restore error window and screen's cursor position.
err_msg()
@ cursor_row, cursor_col SAY ""
RETURN ret
```

Also: ERRORSYS, OPEN_ERROR(), DB_ERROR(), MISC_ERROR(), EXPR_ERROR(), UNDEF_ERRO()

PRIVATE **Memory Command**

Syntax: PRIVATE <array | memvar list>

Action: Declares the variables in the list private to the current program.

Detail: To declare one or more memory variable or array names to be private to the current program, you would use this form of the PRIVATE command. Declaring a PRIVATE memory variable or array means that it is used only by the current routine and any subroutines it calls or its subroutines call.

If a memory variable or array is already in existence and has the same name as one you declare PRIVATE, the first one is preserved so that it remains unaffected by the current program or subsequent subroutine calls.

All PRIVATE variables and arrays are released when the program that created them completes execution, thus they should be initialized in the highest-level routine that uses them. By default, all memory variables are PRIVATE to the routine that originally creates them.

The following example is a partial listing of a subroutine that uses the PRIVATE command. The named memory variables and arrays are used by the subroutine only, and the calling program is unaffected by any changes when the subroutine returns:

```
FUNCTION generic
PRIVATE choice, array1[20], value, array2[50]
.
. <commands>
.
```

When used for arrays, PRIVATE is functionally identical to DECLARE. Array subscripts begin with 1. The number of arrays that can be created depends on the number of available memory variable slots and the amount of free memory. Each array uses a single memory variable slot and may have up to 4096 elements.

Also: PUBLIC, DECLARE, = (store), STORE

PROCEDURE — Program Command

Syntax: PROCEDURE <procedure name>

Action: Names a procedure, and marks its beginning.

Detail: The following is a skeleton of a procedure file. The PROCEDURE commands marks the beginning and gives a name to each procedure in the file:

```
* Business.PRG

PROCEDURE reports
.
. <commands>
.
RETURN

PROCEDURE updates
PARAMETERS filename, index_list
.
. <commands>
.
RETURN
```

Assuming this procedure file is named Business, to execute the procedures stored in it:

```
SET PROCEDURE TO Business
DO reports
DO updates WITH "Orders", "Part_No, Cust_No"
```

Procedure files are compiled in with the program that contains the SET PROCEDURE command. Thus, procedures do not have to be in a separate procedure file. Instead, you can simply place them at the end of the program that calls them. For example:

```
* Business.PRG
DO reports
DO updates WITH "Orders", "Part_No, Cust_No"

PROCEDURE reports
.
. <commands>
.
RETURN

PROCEDURE updates
PARAMETERS filename, index_list
.
. <commands>
.
RETURN
```

Also: SET PROCEDURE TO, DO, PARAMETERS, FUNCTION

PROCLINE() — Debug Function

Syntax: PROCLINE()

Action: Evaluates the line number in the source code of the current command.

Return: <expN> line number relative to the beginning of the current program.

Detail: PROCLINE() is useful if you are debugging a program and need to know the current line number. To query the current line number, use:

```
? PROCLINE()
```

Note that PROCLINE() does not work properly if the -l option was used at compile time to exclude line numbers.

Also: PROCNAME()

PROCNAME() Debug Function

Syntax: PROCNAME()

Action: Evaluates the name of the current program or procedure.

Return: <expC> program, procedure, or function name.

Detail: PROCNAME() is useful if you are debugging a program and need to know the current procedure name. To query this function, use:

```
? PROCNAME()
```

If a subroutine needs to know who calls it, pass PROCNAME() to it as a parameter:

```
DO subroutine WITH PROCNAME()
```

Also: PROCLINE()

PROW() Environment Function

Syntax: PROW()

Action: Evaluates the current printer row position.

Return: <expN> representing the printer row position.

Detail: PROW() is most often used with the @...SAY command when SET DEVICE TO PRINTER is in effect. The function is used to position information on the printer relative to the location of previously printed information. For example, to begin printing at the current print location, you could use:

```
SET DEVICE TO PRINTER
@ PROW(), PCOL() SAY "This begins at current location."
SET DEVICE TO SCREEN
```

The EJECT command reset PROW() to zero.

The SETPRC() function allows you to reset PROW() to any value.

Also: PCOL(), COL(), ROW(), @...SAY, SETPRC(), EJECT, SET DEVICE TO

PUBLIC — Memory Command

Syntax: PUBLIC <array | memvar list> [, CLIPPER]

Action: Declares the variables in the list for global use by all programs.

Detail: PUBLIC variables are available to all routines in an application and must be explicitly released from memory. To make one or more arrays or memory variables public, or global, use the PUBLIC command.

The following program skeleton uses the PUBLIC command to declare the variables named balance and check_no. When this program RETURNs, these two variables remain in memory for use by higher-level routines:

```
PUBLIC balance, check_no
RESTORE FROM Checks ADDITIVE   && get old values
.
. <commands to compute new balance and check_no>
.
SAVE TO Checks                 && save new values
RETURN
```

This, however, is poor form. It is best to initialize all variables in the highest-level routine in which they are used. Thus, well written programs have little use for the PUBLIC command as variables initialized in the higest-level routine are functionally public.

Note that the PRIVATE command can be used to create a private variable with the same name as a public variable. If you do this, the value of the public variable is saved and hidden so that any changes made to the new, private variable do not affect the original. When the subroutine RETURNs, the private variable is released, and the value of the original variable is restored in memory.

Memory variables declared PUBLIC are intiialized with a logical value of false. Elements in PUBLIC arrays are unitialized.

The CLIPPER variable name, if used, is initialized to a logical value of true. You can use this variable in your programs by placing IF CLIPPER...ENDIF constructs around Clipper specific code. In this way, you can make your programs compatible with other dialects of the Dbase language because they will initialize the CLIPPER variable to false like all other PUBLIC variables. For example:

```
* Set true by Clipper, false by other software.
PUBLIC CLIPPER

IF CLIPPER
    .
    . <Clipper specific code>
    .
ELSE
    .
    . <code to run in another dialect>
    .
ENDIF
```

Also: PRIVATE, DECLARE, PARAMETERS, RELEASE, RESTORE, STORE, = (store)

QUIT

OS Command

Syntax: QUIT

Action: Returns control of your computer to the operating system.

Detail: The following example uses QUIT as the menu action that terminates the main program:

```
DO WHILE .T.
   *
   * <commands to display menu and get selection>
   *
   DO CASE
      CASE selection = 0  && selection 0 is Exit on menu
         QUIT
      CASE selection = 1
         DO <program one>
      CASE selection = 2
         DO <program two>
   ENDCASE
ENDDO
```

Also: RETURN, CANCEL

RANGE

Input Keyword

Syntax: @...GET...RANGE <N | D minimum>, <N | D maximum>

Action: Specifies a minimum and/or maximum value for a numeric or date GET variable.

Detail: Neither RANGE value can be omitted to indicate no lower or upper boundary. The following example illustrates RANGE:

```
number = 0
due_date = CTOD("  /  /  ")

* number must be a positive value
@ 10, 5 GET number PICTURE "99999" RANGE 0, 99999

* due_date must be greater than today
* and less than 12/31/99.
@ 11, 5 GET due_date RANGE DATE()+1, CTOD("12/31/99")

READ
```

Also: @...GET, @...SAY...GET, PICTURE, VALID

RAT() Character Function

Syntax: RAT(<C search>, <C target>)

Action: Evaluates the starting position of the last occurence of the search string.

Detail: RAT() is identical to AT(), except it works from the right of the string instead of from the left. For example, to extract the last item in a field that contains a list of items separated by commas:

```
? SUBSTR(<field>, RAT(",", <field>) + 1)
```

Also: AT(), SUBSTR(), $

READ Input Command

Syntax: READ [SAVE]

Action: Activates all pending @...GET variables for editing.

Detail: The following commands might be used as part of a menu program to allow the user to make a selection between zero and 9:

```
selection = 0
@ 10, 0 SAY "Enter your selection" GET selection;
                                  PICTURE "9" RANGE 0,9
READ
```

Use READ SAVE if you want to be able to reedit the GET variables. If you use READ SAVE, make sure that you use CLEAR GETS when you no longer want access to the GET variables.

This function allows you the choice of changing, saving, or undoing the GETs you are editing.

```
FUNCTION editor
* Syntax: editor()
* Return: True if saved, otherwise false.
* Action: Read current GETs.  User chooses save, change,
*         or undo
*
PRIVATE action, ret
DO WHILE .T.
   @ 1, 5 SAY "Editing current record.  "+;
              "Press PgDn to end, Esc to cancel."
   READ SAVE

   * Force Undo if Esc is pressed to exit READ.
   IF LASTKEY() == 27
      action = 3
      KEYBOARD CHR(13)
   ENDIF

   * Lightbar menu:    Change     Save     Undo
   @ 1,1 CLEAR TO 1,78
   @ 1, 5 PROMPT "Change" MESSAGE "Edit again."
   @ 1,16 PROMPT "Save"   MESSAGE "Save changes."
   @ 1,25 PROMPT "Undo"   MESSAGE "Discard changes."
   MENU TO action

   * Stay in loop to Change if action=1, otherwise exit.
   IF action != 1
      ret = (action==2)   && true if 2, otherwise false
      EXIT
   ENDIF
ENDDO
CLEAR GETS   && left by READ SAVE
RETURN ret
```

To use the editor() function, query it after you do the GETs:

```
memvar = SPACE(10)
@ 2,3 GET memvar
IF editor()
   DO save_edit
ELSE
   RETURN
ENDIF
```

Also: @...GET, @...SAY, READEXIT(), READINSERT(), READVAR(), SET FORMAT TO, CLEAR GETS

READEXIT() — Input Function

Syntax: READEXIT([<L on | OFF>])

Action: Determines whether Up Arrow and Down Arrow can be used as READ exit keys.

Return: <expL> current READEXIT() setting.

Detail: Normally, you cannot use Up Arrow and Down Arrow to exit a READ. These keys, when pressed in the first and last field, respectively, are ignored. To enable these keys, use:

```
READEXIT(.T.)
```

To disable them, use:

```
READEXIT(.F.)
```

To save and restore the current setting, use:

```
old_set = READEXIT(.T.)  && save setting and reset
.
. <commands>
.
READEXIT(old_set)        && restore saved setting
```

Also: READ, READINSERT()

READINSERT() Input Function

Syntax: READINSERT([<L on | off>])

Action: Toggles the insert mode on and off.

Return: <expL> current insert modes setting.

Detail: Normally, when you enter the edit mode with READ or MEMOEDIT(), you are in overwrite mode. To turn on the insert mode, use:

```
READINSERT(.T.)
```

To go back to overwrite mode, use:

```
READINSERT(.F.)
```

To save and restore the current setting, use:

```
old_set = READINSERT(.T.)  && save setting and reset
.
. <commands>
.
READINSERT(old_set)        && restore saved setting
```

Also: READ, MEMOEDIT(), READEXIT()

READVAR() Input Function

Syntax: READVAR()

Action: Evaluates the name of the current GET or MENU variable.

Return: <expC> variable name in uppercase letters.

Detail: The following example uses READVAR() in a user-defined function that is called by VALID to use the variable name in a message to the user:

```
even = 0
@ 10, 0 GET even VALID check(even)
READ

FUNCTION check
PARAMETERS number
IF number/2 != INT(number/2)
   @ 15, 0 SAY READVAR() + " must be an even number."
   RETURN .F.
ELSE
   RETURN .T.
ENDIF
```

Also: @...GET, MENU TO

RECALL — Database Command

Syntax: RECALL [<scope>]

Action: Reinstates records in the active file that have been marked for deletion.

Detail: If you have marked certain records for deletion that you want to reinstate to a non-deleted status, use RECALL. The following example reinstates all deleted records in the Orders database file:

```
USE Orders
RECALL ALL
CLOSE DATABASES
```

The next example reinstates the records in the Customer file that meet a particular condition:

```
USE Customer
RECALL FOR Due_Date < DATE()
CLOSE DATABASES
```

The final example recalls a single record in the Mailing list:

```
USE Mailing
RECALL RECORD 7
CLOSE DATABASES
```

Also: DELETE, DELETED(), SET DELETED, PACK

RECCOUNT() Database Function

Syntax: RECCOUNT()

Action: Evaluates the number of records in a database file.

Return: <expN> representing the number of records in the file.

Detail: RECCOUNT() is a quick way of telling how many records are in the active database file. The function is sometimes used to calculate the size of a database file before copying it. The following formula gives the size of a resulting SDF text file:

```
RECCOUNT() * RECSIZE()
```

Before copying an SDF file to drive A:, you could first check to see if there is enough free disk space with the following routine:

```
USE <database file>
IF DISKSPACE(1) >= RECCOUNT() * RECSIZE()
   COPY TO A:<text file> SDF
ELSE
   ? "Not enough free disk space for copy."
ENDIF
CLOSE DATABASES
```

Note that the return value of RECCOUNT() is not affected by any filter condition that might be in effect. This function returns the actual number of physical records in the database file.

To check the record count in an unselected database file, use the alias name and pointer with the function. For example:

```
? Orders->(RECCOUNT())  && check RECCOUNT() for Orders
```

LASTREC() and RECCOUNT() are functionally identical.

Also: RECNO(), RECSIZE(), COUNT, LASTREC(), ->, HEADER()

RECNO() — Database Function

Syntax: RECNO()

Action: Evaluates the current record number in a database file.

Return: <expN> representing the current record number.

Detail: The following example uses the RECNO() function to keep track of your place in the active database file before issuing a command that moves the record pointer:

```
old_recno = RECNO()
REPORT FORM Daily TO PRINTER
GO old_recno
RETURN
```

Assuming that this routine is called with a database file in use, the record pointer will appear undisturbed when the report is finished printing.

To check the record number for an unselected database file, use the alias name and pointer with the function. For example:

```
? Orders->(RECNO())  && Check RECNO() for Orders
```

Also: RECCOUNT(), RECSIZE(), ->

RECSIZE() — Database Function

Syntax: RECSIZE()

Action: Evaluates the record length of a database file.

Return: <expN> representing the record size for the active file.

Detail: The following example uses the RECSIZE() function to help determine if there is enough free space before copying an SDF file to drive A:

```
USE <database file>
IF DISKSPACE(1) >= RECCOUNT() * RECSIZE()
   COPY TO A:<text file> SDF
ELSE
   ? "Not enough free disk space for copy."
ENDIF
CLOSE DATABASES
```

To check the record size of an unselected database file, use the alias name and pointer with the function. For example:

```
? Orders->(RECSIZE())  && check RECSIZE() of Orders
```

Also: RECCOUNT(), RECNO(), ->

REINDEX — Index Command

Syntax: REINDEX

Action: Rebuilds all open index files for the active database file.

Detail: Normally, you maintain index files along with the database file by making sure that all files are open whenever any changes are made. However, if for any reason an index file becomes outdated, REINDEX recreates the file using the key expression with which it was originally created.

For example, suppose that you added some Orders without opening the index files that belong to the file. The following routine recreates them:

```
USE Orders INDEX Part_No, Cust_No
REINDEX
CLOSE DATABASES
```

In maintenance routines that recreate index files, it is better to use the original INDEX ON command rather than REINDEX. This way, if an index file gets corrupted or erased, the routine can recreate it without being dependent on the original index file. For example:

```
PROCEDURE reindex
USE File1
INDEX ON Field1 TO F1_1
INDEX ON Field2 TO F1_2
USE File2
INDEX ON Field1 + Field2 TO F2_1
RETURN
```

Also: INDEX, SET INDEX TO, USE

RELEASE — Memory Command

Syntax: RELEASE <memory variable list>

Action: Releases the named memory variables from memory.

Detail: The following example creates and erases several memory variables:

```
STORE 0 TO num1, num2, num3    && three numeric memvars
boolean = .T.                  && one logical memvar
my_name = "Debby Moody"        && one character memvar
today = DATE()                 && one date memvar

RELEASE num2, num3             && erase two memvars
RELEASE ALL                    && erase remaining memvars
```

Also: RELEASE ALL, CLEAR MEMORY, PUBLIC, PRIVATE, = (store), STORE

RELEASE ALL — Memory Command

Syntax: RELEASE ALL [LIKE | EXCEPT <skeleton>]

Action: Releases all memory variables, or a group of them, from memory.

Also: RELEASE, CLEAR MEMORY, PUBLIC, PRIVATE, = (store), STORE

RENAME — OS Command

Syntax: RENAME <filename> | (<C filename>) TO <filename> | (<C filename>)

Action: Changes the name of a disk file from the first file name to the second.

Detail: The RENAME command is similar to the DOS Rename command, except that it does not allow the use of wildcard characters. It is used to rename files on the disk, one at a time. In order to RENAME a file, it must be closed and you must specify the entire file name, including the extension.

The following example uses the RENAME command to change the name of a database file and its corresponding memo file:

```
CLOSE DATABASES          && make sure files are not open
RENAME Mailing.DBF TO MailList.DBF
RENAME Mailing.DBT TO MailList.DBT
```

RENAME can be used to move a file from one directory to another one on the same disk drive by specifying the new directory name as part of the TO file name. For example, to move a database file from its current directory to one called \Data, you could use:

```
RENAME Orders.DBF TO \Data\Orders.DBF
```

Both file names can be specified as character expressions by enclosing the expression in parentheses. For example:

```
from_file = "Test.TXT"
to_file   = "New.TXT"
RENAME (from_file) TO (to_file)
```

Also: COPY FILE, DIR, ERASE, CLOSE

REPLACE **Database Command**

Syntax: REPLACE [<scope>] <field> WITH <expression>
[, <field> WITH <expression> ...]

Action: Replaces the named fields with the specified expressions.

Detail: The following example changes the area code for all people with a particular zip code:

```
USE Mailing
REPLACE Phone WITH "(617)" + RIGHT(Phone, 8);
              FOR Zip = "81267"
```

Using the same file, the following example illustrates how to REPLACE more than a single field at a time:

```
LOCATE FOR First_Name = "Gloria"
REPLACE Address1 WITH "951 Peterson St.",;
        Address2 WITH "# 473",;
        City WITH "San Francisco",;
        Zip WITH "94115"
```

You cannot do a REPLACE that includes more than one record on an index key field while the index file is in use. This is because the first REPLACE may change the position of that record in the index, causing the next record to be other that what you expect. To replace multiple records using a scope, execute the REPLACE command with the index file closed, open the index, and use REINDEX to recreate it. For example:

```
USE Orders
REPLACE Part_No WITH "B123" FOR Part_No = "R123"
SET INDEX TO Part_No
REINDEX
CLOSE DATABASES
```

Also: APPEND BLANK, @...GET, READ, UPDATE, Scope

REPLICATE() — Character Function

Syntax: REPLICATE(<expC>, <N times>)

Action: Concatenates the given string with itself the specified number of times.

Return: <expC> string of replicated strings.

Detail: The following example uses REPLICATE() to aid in the drawing of a shaded, boxed region on the screen:

```
CLEAR
horizontal = REPLICATE(CHR(205), 20)
fill_in    = REPLICATE(CHR(176), 20)
? CHR(213) + horizontal + CHR(184)

FOR i = 1 TO 10
   ? CHR(179) + fill_in + CHR(179)
NEXT

? CHR(212) + horizontal + CHR(190)
```

REPLICATE(SPACE(1),<n>) is functionally identical to SPACE(<n>).

Also: SPACE()

REPORT FORM — Output Command

Syntax: REPORT FORM <frm filename> | (<C filename>) [<scope>]
<scope>
[TO PRINTER [NOEJECT]]
[TO FILE <txt filename> | (<C filename>)]
[HEADING <C heading>] [PLAIN] [SUMMARY]

Action: Displays a report for the active file using the definition in the form file.

Detail: The following example uses a report form that was designed using two related files:

```
USE Orders
SELECT 2
USE Parts INDEX Part_No
SELECT Orders
SET RELATION TO Part_No INTO Parts

* Print report for entire file
REPORT FORM Orders TO PRINTER

* Print report for a particular part number
REPORT FORM Orders TO PRINTER FOR Part_No = "B234"

* Write report to a text file
REPORT FORM Orders TO FILE Orders
CLOSE DATABASES
```

The options that are unique to the REPORT FORM command syntax are described below:

Option	Action
HEADING	Defines a report heading that prints at the top of each report page just before the report title.
NOEJECT	Prevents the initial page eject that occurs before the report starts printing.
PLAIN	Suppresses the page HEADING, date, and page number and causes the report title to appear on the first page of the report only.
SUMMARY	Displays only the subtotal and total lines of the report. Detail lines are not shown.

Also: TO PRINTER, RL

RESTORE **Memory Command**

Syntax: RESTORE FROM <mem filename> | (<C mem filename>) [ADDITIVE]

Action: Restores to memory the memory variables SAVEd in the named file.

Detail: Memory files are created with the SAVE command. The following program skeleton shows how to use the ending values of certain memory variables the next time a program is executed:

```
RESTORE FROM Checks  && Checks.MEM has account balance
.
. <commands to write checks, record deposits, etc.>
.
SAVE TO Checks ALL LIKE balance    && save new balance
```

Restored variables are private to the routine that RESTOREs them. In order for restored memory variables to be declared PUBLIC in a program, issue the PUBLIC command naming those variables and use the ADDITIVE option with the RESTORE command. For example:

```
PUBLIC selection, total_amt
* Assuming that selection and total_amt are in the
* memory file named LastTime.MEM, they will be PUBLIC
* when the file is restored.  All other memvars in the
* file will be PRIVATE to this routine.
RESTORE FROM LastTime ADDITIVE
```

Note that arrays are not saved to the memory file.

Also: SAVE, PRIVATE, PUBLIC

RESTORE SCREEN — Memory Command

Syntax: RESTORE SCREEN [FROM <screen memory variable>]

Action: Restores the screen from a buffer or a memory variable.

Detail: When saving and restoring screen images, you can choose one of two methods. The first and most simple is to work with only a single screen at a time. In this case, you use SAVE SCREEN with no parameters to save the current image to a buffer that does not have a name and RESTORE SCREEN with no parameters to restore the image from the buffer. For example:

```
SAVE SCREEN     && save current screen image to buffer
.
. <commands that change screen>
.
RESTORE SCREEN  && restore screen from buffer
```

The second method is to save multiple screens to named memory variables. In this case, you name the screen images when you issue SAVE SCREEN TO <memory variable>. Then, you retrieve screen images by name with RESTORE SCREEN FROM <memory variable>. For example:

```
SAVE SCREEN TO screen1
.
. <commands that change screen>
.
SAVE SCREEN TO screen2
.
. <more screen commands>
.
IF <condition>
   RESTORE SCREEN FROM screen1
ELSE
   RESTORE SCREEN FROM screen2
ENDIF
```

Each screen variable saves the full 25 by 80 screen and uses a single memory variable slot of 4000 bytes. To save and restore partial screens, or windows, use the SAVESCREEN() and RESTSCREEN() functions.

Like other memory variables, screen variables are affected by such commands as SAVE, STORE, RESTORE, and RELEASE, and follow the same naming conventions as other memory variables.

Also: SAVE SCREEN, SAVESCREEN(), RESTSCREEN()

RESTSCREEN() — Memory Function

Syntax: RESTSCREEN(<N top row>, <N left col>,
<N bottom row>, <N right col>,
<screen memory variable>)

Action: Restores a previously saved screen using the specified coordinates.

Return: Nothing.

Detail: The following example saves a portion of the screen before using it for another purpose. Afterwards, the old screen is restored and the new screen is moved:

```
* Save current screen.
old_screen = SAVESCREEN(7, 10, 14, 50)

* Use area of screen.
@ 7, 10 TO 14, 50 DOUBLE
@ 8, 11 CLEAR TO 13, 49
.
. <commands to write in box>
.
@ 12, 12 SAY "Press any key to move box"
INKEY(0)

* Save new screen.
new_screen = SAVESCREEN(7, 10, 14, 50)

* Restore old screen.
RESTSCREEN(7, 10, 14, 50, old_screen)

* Move new screen to upper-left of screen.
RESTSCREEN(0, 0, 7, 40, new_screen)
```

Also: SAVE SCREEN, RESTORE SCREEN, SAVESCREEN()

RETURN **Program Command**

Syntax: RETURN

Action: Returns control to the calling program starting with the command following the call to the subroutine.

Detail: The following menu program uses RETURN to return control to the operating system when the user selects the Exit menu option:

```
DO WHILE .T.
   CLEAR
   selection = 0
   @  6, 29 SAY "0 - Exit"
   @  8, 29 SAY "1 - Add Records"
   @ 10, 29 SAY "2 - Edit Records"
   @  4, 20 TO 14, 54 DOUBLE
   @ 14, 37 GET choice PICTURE "9" RANGE 0, 2
   READ
   DO CASE
      CASE choice = 0
         RETURN    && return control to operating system
      CASE choice = 1
         DO Add_Recs
      CASE choice = 2
         DO EditRecs
   ENDCASE
ENDDO
```

Note that in this example, QUIT or CANCEL could be substituted for RETURN to pass control back to the operating system. For procedures that are not at the top level, use RETURN to transfer control to the calling procedure. The dBASE option RETURN TO MASTER is not supported.

Also: CANCEL, QUIT, RETURN Value

RETURN Value — Program Command

Syntax: RETURN <expression>

Action: Returns the value of the expression from a user-defined function.

Detail: The following program has an internal user-defined function that illustrates the use of RETURN with a value:

```
CLEAR
name = SPACE(50)
@ 10, 0 SAY "Enter your first name" GET name
READ
? capital(name)

FUNCTION capital
* Syntax: capital(<C name>)
* Action: Capitalizes first letter of parameter, and
*         converts remaining characters to lowercase.
PARAMETERS first_name
RETURN UPPER(SUBSTR(first_name, 1, 1)) + ;
       LOWER(SUBSTR(first_name, 2))
```

If the RETURN command is omitted, the function returns <expL> false by default. Using RETURN without a return expression produces a compile-time error.

Also: FUNCTION, PARAMETERS, RETURN

RIGHT() — Character Function

Syntax: RIGHT(<expC>, <N length>)

Action: Extracts a substring of designated length starting with the last character.

Return: <expC> substring.

Detail: The following routine uses RIGHT() to extract all characters in a string past a specified character in the string:

```
PROCEDURE extract
PARAMETERS string, character, result
result_len = LEN(string) - AT(character, string)
result = RIGHT(string, result_len)
RETURN
```

For example, to extract all of the characters in the First_Name field after the first period:

```
USE Mailing
name     = First_Name
search   = "."
new_name = ""
DO Extract WITH name, search, new_name
? new_name
```

Also: LEFT(), SUBSTR()

RL — External Program

Syntax: RL

Action: Allows you to design report and label form files using a menu-driven system.

Detail: Before you can use the RL utility, you must compile and link the programs that it comprises. For your convenience, Clipper includes a batch file called MakeRL.BAT to do this. Once all of the programs are compiled, you execute RL.EXE to access the report and label design system.

The reports and label forms that you design can be viewed with the REPORT FORM and LABEL FORM commands.

Also: REPORT FORM, LABEL FORM

RLOCK() **Network Function**

Syntax: RLOCK()

Action: Attempts a record lock, and returns the result of that attempt.

Return: <expL> true if the record lock is successful, otherwise false.

Detail: RLOCK() and LOCK() are identical functions. The following example illustrates the use of RLOCK() to obtain a record lock before editing a record with an @...GET...READ sequence of commands:

```
SET EXCLUSIVE OFF  && locking unnecessary if ON
USE Mailing
LOCATE FOR First_Name = "Gloria"
IF FOUND()
   * This loop tries to lock the record 200 times,
   * then prompts you.
   times = 0
   DO WHILE times < 200 .AND. (!RLOCK())
      times = times + 1
      IF times = 200
         WAIT "Try record lock again? (Y/N)" TO response
         IF UPPER(response) = "Y"
            times = 0
         ELSE
            RETURN  && to try a different record
         ENDIF
      ENDIF
   ENDDO
   @ 10, 5 SAY "First Name " GET First_Name
   @ 17, 5 SAY "Phone      " GET Phone
   READ
ENDIF
UNLOCK  && releases record lock and program continues...
```

Also: Networking, LOCK(), FLOCK(), UNLOCK, SET EXCLUSIVE, USE

ROUND() **Numeric Function**

Syntax: ROUND(<N number>, <N decimal places>)

Action: Rounds the specified number using the indicated number of decimal places.

Return: <expN> rounded number.

Detail: The following example rounds the result of a calculation to two decimal places (i.e., dollars and cents):

```
INPUT "Enter the initial amount " TO amount
INPUT "Enter the sales tax rate " TO tax
amount = amount + ROUND(amount * tax, 2)
```

To round a number to the left of the decimal, use a negative number of decimals with the ROUND() function. For example:

```
x = 15367.895
? ROUND(x, -1)     && returns 15370.000
? ROUND(x, -2)     && returns 15400.000
? ROUND(x, -3)     && returns 15000.000
```

Also: INT()

ROW() **Environment Function**

Syntax: ROW()

Action: Evaluates the current screen row position.

Return: <expN> representing the screen row number.

Detail: ROW() is most often used with the @ commands when SET DEVICE TO SCREEN is in effect to position information on the screen relative to the location of previously displayed information.

For example, to begin displaying at the current screen location, you could use:

```
@ ROW(), COL() SAY "This begins at current location."
```

The CLEAR command resets ROW() to zero.

Also: COL(), PROW(), PCOL(), @...SAY, @...GET, SET DEVICE TO

RTRIM() — Character Function

Syntax: RTRIM(<expC>)

Action: Removes trailing blank spaces from the specified character string.

Return: <expC> string with no trailing blanks.

Detail: RTRIM() and TRIM() are functionally identical. The following example uses RTRIM() to display the first and last name fields in the Mailing list side by side:

```
USE Mailing
? RTRIM(First_Name) + " " + Last_Name
CLOSE DATABASES
```

Also: TRIM(), LTRIM(), LEN(), ALLTRIM()

RUN — OS Command

Syntax: RUN <OS command> | <com filename> | <exe filename> |
<bat filename> | (<expC>)

Action: Executes an external program.

Detail: The RUN command is used to execute external programs. All active memory variables, environment settings, and open files remain intact when control is returned. Note that you must have enough available memory to load the DOS command processor, Command.COM, plus the program that you are attempting to execute. Otherwise, RUN results in an error message such as "Insufficient memory." For example, to change the current directory you could use:

```
RUN cd\dos
```

You can specify the program name that you want to run as a character expression. To do this, enclose the expression in parentheses. For example, to gain DOS access:

```
cmd_name = "Command"
RUN (cmd_name)
```

Type EXIT at the DOS prompt to return to the program.

The order of precedence used by the RUN command is indicated in the command syntax. For example, if there is a .COM and a .BAT file named Test:

```
! Test
```

executes the .COM file, not the .BAT file.

RUN is functionally identical to !, the bang command.

Do not execute memory resident programs with the RUN command.

Also: ! (run), CALL

SAVE **Memory Command**

Syntax: SAVE TO <mem filename> | (<C mem filename>)
[ALL LIKE | EXCEPT <skeleton>]

Action: Saves all memory variables, or a group of them, to a memory file.

Detail: Memory files are created with the SAVE command. The following program skeleton shows how to save the ending values of certain memory variables so that they can be used the next time a program is executed:

```
RESTORE FROM Checks  && Checks.MEM has account balance
.
. <commands to write checks, record deposits, etc.>
.
SAVE TO Checks ALL LIKE balance    && save new balance
```

SAVE TO <mem filename> with no optional parameters is functionally equivalent to SAVE ALL TO <mem filename>. Both forms of the command save all active memory variables to the named memory file.

The variable's scope, PUBLIC or PRIVATE, is not saved and they become private to the routine that RESTOREs them.

Arrays are not SAVEd in memory files.

Also: RESTORE, = (store), STORE

SAVE SCREEN — Memory Command

Syntax: SAVE SCREEN [TO <screen memory variable>]

Action: Saves the current screen image to a memory buffer or a character type memory variable.

Detail: When saving and restoring screen images, you can choose one of two methods. The first and most simple is to work with only a single screen at a time. In this case, you use SAVE SCREEN with no parameters to save the current image to a buffer that does not have a name and RESTORE SCREEN with no parameters to restore the image from the buffer. For example:

```
SAVE SCREEN     && save current screen image to buffer
.
. <commands that change screen>
.
RESTORE SCREEN  && restore screen from buffer
```

The second method is to save multiple screens to named memory variables. In this case, you name the screen images when you issue SAVE SCREEN TO <memory variable>. Then, you retrieve screen images by name with RESTORE SCREEN FROM <memory variable>. For example:

```
SAVE SCREEN TO screen1
.
. <commands that change screen>
.
SAVE SCREEN TO screen2
.
. <more screen commands>
.
IF <condition>
   RESTORE SCREEN FROM screen1
ELSE
   RESTORE SCREEN FROM screen2
ENDIF
```

Each screen variable saves the full 25 by 80 screen and uses a single memory variable slot of 4000 bytes. To save and restore partial screens, or windows, use the SAVESCREEN() and RESTSCREEN() functions.

Like other memory variables, screen variables are affected by such commands as SAVE, STORE, RESTORE, and RELEASE, and follow the same naming conventions as other memory variables.

Also: RESTORE SCREEN, SAVESCREEN(), RESTSCREEN()

SAVESCREEN() — Memory Function

Syntax: SAVESCREEN(<N top row>, <N left col>,
<N bottom row>, <N right col>)

Action: Saves the specified screen region to a character variable for future use.

Return: <expC> contents of the specified screen region.

Detail: The following example saves a portion of the screen before using it for another purpose. Afterwards, the old screen is restored and the new screen is moved:

```
* Save current screen.
old_screen = SAVESCREEN(7, 10, 14, 50)

* Use area of screen.
@ 7, 10 TO 14, 50 DOUBLE
@ 8, 11 CLEAR TO 13, 49
.
. <commands to write in box>
.
@ 12, 12 SAY "Press any key to move box"
INKEY(0)
```

```
* Save new screen.
new_screen = SAVESCREEN(7, 10, 14, 50)

* Restore old screen.
RESTSCREEN(7, 10, 14, 50, old_screen)

* Move new screen to upper-left of screen.
RESTSCREEN(0, 0, 7, 40, new_screen)
```

Also: SAVE SCREEN, RESTORE SCREEN, RESTSCREEN()

Scope — Database Parameter

Syntax: <command> [ALL | NEXT <expN> | [RECORD] <expN> | REST]
[WHILE <L condition>]
[FOR <L condition>]

Action: Limits the records that a command processes.

Detail: Scope is used to specify which records in the active database file are to be processed by a command. There are three ways to specify a scope, and they are described below in order of their precedence.

The first way is to specify a single record or a group of records based on their position in the database file. This is done using one of these clauses:

Clause	Scope
ALL	All records in the file are processed beginning with the first record.
NEXT <expN>	The specified number of records are processed beginning with the current record.
[RECORD] <expN>	The specified record is processed.
REST	The remaining records in the file are processed beginning with the current record.

The second way is to specify a WHILE condition that each record must meet in order for the command to continue. WHILE is used when the database file is known to be in a particular order (see INDEX, SORT).

The final way is to specify a FOR condition that each record must meet in order to be processed by the command.

You can specify any of the three types of scope separately or use any combination. For example, to list from the first ten records in the mailing list those with the last name Adams:

```
USE Mailing
LIST Last_Name NEXT 10 FOR Last_Name = "Adams"
```

The next example lists all records in the file with the last name Adams rather than limiting the listing to the first ten records. Note that a FOR condition, used alone, implies ALL records:

```
USE Mailing
LIST Last_Name FOR Last_Name = "Adams"
```

The next example uses an index file keyed on Last_Name to list all records with the last name Adams. This method is faster than the one used in the previous example. Note that a WHILE condition, used alone, implies the REST of the records in the file:

```
USE Mailing INDEX Last
SEEK "Adams"
LIST Last_Name WHILE Last_Name = "Adams"
```

The final example illustrates all three types of scope used together and clearly demonstrates their order of precedence. This example finds the first record in the mailing list with the last name Adams and lists from the next five records those that also have an Age value less than 30:

```
USE Mailing INDEX Last
SEEK "Adams"
LIST Last_Name, Age NEXT 5;
                    WHILE Last_Name = "Adams";
                    FOR Age < 30
```

SCROLL() Output Function

Syntax: SCROLL(<N top row>, <N left col>,
<N bottom row>, <N right col>, <N lines>)

Action: Causes the specified screen region to scroll a particular number of lines.

Return: Nothing.

Detail: The lines parameter specifies how many lines to scroll, and in which direction, up or down. Positive numbers scroll up, leaving blank lines at window bottom. Negative numbers scroll down leaving blank lines at window top. A lines parameter of zero clears the entire window.

The following example displays eight records in a window, and assumes there are always at least eight records in the database file. Scrolling is one record at a time based on user keypress.

```
* Set up parameters.
num_lines = 8         && number of lines in window
t_row =  7            && top row of window
b_row = 14            && bottom row of window
l_col = 30            && left column of window
r_col = 50            && right column of window
direction = "D"       && initial direction to scroll

* Open file.
USE Datafile          && can be indexed or not

* Paint window full of records.
i = 1
DO WHILE i <= num_lines .AND. .NOT. EOF()
   @ (t_row-1)+i, l_col SAY Field
   SKIP
   i = i+1
ENDDO

* Position pointer at first record.
GO TOP
```

```
* Loop for window display according to user keypress.
DO WHILE .T.
   key = INKEY()          && get keypress
   DO CASE
      CASE key == 18 .AND. .NOT. BOF()   && PgUp
         IF direction == "D"
            SKIP -1
            IF BOF()
               LOOP   && still at top, no skip necessary
            ENDIF
         ELSE
            SKIP -num_lines
         ENDIF
         direction = "D"
         row = t_row
      CASE key == 3 .AND. .NOT. EOF()   && PgDn
         IF direction == "U"
            SKIP 1
            IF EOF()
               SKIP -1    && recovery from EOF condition
               LOOP
            ENDIF
         ELSE
            SKIP num_lines
         ENDIF
         direction = "U"  && move down = scroll up
         row = b_row
      CASE key == 27      && Esc key exits
         USE              && close files when done
         RETURN
      OTHERWISE
         LOOP
   ENDCASE
   * Scroll the screen one line and
   * repaint the top or bottom line.
   SCROLL( t_row, l_col, b_row, r_col,;
          IF(direction=="U", 1, -1) )
   @ row, l_col SAY Field
ENDDO
```

SECONDS() **Environment Function**

Syntax: SECONDS()

Action: Evaluates the number of seconds that have elapsed since midnight.

Return: <expN> number of seconds.

Detail: SECONDS() is a convenient function if you are doing benchmark tests. For example, the following routine evaluates which is faster, COUNT or a DO WHILE loop that does the counting:

```
USE Mailing

beg_count = SECONDS()
COUNT TO i
end_count = SECONDS()
time_count = end_count - beg_count

GO TOP
beg_do = SECONDS()
i = 0
DO WHILE .NOT. EOF()
   i = i + 1
   SKIP
ENDDO
end_do = SECONDS()
time_do = end_do - beg_do

? "COUNT took", time_count, "seconds."
? "DO took", time_do, "seconds."
difference = IF(time_count>time_do,;
                time_count-time_do, time_do-time_count)
? "Difference is", difference
```

Also: TIME(), DATE()

SEEK **Search Command**

Syntax: SEEK <expression>

Action: Finds the first record in an indexed file whose key matches the expression.

Detail: The following example prompts the user for a part number and uses the SEEK command to locate the correct record:

```
USE Orders INDEX Part_No
DO WHILE .T.
   CLEAR
   part = SPACE(4)
   @ 10, 0 SAY "Enter the part number to view:";
           GET part PICTURE "A999"
   READ
   IF EMPTY(part)
      EXIT
   ENDIF
   SEEK part
   IF FOUND()
      DISPLAY
   ENDIF
ENDDO
CLOSE DATABASES
```

If SEEK does not find a match, the record pointer will be at EOF() unless SOFTSEEK is SET ON.

Also: FOUND(), SET EXACT, SET SOFTSEEK, SET INDEX TO, USE, INDEX, SET ORDER TO, SET SOFTSEEK, FIND

SELECT **Database Command**

Syntax: SELECT <alias> | <work area number> | (<N work area number>)

Action: Activates the specified database file work area.

Detail: The following example sets up a relationship between the Orders and Customer database files:

```
USE Orders
SELECT 2            && SELECT using work area number
USE Customer INDEX Cust_No
SELECT Orders       && SELECT using alias name
SET RELATION TO Cust_No INTO Customer
LIST Part_No, Amount, Customer->Last_Name,;
                      Customer->Phone
```

Once a work area is occupied, always refer to it by alias name to make your code more readable.

Note that using a work area number of zero with SELECT activates the first available (unoccupied) work area:

```
SELECT 0       && selects lowest available work area
```

There are 250 work areas available for your use. To use more than 15 of these simultaneously, you must have DOS version 3.3 or higher and set files to the number you want plus 5 in your Config.SYS file. For example, to span 30 files at once:

```
FILES=35
```

You must also set a DOS environmental variable called Clipper to the number you want to open. For example, to have 30 areas open at once:

```
SET CLIPPER=F30
```

Also: USE, SET RELATION TO, ALIAS(), SELECT(), Config.sys

SELECT() Database Function

Syntax: SELECT([<C alias>])

Action: Evaluates the work area number of the currently selected database file.

Return: <expN> representing the current work area number.

Detail: The following example illustrates how to use SELECT():

```
USE Orders
SELECT 2
USE Customer
? SELECT()              && returns 2
SELECT Orders
? SELECT()              && returns 1
? SELECT("Customer")    && returns 2
```

The next example saves the number of the current work area, opens a file in the next available work area, and re-activates the old work area:

```
PROCEDURE generic
PRIVATE old_area
old_area = SELECT()
SELECT 0
USE Newfile
.
. <commands>
.
USE
SELECT (old_area) && use extended expression parentheses
RETURN
```

Also: ALIAS(), SELECT

SET ALTERNATE — Output Command

Syntax: SET ALTERNATE on | OFF | (<L switch>)

Action: Controls whether or not output is sent to the open alternate file.

Detail: Output from the @...SAY command is not recorded in the alternate file. To record this output, use SET PRINTER TO <file> in conjunction with SET DEVICE TO PRINTER.

The following program skeleton shows you how to work with an alternate text file:

```
SET ALTERNATE TO Output  && open file
SET ALTERNATE ON         && begin recording output
.
. <commands whose output you want to record>
.
SET ALTERNATE OFF        && suspend recording output
.
. <commands whose output you do not want to record>
.
SET ALTERNATE ON         && resume recording output
.
. <more commands to record>
.
SET ALTERNATE OFF        && stop recording output
CLOSE ALTERNATE          && close file
```

You must issue SET ALTERNATE OFF either before or after closing the alternate file, as this operation is not performed automatically, and any new alternate file opened will begin receiving output immediately.

You can specify this SET command using a logical expression by enclosing the expression in parentheses. An expression that evaluates true is interpreted as ON and one that evaluates false is interpreted as OFF. For example:

```
SET ALTERNATE TO Letter
answer = .F.
@ 10, 0 SAY "Write this letter to a file? (Y/N)";
        GET answer PICTURE "Y"
READ
SET ALTERNATE (answer)
TYPE Letter.TXT TO PRINTER
SET ALTERNATE OFF
CLOSE ALTERNATE
```

Also: SET ALTERNATE TO, CLOSE ALTERNATE, SET DEVICE TO, SET PRINTER TO (file), FWRITE()

SET ALTERNATE TO **Output Command**

Syntax: SET ALTERNATE TO [<txt filename> | (<C txt filename>)]

Action: Creates and opens a text file that records output.

Detail: Output from the @...SAY command is not recorded in the alternate file. To record this output, use SET PRINTER TO <file> in conjunction with SET DEVICE TO PRINTER.

The following program skeleton shows you how to work with an alternate text file:

```
SET ALTERNATE TO Output   && open file
SET ALTERNATE ON          && begin recording output
.
. <commands whose output you want to record>
.
SET ALTERNATE OFF         && suspend recording output
.
. <commands whose output you do not want to record>
.
SET ALTERNATE ON          && resume recording output
.
. <more commands to record>
.
SET ALTERNATE OFF         && stop recording output
CLOSE ALTERNATE           && close file
```

You must issue SET ALTERNATE OFF either before or after closing the alternate file, as this operation is not performed automatically, and any new alternate file opened will begin receiving output immediately.

You can specify the file name as a character expression by enclosing the expression in parentheses. For example:

```
alt_file = "Letter"
SET ALTERNATE TO (alt_file)
```

Also: SET ALTERNATE, CLOSE ALTERNATE, SET DEVICE TO, SET PRINTER TO (file), FWRITE()

SET BELL

Environment Command

Syntax: SET BELL on | OFF | (<L switch>)

Action: Controls whether or not the bell rings during data entry.

Detail: During data entry, there is no audible indication when you make an input error. To cause the bell to ring when you type past the end of a field or when you make a data entry error (e.g., typing a value that does not fit the specified PICTURE or RANGE), use:

```
SET BELL ON
```

You can make the bell ring using the command ?? CHR(7), even when SET BELL is OFF.

You can specify this SET command using a logical expression by enclosing the expression in parentheses. An expression that evaluates true is interpreted as ON and one that evaluates false is interpreted as OFF.

```
is_bell = <L condition>
SET BELL (is_bell)
```

Also: READ, SET CONFIRM

SET CARRY

Database Command

Syntax: SET CARRY on | off

Action: This command is not operational.

Detail: Although use of SET CARRY is allowed in programs for compatibility with other dialects, the command is not operational in Clipper.

SET CENTURY **Date Command**

Syntax: SET CENTURY on | OFF | (<L switch>)

Action: Controls whether or not the century is used as part of date displays.

Detail: When SET CENTURY is ON, all date displays include the century and have 4-digit years. When OFF, the years are 2 digits.

The following example queries the system date with SET CENTURY ON and OFF:

```
* Default is SET CENTURY OFF
? DATE()   && returns 12/25/89
SET CENTURY ON
? DATE()   && returns 12/25/1989
```

You can specify this SET command using a logical expression by enclosing the expression in parentheses. An expression that evaluates true is interpreted as ON and one that evaluates false is interpreted as OFF.

```
is_century = <L condition>
SET CENTURY (is_century)
```

When SET CENTURY is ON during data entry, dates may be entered as two-digit years and the twentieth century will be assumed.

Also: SET DATE, DATE()

Set Clipper **OS Command**

Syntax: Set Clipper=[V<memvar Kbytes>]
[;R<run Kbytes>]
[;E<expanded memory Kbytes>]
[;X<exclude Kbytes>]
[;F<open files>]

Action: Create an operating system environmental variable for run-time configuration of the compiled application program.

Detail: Each time a Clipper compiled program executes, it checks the operating system for an environmental variable called Clipper. If it finds one, it uses the numbers specified in the parameter list to configure certain run-time settings.

Parameter	Description
V	Set maximum memory available for memory variables
R	Reserve memory for RUN command
E	Set amount of expanded memory used for index buffers
X	Exclude (hide) memory from your program
F	Set maximum number of files your program will open

Use the V parameter to limit the maximum memory your program will allocate to memory variable storage. Each memvar requires 22 bytes and the default number of memvars is 2048, requiring 44K of memory storage. If your program uses a maximum of only 500 variables at one time, it does not need 44K. 500 times 22 is 11,000 bytes, so you could SET CLIPPER=V11 and have an additional 33K of run-time memory available.

Use the R parameter to reserve a specific amount of memory for the RUN command. SET CLIPPER=R128 insures that your program will always have 128K of memory available to RUN external programs. If you are running without expanded memory, this area is shared by index buffers.

Use the E parameter to limit the maximum amount of expanded memory your program will use (if it exists) for index buffers. The default is one megabyte, but if you need to reserve 500K for another purpose, you could SET CLIPPER=E500.

Use the X parameter to exclude or hide memory from your program. If you are developing on a 640K machine but your program must run on 512K machines, you could SET CLIPPER=X128 for testing. Note that this excludes memory only from your program, but not for external programs executed by a RUN command in your program.

Use the F parameter to set the maximum number of files your program will open. The default is five less than specified in your Config.sys file up to 15 maximum. Under versions of DOS from 3.3 and higher, you can increase this up to a maximum of 250. To set your maximum number of open files to 30, put FILES=35 in Config.sys and SET CLIPPER=F30.

To set multiple parameters, separate each with a semicolon:

```
SET CLIPPER=F30;V20;E900
```

Also: Config.sys

SET COLOR TO — Display Command

Syntax: SET COLOR | COLOUR TO [<standard> [, <enhanced>
[, <border> [, <background>
[, <unselected>]]]]]
| [(<C attribute list>)]

Action: Defines the color attributes that you see on your screen.

Detail: The following tables show the codes that can be used with SET COLOR TO for color and monochrome monitors.

Color

Code	Number	Effect
N | (space)	0	Black
B	1	Blue
G	2	Green
BG	3	Cyan
R	4	Red
BR	5	Magenta
GR	6	Brown
W	7	White
X	n/a	Blank

Monochrome

Code	Number	Effect
N | (space)	0	Black
U	1	Underline
W	7	White
I	n/a	Inverse
X	n/a	Blank

Attributes

Two attributes can be added to either the color or monochrome codes in order to produce bright and blinking effects:

Code	Number	Effect
+	8	Bright
*	128	Blinking

The standard and enhanced options in the syntax are represented by pair of these codes separated by a slash (/). The first is the foreground and the second is the background and both are optional. Omitting any option, or any part of an option, leaves it unchanged. For example, this command does not affect the enhanced display:

```
* Standard is yellow on blue, border is red
SET COLOR TO GR+/B, , R
```

You can represent the color attributes as a character expression by enclosing the expression in parentheses. For example:

```
newcolor = "GR+/B, , R"
SET COLOR TO (newcolor)
```

The unselected option refers to the color of unavailable menu selections.

It is best to assign color values to memvars at the start of your application, and use the memvars to change colors everywhere. This way, if you want to change a color value, you can to do it in one place only.

The following section of code tests the ISCOLOR() function before using SET COLOR TO. Using this code in the setup portion of an application, you can use the application on either a monochrome or a color system:

```
* Program: Main.PRG
* Syntax : Main [MONO]
* Action : Application start-up.
* Note   : Optional MONO parameter forces monochrome
*        : attributes on color systems.  This is useful
*        : on systems with color cards and monochrome
*        : monitors, or anywhere color attributes fail.
*
PARAMETERS param1
sys_mono = IF(PCOUNT()==1, UPPER(param1)=="MONO", .F.)

IF ISCOLOR() .AND. (!sys_mono)
   s_standard = "W+/B"          && standard SAY
   s_enhanced = "W+/G"          && enhanced GET
   s_backgr   = "B"             && background
   s_border   = "G"             && border
   s_unselect = "W+/BG"         && active unselected GET
   s_noprompt = "W/B"           && inaccessible prompts
   s_warning  = "W+/R*"         && warning message
   s_blank    = "G/G"           && blank, for password
ELSE           && monochrome
   s_standard = "W+"            && standard SAY
   s_enhanced = "I"             && enhanced GET
   s_backgr   = "N"             && background
   s_border   = "N"             && border
   s_unselect = "I"             && active unselected GET
   s_noprompt = "W"             && inaccessible prompts
   s_warning  = "W+*"           && warning message
   s_blank    = "X"             && blank, for password
ENDIF

* Save user's screen attributes and set ours.
user_row = ROW()
SAVE SCREEN TO scr_user
SET COLOR TO (s_standard +","+ s_enhanced +","+;
              s_backgr   +","+ s_border   +","+;
              s_unselect)
```

```
* Begin application.
DO main_menu && application's top level until user quits

* Quit to the operating system.
RESTORE SCREEN FROM scr_user
@ user_row-1, 0 SAY ""          && reposition cursor
QUIT
```

Also: ISCOLOR(), SET INTENSITY

SET CONFIRM — Database Command

Syntax: SET CONFIRM on | OFF | (<L switch>)

Action: Controls whether or not you must press Enter after each field when typing.

Detail: To force the user to confirm each field entry by pressing Enter when adding records to the Mailing list:

```
USE Mailing
SET FORMAT TO Mailing
SET CONFIRM ON
APPEND BLANK
READ
SET CONFIRM OFF
CLOSE DATABASES
```

You can specify this SET command using a logical expression by enclosing the expression in parentheses. An expression that evaluates true is interpreted as ON and one that evaluates false is interpreted as OFF.

```
is_confirm = <L condition>
SET CONFIRM (is_confirm)
```

Also: READ, SET BELL

SET CONSOLE **Display Command**

Syntax: SET CONSOLE ON | off | (<L switch>)

Action: Controls whether or not output (except full-screen mode) is seen on the screen.

Detail: The following example uses SET CONSOLE to suppress the display of a report on the screen while it is being printed:

```
USE Orders
SET CONSOLE OFF
REPORT FORM Daily TO PRINTER
SET CONSOLE ON
CLOSE DATABASES
```

You can specify this SET command using a logical expression by enclosing the expression in parentheses. An expression that evaluates true is interpreted as ON and one that evaluates false is interpreted as OFF. For example, to query the user as to whether or not the report is to be displayed on the screen while it is printed:

```
@ 10,5 SAY "Show report on screen while printing? (Y/N)"
SET CONSOLE (CHR(INKEY(0)) $ "yY")
REPORT FORM Daily TO PRINTER
SET CONSOLE ON
CLOSE DATABASES
```

Also: TO PRINTER, SET PRINTER

SET CURSOR **Display Command**

Syntax: SET CURSOR ON | off | (<L switch>)

Action: Determines whether or not the cursor is displayed on the screen.

Detail: The following example turns the cursor off while the data entry screen is being painted and turns it on again before the READ:

```
CLEAR
USE Mailing
SET CURSOR OFF
@  0,  0 SAY "First Name" GET First_Name
@  1,  0 SAY "Last Name " GET Last_Name
@  2,  0 SAY "Address   " GET Address
@  3,  0 SAY "City      " GET City
@  4,  0 SAY "State     " GET State
@  5,  0 SAY "Zip       " GET Zip
SET CURSOR ON
READ
```

You can specify this SET command using a logical expression by enclosing the expression in parentheses. An expression that evaluates true is interpreted as ON and one that evaluates false is interpreted as OFF.

Also: ACCEPT, INPUT, WAIT, READ

SET DATE — Date Command

Syntax: SET DATE AMERICAN | ansi | british | french | german | italian

Action: Determines the default format for date displays.

Detail: The date formats are shown below for each SET DATE command line option:

Option	Format
AMERICAN	MM/DD/[CC]YY
ANSI	[CC]YY.MM.DD
BRITISH	DD/MM/[CC]YY
FRENCH	DD/MM/[CC]YY
GERMAN	DD.MM.[CC]YY
ITALIAN	DD-MM-[CC]YY

In each case, MM represents the month, DD the day, and YY the year. [CC] represents the optional century that is a part of the date display only if SET CENTURY is ON.

For example, to use the British date format, use:

```
SET DATE BRITISH
```

Also: PICTURE, SET CENTURY, DATE()

SET DEBUG **Debug Command**

Syntax: SET DEBUG on | off

Action: This command is not operational.

Detail: Although use of SET DEBUG is allowed in programs for compatibility with other dialects, the command is not operational in Clipper.

Clipper's debugger is contained in DEBUG.OBJ which must be linked with your program.

Also: Debugging

SET DECIMALS TO **Numeric Command**

Syntax: SET DECIMALS TO [<N decimals>]

Action: Defines the minimum number of decimal places for numeric displays.

Detail: To fix the number of decimal places to 2 when you are dealing with currency:

```
SET DECIMALS TO 2
SET FIXED ON
```

Used with no parameters, SET DECIMALS TO changes the number of decimals to zero.

Also: SET FIXED

SET DEFAULT TO **OS Command**

Syntax: SET DEFAULT TO [<drive letter> [:<path>]]

Action: Changes the disk that is used as the default drive.

Detail: To work with files on the floppy drive A: rather than the default hard disk drive C:

```
SET DEFAULT TO A
.
. <commands to use files on drive A:>
.
```

With this command, you can also change the default directory. For example:

```
SET DEFAULT TO C:\  && changes default to root directory
```

If used with no parameters, SET DEFAULT TO changes the default drive to the logged-in drive and directory when you entered the program. In keeping with the above example where the original default drive was C:

```
SET DEFAULT TO  && returns C: to the default drive
```

Also: SET PATH TO

SET DELETED **Database Command**

Syntax: SET DELETED on | OFF | (<L switch>)

Action: Controls whether or not deleted records are processed.

Detail: To print a report for the Orders database file that ignores deleted records:

```
USE Orders
SET DELETED ON
REPORT FORM Daily TO PRINTER
SET DELETED OFF
CLOSE DATABASES
```

You can specify this SET command using a logical expression by enclosing the expression in parentheses. An expression that evaluates true is interpreted as ON and one that evaluates false is interpreted as OFF. For example:

```
@ 10, 0 SAY "Ignore deleted records? (Y/N)"
SET DELETED (CHR(INKEY(0)) $ "yY")
REPORT FORM Daily TO PRINTER
SET DELTED OFF
CLOSE DATABASES
```

Also: DELETE, DELETED(), RECALL, PACK

SET DELIMITERS **Display Command**

Syntax: SET DELIMITERS on | OFF | (<L switch>)

Action: Controls whether or not data entry areas are surrounded by delimiters.

Detail: To change the delimiters to angle brackets when you edit the Orders database file:

```
USE Orders INDEX Part_No, Cust_No
SET FORMAT TO EditRecs
SET DELIMITERS TO "<>"     && define delimiter characters
SET DELIMITERS ON          && use delimiters
APPEND BLANK
READ            && fields are enclosed in angle brackets
SET DELIMITERS OFF
SET DELIMITERS TO DEFAULT && change back to colons
CLOSE DATABASES
```

You can specify this SET command using a logical expression by enclosing the expression in parentheses. An expression that evaluates true is interpreted as ON and one that evaluates false is interpreted as OFF.

```
is_delims = <L condition>
SET DELIMITERS (is_delims)
```

Also: SET DELIMITERS TO, READ

SET DELIMITERS TO **Display Command**

Syntax: SET DELIMITERS TO [<C delimiter characters> | DEFAULT]

Action: Determines the delimiters used for data entry areas with SET DELIMITERS ON

Detail: The default delimiters are colons (:).

If only one <delimiter character> is specified, it is used for both the left and right delimiters.

To change the delimiters to angle brackets when you edit the Orders database file:

```
USE Orders INDEX Part_No, Cust_No
SET FORMAT TO EditRecs
SET DELIMITERS TO "<>"  && define delimiter characters
SET DELIMITERS ON       && use delimiters
APPEND BLANK
READ            && fields are enclosed in angle brackets
SET DELIMITERS OFF
SET DELIMITERS TO DEFAULT       && change back to colons
CLOSE DATABASES
```

SET DELIMITERS TO with no other parameters is functionally equivalent to SET DELIMITERS TO DEFAULT, and restores the colon as left and right delimiter characters.

Also: SET DELIMITERS, READ

SET DEVICE TO **Output Command**

Syntax: SET DEVICE TO SCREEN | printer

Action: Defines the output device for subsequent @...SAY commands.

Detail: The following example uses SET DEVICE TO PRINTER to print invoices:

```
USE Invoices
SET DEVICE TO PRINTER

DO WHILE .NOT. EOF()
   * These @...SAY commands are printed.
   @  2, 60 SAY DATE()
   @  4,  5 SAY TRIM(First_Name) + " " + Last_Name
   @  5,  5 SAY Address1
   @  6,  5 SAY TRIM(City) + ", " + State + "  " + Zip
   @ 10,  8 SAY Quantity PICTURE "999"
   @ 10, 15 SAY SUBSTR(Descrip, 1, 40)
   @ 10, 60 SAY Price PICTURE "999999.99"
   @ 10, 70 SAY Quantity * Price PICTURE "999999.99"
   SKIP
ENDDO

SET DEVICE TO SCREEN
CLOSE DATABASES
```

To send output from @...SAY to a text file, use SET PRINTER TO <filename> to redirect the output from SET DEVICE TO PRINTER.

Also: @...SAY, SET PRINTER TO (file)

SET ECHO — Debug Command

Syntax: SET ECHO on | off

Action: This command is not operational.

Detail: Although use of SET ECHO is allowed in programs for compatibility with other dialects, the command is not operational in Clipper.

SET ESCAPE **Program Command**

Syntax: SET ESCAPE ON | off | (<L switch>)

Action: Controls whether or not Esc can be used to interrupt the currently active @...GET.

Detail: Normally, users are at liberty to exit from any @...GET/READ by pressing the Esc key. When a user does this, the RANGE and VALID clauses for the @...GET variable are ignored and the READ is terminated. This means that @...GET variables remaining on the screen are also terminated. To eliminate this possibility, use:

```
SET ESCAPE OFF
```

You can specify this SET command using a logical expression by enclosing the expression in parentheses. An expression that evaluates true is interpreted as ON and one that evaluates false is interpreted as OFF.

```
is_escape = <L condition>
SET ESCAPE (is_escape)
```

Also: READ, SET KEY, SETCANCEL()

SET EXACT **Comparison Command**

Syntax: SET EXACT on | OFF | (<L switch>)

Action: Determines how comparison operations are performed.

Detail: SET EXACT affects all forms of string comparison in all commands except == double equals.

Normally, when character strings are compared for equality, the strings are compared until the one on the right side of the equals sign (=) runs out of characters. If the strings are equal up until that point, the comparison produces a logical true. For example, look at the following query results:

```
? "Are you sleeping?" = "Are"   && returns .T.
? "Are" = "Are you sleeping?"   && returns .F.
```

If you want to compare strings for length as well as equality, use:

```
SET EXACT ON       && strings must be exactly the same
? "Are you sleeping?" = "Are"    && returns .F.
? "Are" = "Are"                  && returns .T.
```

Note that trailing blank spaces are insignificant when SET EXACT is ON. For example:

```
? "Are" = "Are    "                && returns .T.
SET EXACT OFF
? "Are" = "Are    "                && returns .F.
```

You can specify this SET command using a logical expression by enclosing the expression in parentheses. An expression that evaluates true is interpreted as ON and one that evaluates false is interpreted as OFF.

```
is_exact = <L condition>
SET EXACT (is_exact)
```

Also: = (compare), SEEK, FIND, LOCATE, ASCAN(), ==

SET EXCLUSIVE — Network Command

Syntax: SET EXCLUSIVE ON | off | (<L switch>)

Action: Determines the open attribute for subsequently opened database files.

Detail: You need to SET EXCLUSIVE OFF in order to allow file and record sharing in a network environment. Otherwise, each file is opened for the sole use of whoever opens it first, and other users are denied access.

When you open a file with SET EXCLUSIVE OFF, you must obtain the appropriate file or record locks before allowing any changes to the data. For example:

```
SET EXCLUSIVE OFF
USE Orders
SELECT 2
USE Customer INDEX Cust_No
.
. <commands to obtain file/record locks>
.
```

You can specify this SET command using a logical expression by enclosing the expression in parentheses. An expression that evaluates true is interpreted as ON and one that evaluates false is interpreted as OFF.

```
is_excl = <L condition>
SET EXCLUSIVE (is_excl)
```

Also: Networking, USE, FLOCK(), LOCK(), RLOCK()

SET FILTER TO — Database Command

Syntax: SET FILTER TO [<L condition>]

Action: Imposes a filter condition on the active database file.

Detail: The following example uses SET FILTER TO to print two different versions of the same report form:

```
USE Orders
SET FILTER TO ! DELETED()  && filter out deleted records
REPORT FORM Daily TO PRINTER
SET FILTER TO              && drop filter to see all records
REPORT FORM Daily TO PRINTER HEADING "All Orders"
CLOSE DATABASE
```

Unless the command immediately following the SET FILTER TO command moves the record pointer, you should issue a GO TOP to make sure that the filter condition is activated. Otherwise, the current record will be processed even if it does not meet the filter condition.

GO <record number> ignores the status of SET DELETED.

Also: GO

SET FIXED **Numeric Command**

Syntax: SET FIXED on | OFF | (<L switch>)

Action: Determines whether the number of decimals displayed is fixed or variable.

Detail: To fix the number of decimal places to 2 when you are dealing with currency:

```
SET DECIMALS TO 2
SET FIXED ON
```

You can specify this SET command using a logical expression by enclosing the expression in parentheses. An expression that evaluates true is interpreted as ON and one that evaluates false is interpreted as OFF.

```
is_fixed = <L condition>
SET FIXED (is_fixed)
```

Also: SET DECIMALS TO

SET FORMAT TO **Input Command**

Syntax: SET FORMAT TO [<fmt filename>]

Action: Opens a format file to be used by subsequent full-screen editing commands.

Detail: Format files are compiled into the calling object file and can contain any valid Clipper command or function.

The following example shows how to use a format file to edit records in the Orders database file:

```
USE Orders INDEX Part_No, Cust_No
SET FORMAT TO EditRecs
.
. <commands to locate the record you want to edit>
.
```

```
READ
CLOSE DATABASES  && also closes index and format files
```

EditRecs.FMT is listed below:

```
* EditRecs.FMT
@ 5, 5 SAY "Customer Number" GET Cust_No;
                             PICTURE "@! A999"
@ 6, 5 SAY "Part Number    " GET Part_No;
                             PICTURE "@! A9999"
@ 7, 5 SAY "Quantity       " GET Quantity;
```

SET FORMAT TO with no parameters closes the format file in the current work area.

Also: @...SAY, @...GET, @...SAY...GET, @...TO, @...CLEAR, READ, @...BOX, CLOSE FORMAT

SET FUNCTION TO — Environment Command

Syntax: SET FUNCTION <N key number> TO [<expC>]

Action: Programs the designated function key with the specified character string.

Detail: The following example prompts you and reprograms all of the available function keys according to your responses:

```
FOR number = 1 TO FKMAX()
   response = SPACE(2000)
   @ 6, 0 SAY "Enter the contents for function key " +;
              FKLABEL(number) GET response
   READ
   SET FUNCTION number TO response
NEXT
```

To cause an automatic carriage return after the function key is pressed, use a semicolon as the last character in the function key definition. For example:

```
SET FUNCTION 3 TO; "LIST FOR Last_Name = 'SMITH';"
```

Note that SET KEY takes precedence over SET FUNCTION when there is a conflict.

The available function keys are listed below:

Key Number	Key Label
1 - 10	F1 - F10
11 - 20	Shift-F1 - Shift-F10
21 - 30	Ctrl-F1 - Ctrl-F10
31 - 40	Alt-F1 - Alt-F10

Also: SET KEY, FKLABEL(), FKMAX(), ;

SET HEADING — Output Command

Syntax: SET HEADING on | off

Action: This command is not operational.

Detail: Although use of SET HEADING is allowed in programs for compatibility with other dialects, the command is not operational in Clipper.

SET HEADINGS is the actual syntax in other dialects, but this produces a compile-time error in Clipper.

SET INDEX TO — Index Command

Syntax: SET INDEX TO [<index filename list> | (<C index filename list>)]

Action: Opens the named index files for use with the active database file.

Detail: Usually, the database file and its associated index files are opened with a single USE command, but sometimes SET INDEX TO is used to open and close the index files separately. The following example uses SET INDEX TO so that the database file can be viewed in several different orders:

```
USE Orders
REPORT FORM Orders TO PRINTER  && In natural order
SET INDEX TO Part_No, Order_No && Part_No.ntx is master
REPORT FORM ByPart TO PRINTER  && In Part_No order
SET ORDER TO 2                 && Order_No.ntx is master
REPORT FORM ByOrder TO PRINTER && In Order_No order
CLOSE DATABASES                && all dbf and ntx files
```

SET INDEX TO with no parameters closes all index files in the current work area, and is functionally identical to CLOSE INDEXES.

One or more of the SET INDEX TO file names can be specified as characters expressions by enclosing the expression in parentheses. For example:

```
ntx_file = "Part_No"
SET INDEX TO (ntx_file), Order_No
```

Also: SET ORDER TO, USE, INDEX, CLOSE INDEXES

SET INTENSITY — Display Command

Syntax: SET INTENSITY ON | off | (<L switch>)

Action: Controls whether or not you see both a standard and an enhanced display.

Detail: If you do not want a distinction between the standard and enchanced displays, use:

```
SET INTENSITY OFF
```

You can specify this SET command using a logical expression by enclosing the expression in parentheses. An expression that evaluates true is interpreted as ON and one that evaluates false is interpreted as OFF.

```
is_intens = <L condition>
SET INTENSITY (is_intens)
```

Also: SET COLOR TO, @...GET

SET KEY TO — Environment Command

Syntax: SET KEY <N key number> TO [<procedure>]

Action: Causes the named procedure to be executed when the specified key is pressed.

Detail: SET KEY allows you to program a key so that when the key is pressed during a wait state, a procedure is executed. A wait state is produced by executing any command or function that waits for or traps user input. Specifically, these commands and functions are: ACCEPT, ACHOICE(), DBEDIT(), INKEY(), INPUT, MENU TO, MEMOEDIT(), READ, and WAIT.

The key number of any key is equal to its INKEY() value. To disable the SET KEY for a particular key, use SET KEY <N key number> TO with no other parameters.

For example, to display the date and time whenever the F2 function key is pressed:

```
SET KEY -1 TO key_date   && enable F2 keypress
READ                     && enter wait state
SET KEY -1 TO            && disable F2 keypress

PROCEDURE key_date
* Syntax: SET KEY -1 TO key_date
* Action: Display date and time in prompt box.
* Note  : -1 is F2 function key.
*
PRIVATE scr_window
* Save message window, clear it, and redraw box.
scr_window = SAVESCREEN(0, 0, 2, 79)
@ 0, 0 CLEAR TO 2, 79
@ 0, 0 TO 2, 79 DOUBLE
@ 1, 5 SAY "Date: " + CDOW(today)   +", "+;
                      CMONTH(today)   +" "+ ;
               LTRIM(STR(DAY(today))) +", "+;
                    STR(YEAR(today),4)
clock_time = TIME()
```

```
disp_time = IF( VAL(clock_time) < 10,;
                " " + SUBSTR(clock_time,2,4),;
                SUBSTR(clock_time,1,5) )
val_time = VAL(disp_time)
DO CASE
   CASE val_time == zero
      disp_time = "12" + SUBSTR(disp_time, 3) +" a.m."
   CASE val_time < 12
      disp_time = disp_time + " a.m."
   CASE val_time == 12
      disp_time = disp_time + " p.m."
   CASE val_time > 12
      disp_time = STR(val_time-12, 2) +;
                  SUBSTR(disp_time,3) + " p.m."
ENDCASE
@ 1,50 SAY "Time: " + disp_time
KEYBOARD CHR(INKEY(0))                 && wait for keypress
RESTSCREEN(0, 0, 2, 79, scr_window) && restore window
RETURN
```

By default, the F1 key is set to branch to a procedure called help. You can create your own help procedure under this name or redirect the key to a new name:

```
SET KEY 28 TO key_help
```

The following procedure is taken from an actual application of medium size to illustrate what a typical help procedure looks like.

```
PROCEDURE key_help
* Syntax: SET KEY 28 TO key_help
* Action: Display help message(s) in prompt box.
* Note  : 28 is F1 function key.
*
PARAMETERS proc, line, memvar
PRIVATE scr_window, wait_flag

* Save message window, clear it, and redraw box.
scr_window = SAVESCREEN(0, 0, 2, 79)
@ 0, 0 CLEAR TO 2, 79
@ 0, 0 TO 2, 79 DOUBLE
```

```
* Assume a wait after the help message.
wait_flag = true

DO CASE
* From transaction:
   CASE memvar == "M_RESALE_N"
      @ 1,5 SAY [Calif state resale number or "US GOVT"]
   CASE memvar == "M_SPC_DISC"
      @ 1,5 SAY [Discount: "dG" = dGENERATE,] +;
                         [ "FB" = FreeBase,]  +;
                         [ "LB" = Tom Rettig's Library,]
      @ 2,5 SAY [            "HP" = Tom Rettig's HELP,]+;
                         [ "BB" = Bantam Book]
   CASE memvar == "M_TRANS_TY"
      @ 1,5 SAY "C = credit, E = eval, I = info, " +;
                "R = refund"
   CASE memvar == "M_TERMS"
      @ 1,5 SAY "NET = credit, COD = cod" +;
                 "  (cannot be COD if out of U.S.A.)"
   CASE memvar == "M_OTHER_CH"
      @ 1,5 SAY "$2.00 if COD"
   CASE memvar == "M_SHIP_VIA"
      @ 1,5 SAY "UPS, FIRST CLASS MAIL, AIR MAIL, FEDEX"
   CASE memvar == "M_PAID"
      @ 1,5 SAY "Enter here if paid at time of order,"+;
                " otherwise use money window."
   CASE memvar == "M_SOURCE"
      @ 1,5 SAY [Refer to printed "Origin" report ] +;
                "for existing sources."
   CASE memvar = "M_ITEM" .OR. memvar == "REGNUM"
      KEYBOARD "?" + CHR(13)  && brings up list

* From customer:
   CASE memvar == "M_COMPANY"
      @ 1,5 SAY "45-column field will be truncated ",;
           "to: 39 on invoices, 37 on envelopes, " +;
           "35 on package/COD labels."
   CASE memvar == "M_COMMENT"
      @ 1,5 SAY "Ctrl-PgDn to expand comment field."
```

```
   CASE memvar == "M_CATEGORY"
      PRIVATE choice
      choice = menu_codes() && pick list
      IF !EMPTY(choice)
         m_category = choice
         KEYBOARD CHR(13)   && move to next GET
      ENDIF
      wait_flag = false
   CASE memvar == "F_NAME"
      @ 1,5 SAY "Use a comma ',' +;
           " to add a first name to the search."
      @ 2,5 SAY [E.g., "smith,ron"]
   CASE memvar == "M_FNAME" .OR. memvar == "M_LNAME"
      @ 1,5 SAY "The comma ',' "+;
          "symbol cannot be part of a name."

* From customer and reg_ctrl:
   CASE memvar == "REG_NUM"
      @ 1,5 SAY "Serial number must be complete to " +;
                "perform lookup."
      IF proc == "REG_CTRL"
         @ p_row+1, msg_col SAY "Do not specify " +;
             "when registering items without numbers."
      ENDIF

* From money:
   CASE memvar == "M_DETAIL"
      @ 1,5 SAY "W/O = write off, " +;
               "an adjustment for money not collected."
   CASE memvar == "M_AMOUNT"
      @ 1,5 SAY "Positive amount for money received,"+;
               " negative amount for money refunded."

* From get_dates():
   CASE proc == "GET_DATES"
      @ 1,5 SAY "Both dates must be valid." + "  " +;
               "Start date must be at least 1986."
      @ 2,5 SAY "Press Enter to confirm your entry."
```

```
* From item_ctrl:
   CASE memvar == "M_FIELDS"   && really an array
      @ 1,5 SAY "Item_code must be four alpha letters."
      @ 2,5 SAY "Is auto true only if item DOES NOT "+;
                "have serial numbers."

* From set_flags:
   CASE proc == "SET_FLAGS"
      @ 1,5 SAY "Flags act as a filter when set true."
      @ 2,5 SAY "They exclude from invoices and labels."

* From anywhere else:
   OTHERWISE
      @ 1,5 SAY "Help is not available here.  " +;
                "Let me know what you'd like to see."
      @ 2,5 SAY msg_anykey
ENDCASE

IF wait_flag
   CLEAR TYPEAHEAD
   INKEY(0)
ENDIF

RESTSCREEN(0, 0, 2, 79, scr_window)    && restore window
RETURN
```

Also: INKEY(), SET FUNCTION, PROCEDURE

SET MARGIN TO — Output Command

Syntax: SET MARGIN TO [<N left print margin>]

Action: Changes the left margin setting from its default of zero.

Detail: To change the print margin for printing letters:

```
SET MARGIN TO 8
SET PRINTER ON
USE Mailing
DO WHILE .NOT. EOF()
   ? "Dear " + First_Name
   ?
   num_lines = MLCOUNT(Letter, 65)
   FOR x = 1 TO num_lines
      ? MEMOLINE(Letter, 65, x)
   NEXT
   EJECT
   SKIP
ENDDO
CLOSE DATABASES
SET PRINTER OFF
SET MARGIN TO       && reset margin setting to default
```

Note that SET MARGIN TO with no other parameters returns the margin setting to its default value of zero. Functionally, SET MARGIN TO is equivalent to SET MARGIN TO 0.

Also: SET PRINTER, SET DEVICE TO

SET MENUS — Help Command

Syntax: SET MENUS on | off

Action: This command is not operational.

Detail: Although use of SET MENUS is allowed in programs for compatibility with other dialects, the command is not operational in Clipper.

SET MESSAGE TO

Menu Command

Syntax: SET MESSAGE TO [<N row> [CENTER | CENTRE]]

Action: Defines the line on which @...PROMPT...MESSAGEs are displayed.

Detail: The following example illustrates the use of SET MESSAGE TO to define the line on which @...PROMPT messages are displayed:

```
* Menu messages are displayed on line 2.
SET MESSAGE TO 2  && turn on messages

* Allow left/right arrow keys to wrap around.
SET WRAP ON

* Infinite loop for menu display.
DO WHILE .T.
   CLEAR
   @ box_home, 0, 3, 79 BOX box_double
   @ 1, 5 PROMPT "Customer" MESSAGE;
          "Add/search/edit customers and transactions."
   @ 1,17 PROMPT "Invoice"  MESSAGE;
          "Print invoices from customer transactions."
   @ 1,28 PROMPT "Label"    MESSAGE;
          "Print labels from customers or transactions."
   @ 1,37 PROMPT "Report"   MESSAGE;
          "Print reports."
   @ 1,47 PROMPT "Shipping" MESSAGE;
          "Browse ship-to names and companies."
   @ 1,59 PROMPT "Maintain" MESSAGE;
          "File and system maintenance utilities."
   @ 1,71 PROMPT "Quit"     MESSAGE;
          "Quit to the operating system."

   MENU TO action
```

```
* Make decision based on menu option selected.
DO CASE
   CASE action == 1
      DO Customer
   CASE action == 2
      DO Report WITH "INVOICES"
   CASE action == 3
      DO Report WITH "LABELS"
   CASE action == 4
      DO Report
   CASE action == 5
      DO Shipping
   CASE action == 6
      DO Maintain
   CASE action == 7
      SET MESSAGE TO     && turn off messages
      SET WRAP OFF       && turn off menu wrap
      RETURN
 ENDCASE
ENDDO
```

By default, the SET MESSAGE line is zero, and no @...PROMPT MESSAGEs are displayed. SET MESSAGE TO with no parameters returns the message line to zero.

Also: @...PROMPT, MENU TO, SET WRAP

SET ORDER TO — Index Command

Syntax: SET ORDER TO [<N order>]

Action: Determines which open index file is used as the controlling index.

Detail: The following example uses a different index order to print several reports for the Orders database file:

```
USE Orders
REPORT FORM Orders TO PRINTER  && In natural order

SET INDEX TO Part_No, Order_No && Part_No is master ntx
REPORT FORM ByPart TO PRINTER  && In Part_No order

SET ORDER TO 2                 && Order_No is master ntx
REPORT FORM ByOrder TO PRINTER && In Order_No order
CLOSE DATABASES                && all dbf and ntx files
```

Note that FIND and SEEK only work with the controlling index file key. If there are several open index files, use SET ORDER TO to change the controlling index file so that you can find records based on index key values other than those of the first index file in the INDEX list.

SET ORDER TO 0 (or SET ORDER TO with no parameters) ignores all index files without actually closing them so that you can view the file in its natural, record number order. Additions and changes made to the database file with SET ORDER TO 0 are still updated in the open index files.

Also: SET INDEX TO, USE, SEEK, FIND

SET PATH TO — OS Command

Syntax: SET PATH TO [<path list>]

Action: Defines a list of directories that are searched when looking for files.

Detail: To force a path search when files are not found in the current directory, use the SET PATH TO command. The following examples show how to use the SET PATH TO command:

```
SET PATH TO C:\clip; C:\clip\extend; C:\clip\utils
SET PATH TO C:\clip, C:\clip\extend, C:\clip\utils
```

Note that items in the path list can be separated using either semicolons or commas.

After this command is issued, each of the directories in the path setting are searched every time a command attempts to access an existing file (e.g., USE <dbf filename>, DO <prg filename>). Only after the file cannot be found in the current directory or any of those in the path setting is an error triggered.

SET PATH TO with no path setting returns the path search to the current directory only.

To make the path setting the same as the one in DOS:

```
set_path = GETE("Path")
SET PATH TO &set_path
```

Also: SET DEFAULT TO, GETE()

SET PRINTER **Output Command**

Syntax: SET PRINTER on | OFF | (<L switch>)

Action: Controls whether or not screen output (except full-screen) is also printed.

Detail: The SET PRINTER command is commonly used to display the result of the ? and ?? commands. For example:

```
SET PRINTER ON
? "This is the first line to print."
? "This is the second line."
? "Etc..."
SET PRINTER OFF
EJECT
```

Other commands whose result you might want to print (e.g., LIST and DISPLAY commands, LABEL FORM, and REPORT FORM) come equipped with a TO PRINTER option that obviates the need for SET PRINTER. For example:

```
SET PRINTER ON
LIST
SET PRINTER OFF
```

is functionally equivalent to

```
LIST TO PRINTER
```

You can specify this SET command using a logical expression by enclosing the expression in parentheses. An expression that evaluates true is interpreted as ON and one that evaluates false is interpreted as OFF.

```
is_print = <L condition>
SET PRINTER (is_print)
```

Also: SET DEVICE TO, ?, ??, CHR(), SET CONSOLE, TO PRINTER

SET PRINTER TO (device) — Output Command

Syntax: SET PRINTER TO [<device name> | (<C device name>)]

Action: If you have several printers connected, allows you to select which to use.

Detail: If you have more than one printer attached to your computer, this form of the SET PRINTER TO command allows you to select which one you want to use for printed output.

For example, suppose you have a dot matrix printer and a laser printer that are assigned the device names LPT1 and LPT2, respectively. The default printer would be LPT1, and to select the laser printer you would use:

```
SET PRINTER TO LPT2
```

From this point on, all printed output goes to LPT2. To return to using the default dot matrix printer:

```
SET PRINTER TO
```

Also: SET PRINTER, SET DEVICE TO, TO PRINTER

SET PRINTER TO (file) — Output Command

Syntax: SET PRINTER TO [<prn filename> | (<C prn filename>)]

Action: Directs all subsequent printed output to the named text file.

Detail: To write printed output to a file rather than printing it, use this form of the SET PRINTER TO command. Unless you specify a file extension, the default is .PRN. For example:

```
SET PRINTER TO Output
USE Mailing
REPORT FORM MailList TO PRINTER
SET PRINTER TO  && close file and resume printing output
```

To print the file at a later time, you could use:

```
TYPE Output.PRN TO PRINTER
```

All printed output, including @...SAY when you have issued SET DEVICE TO PRINTER, is written to the print file as long as the file is open. To close the print file and resume sending output to the printer, use SET PRINTER TO with no file name.

Also: SET PRINTER, SET DEVICE TO, TO PRINTER, TYPE

SET PROCEDURE TO — Program Command

Syntax: SET PROCEDURE TO [<prg filename>]

Action: Compiles all procedures and user-defined functions in the named file.

Detail: The contents of the <prg filename> are compiled into the object file of the program that has the SET PROCEDURE TO command.

The following is a skeleton of a procedure file containing both procedures and user-defined functions. The PROCEDURE command marks the beginning and gives a name to each procedure in the file and FUNCTION marks the beginning of each user-defined function:

```
PROCEDURE Reports
.
. <commands>
.
RETURN
```

```
PROCEDURE Updates
PARAMETERS filename, index_list
.
. <commands>
.
RETURN

FUNCTION capital
PARAMETERS first_name
RETURN UPPER(SUBSTR(first_name, 1, 1)) + ;
       LOWER(SUBSTR(first_name, 2))
```

Assuming this procedure file is named Business.PRG, to compile each of its procedures and functions:

```
SET PROCEDURE TO Business
DO Reports
DO Updates WITH "Orders", "Part_No, Cust_No"
? capital("DEBBY")
```

In an interpreted language, SET PROCEDURE TO with no parameters, like CLOSE PROCEDURE, would close the open procedure file so that the procedures therein would no longer be accessible. However, in a compiled language, SET PROCEDURE TO opens the file only long enough to compile the procedures and functions. Thus, SET PROCEDURE TO with no parameters is not operational in Clipper.

Also: DO, PROCEDURE, FUNCTION

SET RELATION TO — Database Command

Syntax: SET RELATION [ADDITIVE]
TO [<expression> INTO <alias> | (<C alias>)
[, TO <expression> INTO <alias> | (<C alias>)]...]

Action: Relates the active database file to an unselected one based on a key value.

Detail: The following example sets up a relationship between the Orders file and the Parts and Customer files in order to print invoices:

```
USE Orders INDEX O_Cust
SELECT 2
USE Customer INDEX Cust_No
SELECT 3
USE Parts INDEX Part_No
SELECT Orders
SET RELATION TO Cust_No INTO Customer, ;
          TO Part_No INTO Parts
DO Invoices
CLOSE DATABASES
RETURN

PROCEDURE Invoices
SET DEVICE TO PRINTER
DO WHILE .NOT. EOF()
   @ 1, 0 SAY "Customer"
   @ 1, 9 SAY Customer->Cust_No
   @ 2, 9 SAY TRIM(Customer->First_Name) + " " +;
                Customer->Last_Name
   @ 3, 9 SAY Customer->Address1
   @ 4, 9 SAY TRIM(Customer->City) +", "+;
                Customer->State +"  "+ Customer->Zip
   @ 5, 0 TO 5, 79
   @ 7, 0 SAY "Part  Description + SPACE(31) +;
             "Quantity     Price      Total"
   line = 9
   tot  = 0
   old_cust = Cust_No
   DO WHILE Cust_No == old_cust .AND. (!EOF())
      @ line,  0 SAY Orders->Part_No
      @ line,  7 SAY SUBSTR(Parts->Descrip, 1, 60)
      @ line, 47 SAY Orders->Quantity
      @ line, 58 SAY Parts->Price
      @ line, 69 SAY Orders->Quantity * Parts->Price ;
                PICTURE "99999999.99"
      line = line + 1
      tot  = tot + Orders->Quantity * Parts->Price
      SKIP
   ENDDO
```

```
   @ line+1,57 SAY tot PICTURE "Grand Total $9999999.99"
ENDDO
SET DEVICE TO SCREEN
RETURN
```

Unless the ADDITIVE keyword is used, the SET RELATION TO command destroys existing relations in the current work area before setting up the new relations. Thus, in the above example, the single SET RELATION TO command could be replaced by the following two commands:

```
SET RELATION TO Cust_No INTO Customer
SET RELATION ADDITIVE TO Part_No INTO Parts
```

If the database file that the relation is set into is not indexed, the SET RELATION TO expresssion must be numeric and the database files are linked by matching the record number in the unselected file to the relation expression value for the current record in the active file. Thus, to relate two files based on equal record numbers when the unselected file is not indexed, you would use:

```
SET RELATION TO RECNO() INTO <alias>
```

SET RELATION TO with no parameters destroys all relations from the active database file.

Also: USE, SET INDEX TO, SELECT, RECNO()

SET SAFETY

Help Command

Syntax: SET SAFETY on | off

Action: This command is not operational.

Detail: Although use of SET SAFETY is allowed in programs for compatibility with other dialects, the command is not operational in Clipper.

SET SCOREBOARD **Display Command**

Syntax: SET SCOREBOARD ON | off | (<L switch>)

Action: Controls whether or not line zero is reserved for messages.

Detail: Certain key information (e.g., Ins, and Deleted record status) is displayed on line zero of your screen. This line is referred to as the "scoreboard" and, since it is reserved, you cannot use it without having your display overwritten by the system. To disable the use of line zero by the system, use:

```
SET SCOREBOARD OFF
```

and you will be able to use line zero just as you would any other line. When SET SCOREBOARD is OFF, RANGE and invalid date messages are not displayed. Instead, the cursor moves back to the beginning of the field with no warning, and you must correct the error before leaving the field.

You can specify this SET command using a logical expression by enclosing the expression in parentheses. An expression that evaluates true is interpreted as ON and one that evaluates false is interpreted as OFF.

```
is_score = <L condition>
SET SCOREBOARD (is_score)
```

Also: RANGE, VALID

SET SOFTSEEK **Search Command**

Syntax: SET SOFTSEEK on | OFF | (<L switch>)

Action: Controls the record pointer position if FIND or SEEK does not find what its looking for.

Detail: Normally, if SEEK or FIND results in a no find situation, the record pointer is positioned to the end of file (i.e., EOF() is true). When you SET SOFTSEEK ON and a match for the SEEK or FIND value cannot be found, the record pointer is positioned at the next record with a key value that is greater.

Note that SET SOFTSEEK has no effect on related files when a SET RELATION is in effect.

You can specify this SET command using a logical expression by enclosing the expression in parentheses. An expression that evaluates true is interpreted as ON and one that evaluates false is interpreted as OFF.

```
is_soft = <L condition>
SET SOFTSEEK (is_soft)
```

Also: USE, SET INDEX, SET ORDER, FIND, SEEK

SET STATUS — Display Command

Syntax: SET STATUS on | off

Action: This command is not operational.

Detail: Although use of SET STATUS is allowed in programs for compatibility with other dialects, the command is not operational in Clipper.

SET STEP — Debug Command

Syntax: SET STEP on | off

Action: This command is not operational.

Detail: Although use of SET STEP is allowed in programs for compatibility with other dialects, the command is not operational in Clipper.

SET TALK — Display Command

Syntax: SET TALK on | off

Action: This command is not operational.

Detail: Although use of SET TALK is allowed in programs for compatibility with other dialects, the command is not operational in Clipper.

SET TYPEAHEAD TO — Environment Command

Syntax: SET TYPEAHEAD TO <N keystrokes>

Action: Changes the size of the typeahead buffer.

Detail: If you are able to type very fast, you may want to increase the size of the typeahead buffer. To increase the buffer size to 200 keystrokes, use:

```
SET TYPEAHEAD TO 200
```

To disable the typeahead buffer so that no keystrokes are saved, use:

```
SET TYPEAHEAD TO 0
```

Setting TYPEAHEAD TO zero clears any characters already in the buffer.

Also: CLEAR TYPEAHEAD, INKEY(), KEYBOARD

SET UNIQUE — Index Command

Syntax: SET UNIQUE on | OFF | (<L switch>)

Action: Controls whether or not subsequent index files are created with unique keys.

Detail: Using SET UNIQUE ON forces all subsequently created index files to be flagged as unique. A unique index file keeps track of only the first occurrence of any given key value, and thus ignores duplicate keys. For example:

```
USE Parts
SET UNIQUE ON
INDEX ON Part_No TO Parts && only unique numbers indexed
SET UNIQUE OFF
```

The status of SET UNIQUE does not affect the REINDEX command. REINDEX looks at the index file to determine whether it is unique or not and recreates it accordingly. If you have an index file that is not unique, to make it unique you must recreate it using the INDEX command while SET UNIQUE is ON.

You can specify this SET command using a logical expression by enclosing the expression in parentheses. An expression that evaluates true is interpreted as ON and one that evaluates false is interpreted as OFF.

```
is_unique = <L condition>
SET UNIQUE (is_unique)
```

Also: INDEX

SET WRAP

Menu Command

Syntax: SET WRAP on | OFF | (<L switch>)

Action: Controls whether or not menu highlight wraps when on the first or last option.

Detail: The following example illustrates constructing and activating a lightbar menu. Without SET WRAP ON, the highlight in the menu will not wrap around when the user presses Left Arrow on the first option or Down Arrow on the last option:

```
* Menu messages are displayed on line 2.
SET MESSAGE TO 2  && turn on messages

* Allow left/right arrow keys to wrap around.
SET WRAP ON
```

```
DO WHILE .T.  && infinite loop for menu display
   CLEAR
   @ box_home, 0, 3, 79 BOX box_double
   @ 1, 5 PROMPT "Customer" MESSAGE;
          "Add/search/edit customers and transactions."
   @ 1,17 PROMPT "Invoice"  MESSAGE;
          "Print invoices from customer transactions."
   @ 1,28 PROMPT "Label"    MESSAGE;
          "Print labels from customers or transactions."
   @ 1,37 PROMPT "Report"   MESSAGE;
          "Print reports."
   @ 1,47 PROMPT "Shipping" MESSAGE;
          "Browse ship-to names and companies."
   @ 1,59 PROMPT "Maintain" MESSAGE;
          "File and system maintenance utilities."
   @ 1,71 PROMPT "Quit"     MESSAGE;
          "Quit to the operating system."

   MENU TO action

   DO CASE  && make decision based on option selected
      CASE action == 1
         DO Customer
      CASE action == 2
         DO Report WITH "INVOICES"
      CASE action == 3
         DO Report WITH "LABELS"
      CASE action == 4
         DO Report
      CASE action == 5
         DO Shipping
      CASE action == 6
         DO Maintain
      CASE action == 7
         SET MESSAGE TO   && turn off messages
         SET WRAP OFF     && turn off menu wrap
         RETURN
   ENDCASE
ENDDO
```

You can specify this SET command using a logical expression by enclosing the expression in parentheses. An expression that evaluates true is interpreted as ON and one that evaluates false is interpreted as OFF.

```
is_wrap = <L condition>
SET WRAP (is_wrap)
```

Also: @...PROMPT, MENU TO, SET MESSAGE TO

SETCANCEL() — Program Function

Syntax: SETCANCEL([<L on | off>])

Action: Toggles the ability to terminate a program with Alt-C.

Return: <expL> current SETCANCEL() setting.

Detail: Normally, you can terminate a program by pressing Alt-C while it is executing. To disable Alt-C and then return it to its original status:

```
current = SETCANCEL(.F.)
.
. <commands>
.
SETCANCEL(current)
```

Also: SET KEY TO, SET ESCAPE

SETCOLOR() — Display Function

Syntax: SETCOLOR([<C color settings>])

Action: Evaluates the current color settings and optionally changes them.

Return: <expC> string representing the current color settings.

Detail: The following example uses SETCOLOR() to store the current color settings, change them, and return them to their original setting:

```
current = SETCOLOR("B/R, R/B")
.
. <commands>
.
SETCOLOR(current)
```

Also: SET COLOR TO, ISCOLOR()

SETPRC() Environment Function

Syntax: SETPRC(<N printer row>, <N printer col>)

Action: Sets PROW() and PCOL() to the specified values.

Detail: The following example uses SETPRC() after sending control characters to the printer:

```
SET DEVICE TO PRINTER
@ PROW(), PCOL() SAY CHR(27)+"W"+"1"   && double wide on
SETPRC(0, 0)  && Reset PROW() and PCOL()
.
. <print commands>
.
SET DEVICE TO SCREEN
```

In report loops, you may get an unwanted page eject if you try to @...SAY to a row less than the current PROW() setting. To prevent this, reset PROW() before using the smaller number. For example:

```
DO WHILE <page>
   i = 1
   DO WHILE <item>
      @ i, 0 SAY <whatever>
      IF <page full>
         EXIT
      ENDIF
      i = i+1
   ENDDO
```

```
      * Next page.
      @ page_len, zero SAY page_num
      SETPRC( zero, zero )     && reset Clipper top of form
      page_num = page_num+1
   ENDDO
```

Also: PROW(), PCOL()

SKIP

Database Command

Syntax: SKIP [<N records>]
[ALIAS <alias> | <work area number> | (<N work area number>)]

Action: Moves the record pointer in the active or an unselected database file.

Detail: Always check EOF() when skipping forward with a positive parameter, and check BOF() when skipping backward with a negative parameter.

The following program skeleton demonstrates how to use the SKIP command to process an entire database file:

```
USE <dbf filename>
DO WHILE .NOT. EOF()
   .
   . <commands to process one record>
   .
   SKIP  && skip to the next record
ENDDO
```

The next example shows how to use SKIP with an indexed database file to process all records the same key value:

```
USE <dbf filename> INDEX <ndx filename>
SEEK <key value>
DO WHILE <index key expression> == <key value>
   . <commands to process one record>
   .
   SKIP  && skip to next record in index order
ENDDO
```

To advance the record pointer in an unselected database file, specify the ALIAS keyword. For example:

```
SKIP 2 ALIAS Customer && skip 2 records in customer file

area = 2              && specify work area as expression
SKIP ALIAS (area)     && skip 1 record in work area 2

SKIP 5 ALIAS 2        && skip 5 records in work area 2
```

Use an extended expression to check BOF() or EOF() when skipping in an unselected work area:

```
DO WHILE ! Orders->(EOF())
   .
   . <commands>
   .
   SKIP ALIAS Orders
ENDDO
```

Also: GO, RECNO(), EOF(), BOF(), DO WHILE

SORT — Database Command

Syntax: SORT ON <field> [/[A | D][C]] [, <field> [/[A | D][C]] ...]
TO <dbf filename> | (<C dbf filename>)
[<scope>]

Action: Sorts the active database file to a new file using the indicated key fields.

Detail: The following example sorts the Mailing list using several keys:

```
* Sort by State  - Descending Dictionary sort (/DC)
*         Zip    - Descending sort (/D)
*     Last_Name  - Ascending Dictionary sort (/C or /AC)
*     First_Name - Ascending Dictionary sort (/C or /AC)
USE Mailing
```

```
* Entire file is sorted.
SORT ON State/DC, Zip/D, Last_Name/C, First_Name/C;
     TO MailSort

* Portion of the file is sorted using the same options.
SORT ON State/DC, Zip/D, Last_Name/C, First_Name/C;
     TO PartSort FOR State = "CA" .OR. State = "SC"

* List sorted files.
USE MailSort
LIST OFF State, Zip, Last_Name, First_Name
USE PartSort
LIST OFF State, Zip, Last_Name, First_Name
CLOSE DATABASES
```

You can SORT ON logical fields effectively. False values (.F.) come before true values (.T.). Memo fields are not allowed in the SORT ON field list.

Note that although SORT ON allows a scope, you cannot effectively use a scope that limits records based on their position in the database file. That is, the following scope clauses are not effective:

Clause	**Scope**
ALL	All records in the file are processed beginning with the first record.
NEXT <expN>	The specified number of records are processed beginning with the current record.
[RECORD] <expN>	The specified record is processed.
REST	The remaining records in the file are processed beginning with the current record.

For the most part, these scope clauses are ignored and all records are sorted. Occasionally, however, specfying one of these clauses will cause an inappropriate run-time error.

Also: INDEX, Scope

SOUNDEX() Conversion Function

Syntax: SOUNDEX(<expC>)

Action: Converts the specified string to its soundex equivalent.

Return: <expC> soundex code.

Detail: SOUNDEX() is useful in matching English surnames that are similar, but falls short in other applications. The following example creates an index on the Last_Name field using SOUNDEX() so that you will be able to find names that are close to those in the file:

```
USE Mailing
INDEX ON SOUNDEX(Last_Name) TO NearName
DO WHILE .T.
   name = SPACE(20)
   CLEAR
   @ 10, 0 SAY "Enter a Last_Name" GET name
   READ
   IF name = SPACE(20)
      EXIT
   ENDIF
   SEEK SOUNDEX(name)
   IF FOUND()
      @ 11, 0 SAY "The closest name is " + Last_Name
   ELSE
      @ 11, 0 SAY "Not even close."
   ENDIF
   WAIT
ENDDO
RETURN
```

SOUNDEX codes are in the format “A999”, where A is an uppercase alphabetic letter and 9 is a digit in the range zero through nine.

Also: SEEK, LOCATE, INDEX

SPACE() Character Function

Syntax: SPACE(<N length>)

Action: Creates a string of blanks of the indicated length.

Return: <expC> string consisting solely of blank spaces.

Detail: The following example uses the SPACE() function to initialize a memory variable before using @...GET to allow the user to enter a value:

```
USE Orders INDEX Order_No
key = SPACE(5)  && initialize key to string of 5 spaces
@ 10,5 SAY "Enter the order number to find:" GET key
READ
SEEK ALLTRIM(key)
IF FOUND()
   .
   . <commands to process record>
   .
ENDIF
```

Also: REPLICATE()

SQRT() Numeric Function

Syntax: SQRT(<expN>)

Action: Evaluates the square root of the specified number.

Return: <expN> representing the square root of the number.

Detail: The following example allows you to enter a numeric value and returns the square root of that number:

```
value = 0.00
@ 6,0 SAY "Enter a positive number: " ;
      GET value PICTURE "99999999.99" ;
                RANGE 0, 99999999.99
READ
root = SQRT(value)
@ 6,0 SAY "The square root of " +;
          LTRIM(STR(value, 11, 2)) + " is " +;
          LTRIM(STR(root,  11, 2))
```

Also: **, ^

STORE **Memory Command**

Syntax: STORE <expression> TO <memvar | element list>

Action: Assigns the value of the expression to the memvar or array element. Creates the memvar if it does not exist.

Detail: The STORE command is functionally equivalent to the assignment statement, <memory variable> = <expression>. Use the assignment statement when you want to assign a different value to each variable and the STORE command to assign the same value to many variables. For example:

```
DECLARE temp[3]
STORE SPACE(20) TO m_first, m_last, m_city,;
                   temp[1], temp[2], temp[3]
m_state = SPACE(2)
m_zip   = SPACE(5)
m_phone = SPACE(13)
```

Note that you cannot have an array definition and a memory variable with the same name. For example:

```
DECLARE names[10]            && defines array names[]
STORE "Joe Smith" TO names   && wipes out array names[]
```

Also: = (store), DECLARE, AFILL()

STR() Conversion Function

Syntax: STR(<expN> [, <N length> [, <N decimals>]])

Action: Converts the indicated number to a character string.

Return: <expC> string equivalent of a number.

Detail: The STR() function is most often used when you want to display numbers and text together with the same command. The following example illustrates:

```
value = 0.00
@ 6, 0 SAY "Enter a positive number: " ;
       GET value PICTURE "99999999.99" ;
                 RANGE 0, 99999999.99
READ

* LTRIM() is used with STR() to remove leading blanks so
* that the display does not show large gaps between the
* text and the numbers.
@ 6, 0 SAY "The square root of " +;
          LTRIM(STR(value, 11, 2)) + " is " +;
          LTRIM(STR(SQRT(value) 11, 2))
```

Also: VAL(), LTRIM()

STRTRAN() Character Function

Syntax: STRTRAN(<C target>, <C search>
[, <C replace> [, <N start> [, <N times>]]])

Action: Performs a search and replace on the target character string.

Return: <expC> string with the replacements.

Detail: The following example inserts the word "change" in place of the word "edit" in a character field in the active database file. Each occurrence is replaced:

```
REPLACE ALL Descrip WITH STRTRAN(Descrip, "edit",;
                                           "change")
```

To replace only the first instance of the word:

```
REPLACE ALL Descrip;
        WITH STRTRAN(Descrip, "edit", "change", 1, 1)
```

Note that the default for the replace string is a null string. Thus, if the replace string is not specified, the search string appears removed from the original string.

Also: STUFF(), REPLACE

STUFF() — Character Function

Syntax: STUFF(<expC>, <N begin>, <N remove>, <C insert>)

Action: Inserts one string into another beginning at a particular location.

Return: <expC> string with the replacements.

Detail: The following example inserts the word "change" in place of the word "edit" in a character field in the active database file:

```
REPLACE Descrip WITH ;
        STUFF(Descrip, AT("edit",Descrip), 4, "change");
        FOR "edit" $ Descrip
```

Use an <N remove> parameter equal to the length of the <C insert> parameter (i.e., LEN(<C insert>) to overwrite the new value on top of the original string rather than actually inserting it.

Use an <N remove> parameter equal to zero to insert the new value beginning at the specified location.

Also: STRTRAN(), REPLACE

SUBSTR() — Character Function

Syntax: SUBSTR(<C string>, <N start> [, <N length>])

Action: Extracts a specified portion of the character string.

Return: <expC> substring.

Detail: Use the SUBSTR() function when you want to work with a portion of an existing string. For example, if you only want to see only the first 40 characters of a field named Address, you would use:

```
SUBSTR(Address, 1, 40)
```

If you want to see the contents of the Address field past the first comma in the field, use:

```
SUBSTR(Address, AT(",", Address) + 1)
```

As in the last example, if you do not specify a value for the <N length> parameter, the remainder of the original string is assumed.

If the <N start> parameter is negative, the start position is taken from the right side of the string. For example:

```
? SUBSTR("abcdef", -3, 2)   && returns "de"
```

Also: LEFT(), RIGHT(), $

SUM — Database Command

Syntax: SUM [<scope>] [<expN list> TO <memory variable list>]

Action: Evaluates the total of each specified number in the active file.

Detail: To determine the total Sales of a particular sales person on your staff and save the results:

```
USE Sales
SUM Sales FOR SaleCode = "A154" TO avg_sale
```

For compatibility with other Dbase dialects, it is syntactically correct to use SUM with no parameters, although such a command accomplishes nothing but a waste of time since it gives you no result.

Also: COUNT, AVERAGE, TOTAL

Switch — External Program

Syntax: Switch <exe filename list>

Action: Chains from one executable file to another.

Detail: The DOS error level provides a way for a program to terminate execution and pass a message to the next program to execute. Thus, Switch.EXE is used almost exclusively with the ERRORLEVEL() function.

You set this function to tell Switch.EXE which program it is supposed to execute. The following example chains several programs together, assuming that only one can fit into memory at once:

```
* Menu.PRG
SET MESSAGE TO 24     && menu messages display on line 24

CLEAR
* Display menu prompts and messages.
@ 10,2 PROMPT "Exit";
       MESSAGE "Leave main menu."
@ 11,2 PROMPT "Add Records";
       MESSAGE "Append records to active database file."
@ 12,2 PROMPT "Edit Records";
       MESSAGE "Edit records in active database file."
@ 13,2 PROMPT "Print Labels";
       MESSAGE "Print mailing labels."
@ 14,2 PROMPT "Print Reports";
       MESSAGE "Print reports for active database file."
* Activate menu.
MENU TO choice
```

```
* Set ERRORLEVEL based on menu choice.
ERRORLEVEL(choice - 1)

* Quit back to Switch.
RETURN
```

Once Menu.PRG, Add.PRG, Edit.PRG, Labels.PRG, and Reports.PRG are compiled and linked as separate programs, you would issue at the DOS prompt to begin the application:

```
C> SWITCH Menu Add Edit Labels Reports
```

Each subprogram would use the function ERRORLEVEL(0) to recall the main menu program. The main menu would use ERRORLEVEL(0) to return to DOS.

Also: ERRORLEVEL()

TEXT

Output Command

Syntax: TEXT [TO PRINTER] [TO FILE <txt filename> | (<C txt filename>)]
<text>
ENDTEXT

Action: Displays the indicated <text>.

Detail: The following program skeleton uses a TEXT...ENDTEXT construction to display a very simple menu on the screen:

```
TEXT

                0 - Exit
                1 - Add Records
                2 - Edit Records
                3 - Search
                4 - Reports
                5 - Labels

ENDTEXT
INPUT "Select an option by number " TO choice
.
. <commands to check and process choice>
.
```

To print the text in the TEXT...ENDTEXT construction, use the TO PRINTER option with the TEXT command. For example:

```
TEXT TO PRINTER
   This text will be printed as well
   as displayed on the screen.
ENDTEXT
```

Similarly, to write the text to a text file use the TO FILE option:

```
txt_file = "Output"
TEXT TO FILE(txt_file)
   This text will be written to the named
   text file as well as displayed on the screen.
ENDTEXT
```

Note that ENDTEXT cannot be shortened to END.

Also: ?, SET CONSOLE

TIME() — Environment Function

Syntax: TIME()

Action: Evaluates the system time.

Return: <expC> system time in the format hh:mm:ss.

Detail: The following program displays the time in the middle of the screen:

```
DO WHILE INKEY(1) == 0   && changes every second
   @ 12, 35 SAY TIME()
ENDDO
```

To interrupt this program, press any key.

Since there is no time data type, the TIME() function returns a character string representing the time using a 24-hour clock. The format of this string is hh:mm:ss where h stands for hours, m for minutes, and s for seconds. To extract the components of the time and convert them to numbers, use the following formula:

```
hours   = VAL(SUBSTR(TIME(), 1, 2))
minutes = VAL(SUBSTR(TIME(), 4, 2))
seconds = VAL(SUBSTR(TIME(), 7, 2))
```

To display the time using a 12-hour clock:

```
? STR( VAL(TIME())%12 ) + SUBSTR(TIME(), 3)
```

To display the time using a.m. and p.m.:

```
clock_time = TIME()
disp_time  = IF( VAL(clock_time) < 10,;
                   " " + SUBSTR(clock_time,2,4),;
                   SUBSTR(clock_time,1,5) )
val_time = VAL(disp_time)
DO CASE
   CASE val_time == zero
      disp_time = "12" + SUBSTR(disp_time, 3) +" a.m."
   CASE val_time < 12
      disp_time = disp_time + " a.m."
   CASE val_time == 12
      disp_time = disp_time + " p.m."
   CASE val_time > 12
      disp_time = STR(val_time-12, 2) +;
                  SUBSTR(disp_time,3) + " p.m."
ENDCASE
@ 1,50 SAY "Time: " + disp_time
```

Also: DATE(), SECONDS()

Tlink

Link Info

Syntax: TLINK <obj filename list>
[, <exe filename>
[, <map filename>
[, <lib filename list>
[/<option>]]]]

Action: Links the named object files using Borland's Turbo Linker.

Detail: This is the very fast Borland linker from their Turbo C compiler. Common Tlink command line options are described below. Tlink is not case sensitive to these options:

Option	Meaning
/m	Include public symbols in map file
/x	Does not write a map file (faster)

The object and library file name lists are lists in which the file names are separated by a single space or a plus (+) sign. By default, the .EXE and .MAP files that are generated have the same name as the first object file in the list. Any of the optional filename parameters can be omitted using a comma instead of the parameter.

The following example links the file Main.OBJ that is known to reference functions in both Clipper.LIB and Extend.LIB:

```
TLINK Main,,,Clipper Extend
```

The next example links several object files using an additional library file called TR. The MAP file is given a different name.

```
TLINK Main AddRecs EditRecs,,Map_Out,CLIPPER TR EXTEND
```

The next example links several object files using an additional library file called TR. No MAP file is generated for faster operation.

```
TLINK Main AddRecs EditRecs,,,CLIPPER TR EXTEND /x
```

The TLINK parameters can be taken from one or more ASCII text files called response files by preceding the file name with an @ symbol. No file extension is assumed for response files. When you use a response file, each parameter must be on a separate line; however, you can continue a line using a plus sign. For example, the response file, Resp1, listed below:

```
Main + AddRecs +
EditRecs
Exe_Out
Map_Out
Clipper Tr Extend
```

could be used with TLINK as follows:

```
TLINK @Resp1
```

Also: Make

TO PRINTER **Output Keyword**

Syntax: <command> TO PRINTER

Action: Echoes the output of the command to the printer.

Detail: Examples of commands that support the TO PRINTER option follow:

```
LIST TO PRINTER
REPORT FORM <frm filename> TO PRINTER
LABEL FORM <lbl filename> TO PRINTER
```

In each case, the output of the command is printed as well as displayed on the screen. To suppress the screen display, use SET CONSOLE OFF.

Also: SET DEVICE TO, SET CONSOLE, SET PRINTER

TONE() **Output Function**

Syntax: TONE(<N frequency>, <N duration>)

Action: Sounds the bell using the specified frequency and duration.

Detail: TONE() is used to make the bell more pleasant (or more annoying). The duration is specified in increments of 1/18th of a second. Thus, a duration parameter of 36 sounds the specified frequency for 2 seconds. The frequency is measured in cycles per second, or hertz.

The following example plays a musical scale:

```
TONE(261, 10)  && middle C
TONE(293, 10)  && D
TONE(329, 10)  && E
TONE(349, 10)  && F
TONE(392, 10)  && G
TONE(440, 10)  && A
TONE(493, 10)  && B
TONE(523, 10)  && C
```

The following table lists the frequencies for two octaves of the musical scale. Although the frequency of musical notes usually is specified to two decimal places, the TONE() function uses only the integer portion.

Note	Frequency	Note	Frequency
C	130.81	C	261.63 (middle C)
C#	138.59	C#	277.18
D	145.83	D	293.66
D#	155.56	D#	311.13
E	164.81	E	329.63
F	174.61	F	349.23
F#	185.00	F#	369.99
G	196.00	G	392.00
G#	207.65	G#	415.30
A	220.00	A	440.00
A#	233.08	A#	466.16
B	245.94	B	493.88

The following loop sounds a siren-like tone to warn of error:

```
FOR i = 1 TO 3
   TONE(1650-(18*i), 3)
   TONE( 650-( 5*i), 3)
NEXT
```

Also: SET BELL, CHR()

TOTAL **Database Command**

Syntax: TOTAL ON <expression>
TO <dbf filename> | (<C dbf filename>)
[FIELDS <field list>] [<scope>]

Action: Totals the active database file based on a key expression to a new file.

Detail: To TOTAL a file successfully, the file must be in order (either INDEXed or SORTed) by the ON key field. For example:

```
USE Orders INDEX O_Part
* Total by part
TOTAL ON Part_No FIELDS Quantity TO Ord_Part
SET INDEX TO O_Cust
* Total by customer
TOTAL ON Cust_No FIELDS Quantity TO Ord_Cust
CLOSE DATABASES
```

The FIELDS list in this command is used to define which numeric fields are totalled rather than to determine the structure of the resulting file. Although the FIELDS list is optional, without it none of the fields are totalled. The structure of the resulting file is always identical to that of the original file.

Note that you can TOTAL ON an expression that is more complex than a single field. For example, to total the Orders file based on both the Customer and Part numbers:

```
USE Orders INDEX CustPart
TOTAL ON Cust_No + Part_No FIELDS Quantity TO CustPart
CLOSE DATABASES
```

Also: SUM, JOIN, SORT, FIELDS

TRANSFORM() Conversion Function

Syntax: TRANSFORM(<expression>, <C template>)

Action: Converts a value to a character string using a PICTURE function or template.

Return: <expC> string formatted according to the template.

Detail: The TRANSFORM() function allows you to format expression results using PICTURE templates with commands other than @...SAY.

For example, to list the prices in the Parts file as dollar amounts:

```
USE Parts
LIST Part_No, TRANSFORM(Price, "$$$,$$$,$$$.99")
```

To display the names in the mailing list using all capital letters:

```
USE Mailing
LIST TRANSFORM(TRIM(First_Name) + " " + Last_Name, "@!")
```

Also: PICTURE

TRIM() Character Function

Syntax: TRIM(<expC>)

Action: Removes trailing blank spaces from the specified character string.

Return: <expC> string with no trailing blank spaces.

Detail: TRIM() and RTRIM() are functionally identical.

The following example uses TRIM() to display the first and last name fields in the Mailing list side by side:

```
USE Mailing
? TRIM(First_Name) + " " + Last_Name
CLOSE DATABASES
```

Also: LTRIM(), RTRIM(), LEN(), ALLTRIM()

Turbo C **Compile Info**

Syntax: tcc -c -f- -G -ml -O -Z <filename>.c

Action: Compiles the named C program with Borland's Turbo C compiler.

Detail: The Turbo C command line options are described below. These options must be specified when linking with Clipper programs:

Option	Meaning
-c	Compile only (no automatic link)
-f-	Disable floating-point library search
-G	Optimize for execution speed over size
-ml	Large memory model
-O	Optimize loops
-Z	Optimize registers

The following example compiles a C program called Foo.c:

```
tcc -c -f- -G -ml -O -Z Foo.c
```

You must use the Microsoft C compiler, version 5.0 or higher, if your C program contains any double or floating point numbers. Otherwise, you may use the Turbo C compiler.

Also: Make, Microsoft C

TYPE — OS Command

Syntax: TYPE <filename> [TO PRINTER]
[TO FILE <txt filename> | (<C txt filename>)]

Action: Displays the contents of the named ASCII text file.

Detail: The TYPE command is similar to the DOS Type command. It is used to display the contents of an ASCII text file on the screen or the printer.

In order to use TYPE, the file that you want to display must be closed and you must specify the entire file name, including the extension. For example, to print a program file called MainMenu.PRG:

```
TYPE MainMenu.PRG TO PRINTER
```

Although using COPY FILE is more efficient, TYPE can also be used to copy one file to another. To do this, use the TO FILE option:

```
new_file = "Menu.PRG"
TYPE MainMenu.PRG TO (new_file)
```

Avoid trying to TYPE non-ASCII text files such as .DBF and .FRM files as the result will be illegible.

Also: TO PRINTER, COPY FILE

TYPE() — Environment Function

Syntax: TYPE(<C expression>)

Action: Evaluates the data type of the named expression.

Return: <expC> data type of expression as one or two uppercase letters.

Detail: The following example uses the TYPE() function to make sure that the user enters a numeric value in response to the INPUT command:

```
DO WHILE TYPE("age") != "N"
   INPUT "Enter your age " TO age
ENDDO
```

TYPE() can be used with expressions that are more complicated than simple field or memory variable names. For example:

```
USE Mailing
? TYPE("DATE() - Birthday")                       && returns D
? TYPE("TRIM(First_Name) +' '+ Last_Name")  && returns C
? TYPE("SQRT(Age) ** 3")                         && returns N
CLOSE DATABASES
? TYPE("Birthday")                                && returns U
```

TYPE() always returns one of the uppercase letters listed below:

Letter	Meaning
A	Array
C	Character expression
D	Date expression
L	Logical expression
M	Memo field
N	Numeric expression
U	Undefined, cannot evaluate expression
UE	Syntax error in IF() or IIF() functions
UI	Indeterminate error, function not in Clipper.LIB

UNDEF_ERRO() — Error Function

Syntax: UNDEF_ERRO(<C proc name>, <N file line>, <C error info>, <C operation>, <C identifier name>)

Action: Called by Clipper on undefined identifier error.

Return: <expL> true to retry operation, or false to exit to DOS.

Detail: UNDEF_ERRO() is called automatically by Clipper when a name is referenced that is not a field in the currently selected database file or has not been initialized as a memvar.

The error function below is part of the TRHELP high-level error system used to replace Clipper's default EXPR_ERROR() function. It uses the other high-level error functions documented under the ERRORSYS procedure.

Although documented by Nantucket as undef_error(), Clipper keeps track of only ten characters, thus the PROCNAME() function will return "UNDEF_ERRO" when queried.

```
FUNCTION UNDEF_ERRO
* Syntax: <none>, called by Clipper on
*              undefined-variable error.
* Return: True to retry command that caused error,
*              false to exit to the operating system.
```

```
* Action: Handle undefined variable errors.
*
PARAMETERS proc_name, file_line, error_info, operation,;
           var_name

* Sound warning and display error message on screen.
error_tone()
err_msg( "Error accessing variable: " + var_name +;
         " from: " + proc_name + ".  File line: "+;
         LTRIM(STR(file_line)) +".",;
         "Press any key to continue..." )

* Write error details to file; pause for user response.
err_write( PROCNAME(), proc_name, file_line,;
           error_info, operation, var_name )
CLEAR TYPEAHEAD
INKEY(0)
err_msg()  && clear error message

* Activate the debugger if sys_debug is true.
IF sys_debug
   err_msg("Set return value by making logical",;
           "variable 'ret_debug' true or false")
   ALTD()
   err_msg()
   IF TYPE("ret_debug") == "L"
      RETURN ret_debug
   ENDIF
ENDIF

* Without BEGIN/END SEQUENCE around operation that
* caused the error, BREAK behaves the same as RETURN .F.
BREAK
```

Also: ERRORSYS, OPEN_ERROR(), DB_ERROR(), MISC_ERROR(), EXPR_ERROR(), PRINT_ERRO()

UNLOCK **Network Command**

Syntax: UNLOCK [ALL]

Action: Releases all file and record locks held by the current user.

Detail: The following example illustrates the use of UNLOCK to release a record lock:

```
SET EXCLUSIVE OFF  && locking unnecessary if ON
USE Mailing
LOCATE FOR First_Name = "Gloria"
IF FOUND()
   * This loop tries to lock the record 200 times,
   * then prompts you.
   times = 0
   DO WHILE times < 200 .AND. (!RLOCK())
      times = times + 1
      IF times = 200
         WAIT "Try record lock again? (Y/N)" TO response
         IF UPPER(response) = "Y"
            times = 0
         ELSE
            RETURN  && to try a different record
         ENDIF
      ENDIF
   ENDDO
   @ 10, 5 SAY "First Name " GET First_Name
   @ 17, 5 SAY "Phone      " GET Phone
   READ
ENDIF
UNLOCK  && releases record lock and program continues...
```

UNLOCK ALL is used if you have several locks in place for different database files. UNLOCK with no parameters releases only the locks for the active database file, regardless of any relations that might be in effect.

Closing a database file automatically releases all of its locks.

Also: Networking, LOCK(), FLOCK(), RLOCK(), SET EXCLUSIVE, USE, CLOSE DATABASES

UPDATE **Database Command**

Syntax: UPDATE ON <expression> FROM <alias> [RANDOM]
REPLACE <field> WITH <expression>
[, <field> WITH <expression> ...]

Action: Updates a database file with values from another database file based on a key expression.

Detail: The UPDATE command requires two open database files that have the ON <expresion> in common. The active database file (i.e., the one that you want to UPDATE) must be in order (either INDEXed or SORTed) according to the ON <expression>, and the file that you want to UPDATE FROM must also be in order according to that expression unless you use the RANDOM keyword.

If RANDOM is used, it is not necessary for the FROM file to be in order, but the active file must be ordered using an index file. UPDATE is faster when RANDOM is not used.

The UPDATE command replaces the fields that you specify with the REPLACE clause by matching the ON expression in the active and FROM files. Only the first occurrence of any ON expression value in the active file is processed, but multiple occurrences of the same ON expression are processed in the FROM file.

The following example illustrates the UPDATE command with the RANDOM keyword. The Balance field in the Customer database file is updated by subtracting the Payment field in the Payments file:

```
USE Customer INDEX Cust_No
SELECT 2
USE Payments
SELECT Customer
UPDATE FROM Payments ON Cust_No RANDOM;
       REPLACE Balance WITH Balance - Payments->Payment
CLOSE DATABASES
```

The next example is functionally equivalent to the previous one except that the FROM file is indexed so that the RANDOM keyword is not necessary:

```
USE Customer INDEX Cust_No
SELECT 2
USE Payments INDEX PCust_No
SELECT Customer
UPDATE FROM Payments ON Cust_No;
       REPLACE Balance WITH Balance - Payments->Payment
CLOSE DATABASES
```

Also: REPLACE, INDEX, SORT, SELECT

UPDATED() Input Function

Syntax: UPDATED()

Action: Evaluates whether or not any data was changed during the last READ.

Return: <expL> true if any updates were made, otherwise false.

Detail: UPDATED() does not check to see if the new information is the same as the old information, but it simply tests to see if anything was typed. For this reason, pressing Esc to abandon the READ returns an UPDATED() value of true if anything was typed prior to pressing Esc.

The following example illustrates the UPDATED() function in conjunction with the READ command. In this example, a format file is used to add new records to the Orders file:

```
USE Orders
SET FORMAT TO Ord_Add && edit memvars to put into Orders
DO WHILE .T.
   cust = SPACE(4)
   part = SPACE(5)
   amt = 0
   READ
```

```
    IF UPDATED()
       APPEND BLANK
       REPLACE Cust_No WITH cust, Part_No WITH part,;
               Quantity WITH amt
    ELSE
       EXIT
    ENDIF
 ENDDO
 CLOSE DATABASES
```

Also: @...GET, READ, LASTKEY()

UPPER() Character Function

Syntax: UPPER(<expC>)

Action: Converts the specified character string to all uppercase letters.

Return: <expC> string consisting of all uppercase letters.

Detail: The following example uses UPPER() and LOWER() to format the display of the first and last names in the mailing list so that the names appear with an initial capital letter and the rest in lowercase:

```
USE Mailing
LIST UPPER(LEFT( First_Name,  1)) +;
     LOWER(RIGHT(First_Name, 19)), ;
     UPPER(LEFT( Last_Name,   1)) +;
     LOWER(RIGHT(Last_Name,  19))
CLOSE DATABASES
```

There is also a PICTURE function and template symbol, the exclamation point (!), that can be used with the @...SAY command or the TRANSFORM() function to convert strings to uppercase.

Also: ISUPPER(), LOWER(), PICTURE, TRANSFORM()

USE **Database Command**

Syntax: USE [<dbf filename> | (<C dbf filename>)
[INDEX <index filename list> | (<C index filename list>)]
[ALIAS <alias> | (<C alias>)]
[EXCLUSIVE]]

Action: Opens a database file in the current work area.

Detail: The following example of the USE command opens a database file with two index files and assigns an alias name to the database file:

```
USE Mailing INDEX Last, Zip ALIAS MailList
```

The file and alias names can be specified as character expressions by enclosing the expression in parentheses. For example:

```
dbf_file = "Mailing"
ndx_one  = "Last"
aka_name = "MailList"
USE (dbf_file) INDEX (ndx_one), Zip ALIAS (aka_name)
```

A maximum of fifteen index files can be included in the INDEX file list.

The <alias> can be up to ten characters in length. If no ALIAS clause is specified with the USE command, the database file name becomes the default alias for the file.

The EXCLUSIVE keyword is used to override SET EXCLUSIVE OFF on networks.

USE with no parameters closes the open database file in the current work area. This is unlike CLOSE DATABASES which closes all open database files.

Also: SELECT, SET RELATION, CLOSE DATABASES, SET EXCLUSIVE, Networking

USED() — Database Function

Syntax: USED()

Action: Evaluates whether a database file is in use in a particular work area.

Return: <expL> true if there is an open database file, otherwise false.

Detail: The USED() function is used to determine if there is an open database file in the current work area.

```
PROCEDURE generic
IF USED()
   PRIVATE old_area
   old_area = SELECT()
   SELECT 0
ENDIF
USE Newfile
.
. <commands>
.
CLOSE
IF TYPE("old_area") = "N"
   SELECT(old_area)
ENDIF
RETURN
```

To check for an open database file with a particular alias name, use the alias name and pointer with the function. For example:

```
? Orders->(USED())
```

Also: USE, SELECT, SELECT(), ->

User-Defined Function — Language Info

Detail: A user-defined function or "UDF" is very similar to a procedure. The main difference is that it is called from within an expression instead of with the DO command.

A UDF is created in much the same way as any other procedure. To identify it as a function, you use the FUNCTION keyword followed by the name of the function. Then, you specify the function parameter(s) with a PARAMETERS statement, include the commands to compute its value, and return the value using a special form of the RETURN command.

```
FUNCTION capital
PARAMETERS first_name
RETURN UPPER(SUBSTR(first_name, 1, 1)) +;
       LOWER(SUBSTR(first_name, 2))
```

Once a function is defined, you can invoke it using the following syntax:

```
m_fname = "ELLEN"
? capital(m_fname)     && returns "Ellen"
```

Note that the number of parameters that are actually passed to a procedure or UDF does not have to match the number of parameters in the PARAMETERS statement. This allows you to create routines that take a variable number of parameters. PARAMETERS variables that do not receive a passed parameter remain uninitialized.

Numeric, date, and logical parameters are passed to user-defined functions by value. This means that the UDF gets its own private copy of the passed parameter, so any changes made to the PARAMETERS variable in the UDF are not passed back to the calling routine's variable. Preceding a memory variable function parameter with an @ sign passes that parameter by reference, so that changes made will be passed back to the caller's variable.

```
foo = 123
? udf(foo)     && passed by value, foo still equals 123
? udf(@foo)    && passed by reference, foo now equals 456

FUNCTION udf
PARAMETERS number
number = 456
RETURN number
```

String parameters and array references are passed to user-defined functions by reference. If the parameter is an array, the entire array is passed by reference.

The following procedure file contains examples of two user-defined functions:

```
* Function.PRG  -  A procedure file of UDFs

FUNCTION Log10
* Computes the base 10 logarithm of its parameter
PARAMETERS x
RETURN LOG(x) / LOG(10)

FUNCTION Product
* Computes the product of its parameters
PARAMETERS n1, n2
RETURN n1 * n2
```

To following commands illustrate how to use these functions:

```
? Log10(357)      && result is 2.55
? Product(2, 3)   && result is 6
```

User-defined functions can be used in conjunction with the built-in functions as well as other user-defined functions:

```
? SQRT(Product(10, 2))      && result is 4.47
x = -20
? Log10(ABS(x))             && result is 1.30
? Log10(Product(10, 2))     && result is 1.30
```

Also: PARAMETERS, FUNCTION, Expression, VALID

VAL() **Conversion Function**

Syntax: VAL(<C numbers>)

Action: Converts the specified character string to a number.

Return: <expN> equivalent of the character string.

Detail: The following example initializes a pseudo-array of memory variables using macro substitution. Since macro substitution requires a character memory variable, the VAL() function is used to convert the array index so that it can be incremented and compared to a numeric value:

```
USE Mailing
number = "1"
* This loop saves the first ten ages in memory variables
* named age1, age2, ..., age10.
DO WHILE VAL(number) <= 10
   age&number = Age
   number = LTRIM(STR(VAL(number) + 1))
   SKIP
ENDDO
```

Also: STR(), SET DECIMALS

VALID **Input Keyword**

Syntax: @...GET...VALID <L condition>

Action: Validates the GET variable using the specified condition.

Detail: VALID can be used with any logical expression, but its real power comes when using a User-Defined Function or "UDF."

The following example illustrates both forms of the VALID clause. In this example, the first number that you type must be a perfect square and the second number must be less than the first:

```
STORE 0 TO number1, number2
@ 10, 0 SAY "Enter a perfect square" GET number1;
        VALID v_square(@number1)                  && UDF
@ 11, 0 SAY "Enter a smaller number" GET number2;
        VALID number2 < number1                   && <expL>
READ

FUNCTION v_square
* Syntax: square(@<numeric memvar)
* Action: Validation UDF for squaring numbers.
* Return: True for perfect squares and false for other
*         numbers, including negative ones.
*
PARAMETERS n
IF n < 0
   n = 0
   RETURN .F.
ELSE
   ret_val = (SQRT(n) == INT(SQRT(n)))
   IF .NOT. ret_val
      n = 0
   ENDIF
   RETURN ret_val
ENDIF
```

Note that in this example, the user-defined function parameter is preceded by an "@" symbol. This indicates that the variable is being passed to the function by reference, allowing the function to change the parameter. In this case, if the function returns a value of false, the parameter is changed back to zero.

Also: @...GET, RANGE, PICTURE, FUNCTION, User-Defined Function

WAIT

Input Command

Syntax: WAIT [<C prompt>] [TO <memory variable>]

Action: Waits for a single keyboard character and saves it in a memory variable.

Detail: The following program skeleton uses the WAIT command to make sure that the user acknowledges a message on the screen:

```
SET FORMAT TO EditRecs
.
.
.
SEEK key
IF ! FOUND()
   WAIT "Key not on file.  Press any key to continue."
ELSE
   READ
ENDIF
.
.
.
```

Note that single character input can also be obtained with the INKEY() function.

Also: ACCEPT, INPUT, @...GET, INKEY()

WORD() Extend Function

Syntax: WORD(<expN>)

Action: Converts the specified <expN> double to an integer.

Return: <expN> integer.

Detail: WORD() is used almost exclusively for passing parameters with the CALL command to procedures written in C and assembly language.

If the program that you are calling is expecting a type INT number, you must use this function. For example:

```
number = 7030
CALL c_prog WITH WORD(number)
```

Also: CALL

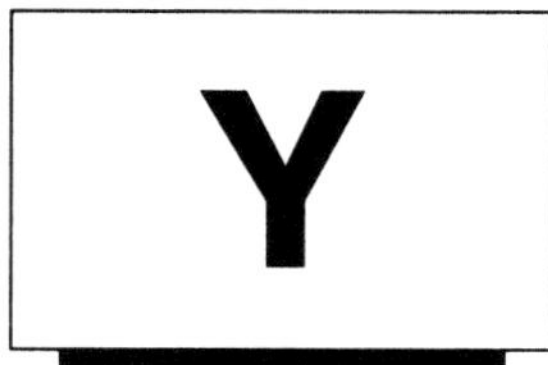

YEAR() — Date Function

Syntax: YEAR(<expD>)

Action: Extracts the year (e.g., 1988) from the specified date.

Return: <expN> representing the year.

Detail: The YEAR() function is used most often with other date conversion functions to create new date display formats.

Regardless of the status of SET CENTURY, YEAR() always returns a four digit year. For this reason, you will usually see YEAR() used with the STR() and SUBSTR() functions. For example, you could extract a two digit year with the following expression:

```
SUBSTR(STR(YEAR(<expD>), 4), 3, 2)
```

To format a particular date using the name of the month followed by the day of the month and the year (e.g., January 23, 1987), use the following expression:

```
CMONTH(<expD>) + " "  + LTRIM(STR( DAY(<expD>)))+;
                 ", " +       STR(YEAR(<expD>), 4)
```

Also: CDOW(), CMONTH(), CTOD(), DAY(), DOW(), DTOC(), DATE(), MONTH()

Y

YEAR()

ZAP

Database Command

Syntax: ZAP

Action: Permanently removes all records from the active database file.

Detail: The following example purges a temporary database file of all of its records while maintaining the open index file:

```
USE Temp INDEX Temp
ZAP
```

Functionally, ZAP is equivalent to DELETE ALL followed by PACK. However, ZAP is much faster because it changes only the header information and the position of the end-of-file marker.

Also: PACK, SET SAFETY

_

(Underscore)

The underscore character is used in naming files, fields, arrays, and memory variables. It makes names easier to read, and may indicate some special use. Internal Clipper functions that begin with the underscore character are described in this chapter.

_exmback() — Extend Function

Syntax: _exmback(unsigned char * <address>, unsigned <bytes>)

Action: Releases the memory allocated by _exmgrab().

Return: Void.

Detail: Whenever an external program allocates memory, it must also release that memory. _exmback() releases the memory that was allocated with _exmgrab(). The following C program illustrates this function:

```
/*********
*  CHAR.C
*
*  Syntax: CHAR( <C string> )
*  Return: <C modified string>
*********/

#include "extend.h"
```

```
CLIPPER char()   /* do not use C parameters */
{
   /* declare variables */
   char *instr, *ret;
   int i;
   unsigned int len;

   /* check syntax */
   if ( PCOUNT==1 && ISCHAR(1) )
   {
      instr = _parc(1);    /* set pointer to parameter */
      len   = _parclen(1)+1;      /* get string length */

      /* allocate memory for return string */
      ret = _exmgrab( len );

      /* check memory allocation */
      if ( ret )
      {
         /* process string, one character at a time */
         for ( i = 0; i < len; i++ )
         {
            if ( <condition> )
               ret[i] = instr[i];
         }

         /* add null string terminator */
         ret[i] = '\0';

         /* return new string to Clipper */
         _retc( ret );

         /* free allocated memory */
         _exmback(ret, len);
      }
      else
         /* never executes - there is no NULL pointer */
         _retc( "Allocation Error" );
   }
```

```
        else
           _retc( "Syntax Error" );
   }
```

The _exmback() function can be called as a procedure from ASM programs by adding an underscore and eliminating the parentheses as follows:

```
; DX:AX contains start address of allocated memory
mov     dx, &lt;segment&gt;
mov     ax, <offset>
mov     cx, <size of allocated memory>
push    cx
push    dx
push    ax
call    __EXMBACK
add     sp, 6
```

_exmgrab() **Extend Function**

Syntax: _exmgrab(unsigned <bytes>)

Action: Allocates the specified amount of memory.

Return: Unsigned character pointer to the starting memory address.

Detail: In order to have a buffer area in which to work, a program must obtain the amount of memory it needs. _exmgrab() allocates memory and returns a pointer to the starting address.

If for any reason _exmgrab() is unable to allocate the needed memory, it does not return a NULL pointer. Instead, it calls an internal Clipper memory-fault handler and triggers a run-time error. If you want to handle memory allocation errors yourself, you must use C's malloc() and free() instead of Clipper's _exmgrab() and _exmback().

The following C program example manipulates a character string without lengthening it. In order to do this, the program needs a maximum amount of memory equal to the length of the string plus its null terminator. The program uses _exmgrab() to obtain the needed memory:

```
/*********
*  CHAR.C
*
*  Syntax: CHAR( <C string> )
*  Return: <C modified string>
*********/

#include "extend.h"

CLIPPER char()
/* do not use C parameters */
{
   /* declare variables */
   char *instr, *ret;
   int i;
   unsigned int len;

   /* check syntax */
   if ( PCOUNT==1 && ISCHAR(1) )
   {
      instr = _parc(1);   /* set pointer to parameter */
      len   = _parclen(1)+1;     /* get string length */

      /* allocate memory for return string */
      ret = _exmgrab( len );

      /* check memory allocation */
      if ( ret )
      {
         /* process string, one character at a time */
         for ( i = 0; i < len; i++ )
         {
            if ( <condition> )
               ret[i] = instr[i];
         }

         /* add null string terminator */
         ret[i] = '\0';
```

```
            /* return new string to Clipper */
            _retc( ret );

            /* free allocated memory */
            _exmback(ret, len);
         }
         else
            /* never executes - there is no NULL pointer */
            _retc( "Allocation Error" );
      }
      else
         _retc( "Syntax Error" );
   }
```

The _exmgrab() function can be called as a procedure from ASM programs by adding an underscore and eliminating the parentheses as follows:

```
mov    ax, <size of memory to allocate>
push   ax
call   __EXMGRAB
add    sp, 2
```

The starting address is returned in DX:AX where DX is the segment and AX is the offset.

_parc() — Extend Function

Syntax: _parc(int <order> [, int <index>])

Action: Allows an external function to access a character parameter.

Return: Pointer to the specified character parameter.

Detail: In order for an external program to manipulate a parameter, the program must have access to that parameter. The _parc() function allows access to a character parameter by providing the address of the character string in memory. The parameters to this function are

Parameter	Data Type	Description
order	int	Represents the position of the parameter in the parameters list when the program is invoked
index	int	Represents the array index of a specific element if the parameter referred to by order is an array

The following C program illustrates _parc():

```
/*********
*  CHAR.C
*
*  Syntax: CHAR( <C string> )
*  Return: <C modified string>
*********/

#include "extend.h"

CLIPPER char()
/* do not use C parameters */
{
   /* declare variables */
   char *instr, *ret;
   int i;
   unsigned int len;

   /* check syntax */
   if ( PCOUNT==1 && ISCHAR(1) )
   {
      instr = _parc(1);   /* set pointer to parameter */
      len   = _parclen(1)+1;     /* get string length */

      /* allocate memory for return string */
      ret = _exmgrab( len );
```

```
            /* check memory allocation */
            if ( ret )
            {
               /* process string, one character at a time */
               for ( i = 0; i < len; i++ )
               {
                  if ( <condition> )
                     ret[i] = instr[i];
               }

               /* add null string terminator */
               ret[i] = '\0';

               /* return new string to Clipper */
               _retc( ret );

               /* free allocated memory */
               _exmback(ret, len);
            }
            else
               /* never executes - there is no NULL pointer */
               _retc( "Allocation Error" );
         }
         else
            _retc( "Syntax Error" );
      }
```

The _parc() function can be called as a procedure from ASM programs by adding an underscore and eliminating the parentheses as follows:

```
mov     ax, <order>
mov     bx, <index>     ; array element index is optional
push    bx              ; omit if optional index is omitted
push    ax
call    __PARC
add     sp, 4    ; use 2 instead of 4 if no optional index
```

The string address is returned in DX:AX where DX is the segment and AX is the offset.

_parclen() Extend Function

Syntax: _parclen(int <order> [, int <index>])

Action: Evaluates the length of a character parameter without the null terminator.

Return: Unsigned integer length of the specified character parameter.

Detail: In order for an external program to manipulate a character parameter, the program may need access to the length of the string. The _parclen() function returns the length of a character parameter. The parameters to this function are

Parameter	Data Type	Description
order	int	Represents the position of the parameter in the parameters list when the program is invoked
index	int	Represents the array index of a specific element if the parameter referred to by order is an array

Use _parclen() instead of the C library function, strlen(), because strlen() does not handle embedded null characters.

The following C program illustrates _parclen():

```
/*********
*  CHAR.C
*
*  Syntax: CHAR( <C string> )
*  Return: <C modified string>
*********/

#include "extend.h"

CLIPPER char()   /* do not use C parameters */
{
   /* declare variables */
   char *instr, *ret;
```

```
        int i;
        unsigned int len;

        /* check syntax */
        if ( PCOUNT==1 && ISCHAR(1) )
        {
           instr = _parc(1);   /* set pointer to parameter */
           len   = _parclen(1)+1;     /* get string length */

           /* allocate memory for return string */
           ret = _exmgrab( len );

           /* check memory allocation */
           if ( ret )
           {
              /* process string, one character at a time */
              for ( i = 0; i < len; i++ )
              {
                 if ( <condition> )
                    ret[i] = instr[i];
              }

              /* add null string terminator */
              ret[i] = '\0';

              /* return new string to Clipper */
              _retc( ret );

              /* free allocated memory */
              _exmback(ret, len);
           }
           else
              /* never executes - there is no NULL pointer */
              _retc( "Allocation Error" );
        }
        else
           _retc( "Syntax Error" );
     }
```

The _parclen() function can be called as a procedure from ASM programs by adding an underscore and eliminating the parentheses as follows:

```
mov     ax, <order>
mov     bx, <index>    ; array element index is optional
push    bx             ; omit if optional index is omitted
push    ax
call    __PARCLEN
add     sp, 4    ; use 2 instead of 4 if no optional index
```

The string length is returned in AX.

_parcsiz() Extend Function

Syntax: _parcsiz(int <order> [, int <index>])

Action: Evaluates the size of a character parameter that is passed by reference.

Return: Unsigned integer number of bytes allocated in memory for the specified parameter.

Detail: In order for an external program to write to a character parameter, the program needs access to its allocated length so as not to overwrite into another part of memory. The _parcsiz() function returns the allocated memory size of a character variable, or zero if passed a constant. The parameters to this function are

Parameter	Data Type	Description
order	int	Represents the position of the parameter in the parameters list when the program is invoked
index	int	Represents the array index of a specific element if the parameter referred to by order is an array

The following C program illustrates _parcsiz():

```
/*********
*  NEWCHAR.C
*
*  Syntax: CHAR( <C string variable> )
*  Return: <expC> null if no error, otherwise syntax
*          error.
*  Note  : Modifies <C string variable>.
*********/

#include "extend.h"

CLIPPER char()
/* do not use C parameters */
{
   /* declare variables */
   char *instr;
   int i;
   unsigned int size;

   /* check syntax */
   if ( PCOUNT==1 && ISCHAR(1) && ISBYREF(1) )
   {
      instr = _parc(1);    /* set pointer to parameter */
      size = _parcsiz(1); /* get max length */

      /* modify string, one character at a time */
      for ( i = 0; i < size; i++ )
          instr[i] = <change>;

      _retc( "" );

   }
   else
      _retc( "Syntax Error" );
}
```

The _parcsiz() function can be called as a procedure from ASM programs by adding an underscore and eliminating the parentheses as follows:

```
mov     ax, <order>
mov     bx, <index>    ; array element index is optional
push    bx             ; omit if optional index is omitted
push    ax
call    __PARCSIZ
add     sp, 4    ; use 2 instead of 4 if no optional index
```

The string length is returned in AX.

_pards() Extend Function

Syntax: _pards(int <order> [, int <index>])

Action: Allows an external function to access a date parameter.

Return: Character pointer to the specified date string parameter.

Detail: In order for an external program to manipulate a parameter, the program must have access to that parameter. The _pards() function allows access to a date parameter by providing the address of the date in memory. The parameters of this function are:

Parameter	Data Type	Description
order	int	Represents the position of the parameter in the parameters list when the program is invoked
index	int	Represents the array index of a specific element if the parameter referred to by order is an array

The date string pointed to is in the format "YYYYMMDD".

The following C program illustrates _pards():

```
/*********
*  DATES.C
*
*  Syntax: DATES( <D date> )
*  Return: <D date>, blank if syntax error.
*  Notes : Received and manipulated in C as a string in
*          the format: "CCYYMMDD"
*********/

#include "extend.h"
#define  DSBLANK  "00000000"  /* blank date for error */
#define  DSLEN    8           /* date string length */

CLIPPER dates()
/* do not use C parameters */
{
   /* declare variables */
   char *instr, *ret;
   int i, len = DSLEN+1;

   /* check syntax */
   if ( PCOUNT==1 && ISDATE(1) )
   {
      instr = _pards(1);  /* set pointer to parameter */

      /* allocate memory for return string */
      ret = _exmgrab( len );

      /* check memory allocation */
      if ( ret )
      {
         /* process date string, one char at a time */
         for ( i = 0; i < DSLEN; i++ )
         {
            ret[i] = instr[i];
         }

         /* add null string terminator */
         ret[i] = '\0';
```

```
            /* return new date string to Clipper */
            _retds( ret );

            /* free allocated memory */
            _exmback(ret, len);
         }
         else
            /* never executes - there is no NULL pointer */
            _retds( DSBLANK );
      }
      else
         _retds( DSBLANK );
   }
```

The _pards() function can be called as a procedure from ASM programs by adding an underscore and eliminating the parentheses as follows:

```
mov     ax, <order>
mov     bx, <index>    ; array element index is optional
push    bx             ; omit if optional index is omitted
push    ax
call    __PARDS
add     sp, 4    ; use 2 instead of 4 if no optional index
```

The string address is returned in DX:AX where DX is the segment and AX is the offset.

Also: DTOS()

_parinfa() — Extend Function

Syntax: _parinfa(int <order>, int <index>)

Action: Evaluates the data type of the specified array element.

Return: Number representing the data type of the specified array element.

Detail: To pass array elements as parameters into C programs, the _parinfa() function provides information the C program must know, such as the number of elements in the array, and their data type. The parameters to this function are

Parameter	Data Type	Description
order	int	Represents the position of the parameter in the parameters list when the program is invoked
index	int	Represents the array index of a specific element

If index is zero, returns the number of elements in the array, otherwise returns the data type of the specified element.

These #defines from Extend.h make it easier to use _parinfa():

```
#define ALENGTH(n)  (_parinfa(n, 0))
#define UNDEF        0
#define CHARACTER    1
#define NUMERIC      2
#define LOGICAL      4
#define DATE         8
#define ALIAS       16
#define MPTR        32
#define MEMO        65
#define WORD       128
#define ARRAY      512
```

```
/*********
*  ARRAY.C
*
*  Syntax: ARRAY( <array name> )
*  Return: <expL> true if all elements are initialized,
*          otherwise false.
*********/

#include "extend.h"
```

```
CLIPPER array()
/* do not use C parameters */
{
   /* declare variables */
   int i, len;

   /* check syntax */
   if ( PCOUNT==1 && ISARRAY(1) )
   {
      len = ALENGTH(1);
      /* process elements one at a time */
      for ( i = 1; i <= len; i++ )
      {
         if (_parinfa(1, i) == UNDEF)
            break;
      }
      _retl( i > len );
   }
   else
      _retl( 0 );     /* syntax error returns false */
}
```

The _parinfa() function can be called as a procedure from ASM programs by adding an underscore and eliminating the parentheses as follows:

```
mov    ax, <order in parameter list>
mov    bx, <element index or zero>
push   bx
push   ax
call   __PARINFA
add    sp, 4
```

If the element index is zero, the number of elements is returned as an integer in AX. If the element index is a valid element number in the array, that element's data type is returned as an integer in AX:

Integer	Meaning
0	undefined
1	character
2	numeric
4	logical
8	date
32	by reference
65	memo
512	array

_parinfo() **Extend Function**

Syntax: _parinfo(int <order>)

Action: Evaluates the data type of the specified parameter.

Return: Number representing the data type of the specified parameter.

Detail: The _parinfo() function provides information the C program must know about parameters: the number of parameters passed and their data types. The parameter to this function is

Parameter	Data Type	Description
order	int	Represents the position of the parameter in the parameters list when the program is invoked

If order is zero, returns the number of parameters passed, otherwise returns the data type of the specified parameter.

The following #defines from Extend.h make it easier to use _parinfo():

```
#define UNDEF          0
#define CHARACTER      1
#define NUMERIC        2
#define LOGICAL        4
#define DATE           8
#define ALIAS         16
#define MPTR          32
#define MEMO          65
#define WORD         128
#define ARRAY        512
#define PCOUNT       (_parinfo(0))
#define ISCHAR(n)    (_parinfo(n) & CHARACTER)
#define ISNUM(n)     (_parinfo(n) & NUMERIC)
#define ISLOG(n)     (_parinfo(n) & LOGICAL)
#define ISDATE(n)    (_parinfo(n) & DATE)
#define ISMEMO(n)    (_parinfo(n) & MEMO)
#define ISBYREF(n)   (_parinfo(n) & MPTR)
#define ISARRAY(n)   (_parinfo(n) & ARRAY)
#define ALENGTH(n)   (_parinfa(n, 0))

********
*  ARRAY.C
*
*  Syntax: ARRAY( <array name> )
*  Return: <expL> true if all elements are initialized,
*          otherwise false.
*********/

#include "extend.h"

CLIPPER array()
/* do not use C parameters */
{
   /* declare variables */
   int i, len;
```

```
      /* check syntax */
      if ( PCOUNT==1 && ISARRAY(1) )
      {
         len = ALENGTH(1);
         /* process elements one at a time */
         for ( i = 1; i <= len; i++ )
         {
            if (_parinfa(1, i) == UNDEF)
               break;
         }
         _retl( i > len );
      }
      else
         _retl( 0 );      /* syntax error returns false */
   }
```

The _parinfo() function can be called as a procedure from ASM programs by adding an underscore and eliminating the parentheses as follows:

```
mov     ax, <order or zero>
push    ax
call    __PARINFO
add     sp, 2
```

If the register pushed is zero, the number of parameters is returned as an integer in AX. If the register pushed is the placement order of a parameter in the list, that parameter's data type is returned as an integer in AX:

Integer	Meaning
0	undefined
1	character
2	numeric
4	logical
8	date
32	by reference
65	memo
512	array

_parl() Extend Function

Syntax: _parl(int <order> [, int <index>])

Action: Converts the specified logical parameter to an integer.

Return: Integer equivalent of the logical value (.T. is 1, .F. is 0).

Detail: In order for an external program to manipulate a parameter, the program must have access to that parameter. The _parl() function allows access to a logical parameter. The parameters to this function are

Parameter	Data Type	Description
order	int	Represents the position of the parameter in the parameters list when the program is invoked
index	int	Represents the array index of a specific element if the parameter referred to by order is an array

```
/*********
*  LOGICAL.C
*
*  Syntax: LOGICAL( <L condition> )
*  Return: <L true or false>
*********/

#include "extend.h"
#define  FALSE  0      /* error always false */

CLIPPER logical()
/* do not use C parameters */
{
   /* declare variables */
   int in;
```

```
        /* check syntax */
        if ( PCOUNT==1 && ISLOG(1) )
        {
           in = _parl(1);          /* get incoming parameter */
           in = <condition>;       /* process condition */
           _retl( in );    /* return new logical to Clipper */
        }
        else
           _retl( FALSE );
     }
```

The _parl() function can be called as a procedure from ASM programs by adding an underscore and eliminating the parentheses as follows:

```
mov    ax, <order>
mov    bx, <index>    ; array element index is optional
push   bx             ; omit if optional index is omitted
push   ax
call   __PARL
add    sp, 4    ; use 2 instead of 4 if no optional index
```

The value of the integer result is returned in AX where one is true and zero is false.

_parnd() Extend Function

Syntax: _parnd(int <order> [, int <index>])

Action: Converts the specified numeric parameter to a double.

Return: Double equivalent of the specified number.

Detail: In order for an external program to manipulate a parameter, the program must have access to that parameter. The _parnd() function allows access to a numeric parameter and converts the number to a double. The parameters to this function are

Parameter	Data Type	Description
order	int	Represents the position of the parameter in the parameters list when the program is invoked
index	int	Represents the array index of a specific element if the parameter referred to by order is an array

```
/*********
*  DOUBLE.C
*
*  Syntax: DOUBLE( <N double> )
*  Return: <N double>
*********/

#include "extend.h"
#define  ERROR  -1.00    /* error value is usually -1 */

CLIPPER double()
/* do not use C parameters */
{
   /* declare variables */
   int in, ret;

   /* check syntax */
   if ( PCOUNT==1 && ISNUM(1) )
   {
      in = _parnd(1);          /* get incoming parameter */
      ret = in;                /* process number */
      _retnd( ret );  /* return new number to Clipper */
   }
   else
      _retnd( ERROR );
}
```

Note that working with doubles in C requires either linking in the Microsoft alternamte floating point library or using undocumented Clipper internal functions.

The _parnd() function can be called as a procedure from ASM programs by adding an underscore and eliminating the parentheses as follows:

```
mov     ax, <order>
mov     bx, <index>    ; array element index is optional
push    bx             ; omit if optional index is omitted
push    ax
call    __PARND
add     sp, 4     ; use 2 instead of 4 if no optional index
```

The address of the double is returned in DX:AX where DX is the segment and AX is the offset.

_parni() — Extend Function

Syntax: _parni(int <order> [, int <index>])

Action: Converts the specified numeric parameter to an integer.

Return: Integer equivalent of the specified number.

Detail: In order for an external program to manipulate a parameter, the program must have access to that parameter. The _parni() function allows access to a numeric parameter and converts the number to an integer. The parameters to this function are

Parameter	Data Type	Description
order	int	Represents the position of the parameter in the parameters list when the program is invoked
index	int	Represents the array index of a specific element if the parameter referred to by order is an array

```
/*********
*  INTEGER.C
*
*  Syntax: INTEGER( <N integer> )
*  Return: <N integer>
*********/

#include "extend.h"
#define  ERROR  -1          /* error value is usually -1 */

CLIPPER integer()
/* do not use C parameters */
{
   /* declare variables */
   int in, ret;

   /* check syntax */
   if ( PCOUNT==1 && ISNUM(1) )
   {
      in = _parni(1);         /* get incoming parameter */
      ret = in;               /* process number */
      _retni( ret );  /* return new number to Clipper */
   }
   else
      _retni( ERROR );
}
```

The _parni() function can be called as a procedure from ASM programs by adding an underscore and eliminating the parentheses as follows:

```
mov     ax, <order>
mov     bx, <index>    ; array element index is optional
push    bx             ; omit if optional index is omitted
push    ax
call    __PARNI
add     sp, 4    ; use 2 instead of 4 if no optional index
```

The value of the integer is returned in AX.

_parnl() Extend Function

Syntax: _parnl(int <order> [, int <index>])

Action: Converts the specified numeric parameter to a long integer.

Return: Long integer equivalent of the specified number.

Detail: In order for an external program to manipulate a parameter, the program must have access to that parameter. The _parnl() function allows access to a numeric parameter and converts the number to a long integer. The parameters to this function are

Parameter	Data Type	Description
order	int	Represents the position of the parameter in the parameters list when the program is invoked
index	int	Represents the array index of a specific element if the parameter referred to by order is an array

```
/*********
*  LONG.C
*
*  Syntax: LONG( <N long> )
*  Return: <N long>
*********/

#include "extend.h"
#define  ERROR  -1        /* error value is usually -1 */

CLIPPER long()
/* do not use C parameters */
{
   /* declare variables */
   long in, ret;

   /* check syntax */
   if ( PCOUNT==1 && ISNUM(1) )
```

```
    {
       in = _parnl(1);        /* get incoming parameter */
       ret = in;              /* process number */
       _retnl( ret );  /* return new number to Clipper */
    }
    else
       _retnl( ERROR );
}
```

The _parnl() function can be called as a procedure from ASM programs by adding an underscore and eliminating the parentheses as follows:

```
mov     ax, <order>
mov     bx, <index>    ; array element index is optional
push    bx             ; omit if optional index is omitted
push    ax
call    __PARNL
add     sp, 4    ; use 2 instead of 4 if no optional index
```

The value of the long is returned in DX:AX.

_ret() Extend Function

Syntax: _ret()

Action: Returns to the calling program without a return value.

Detail: The _ret() function allows a C function to be called as a DO procedure, but is not very useful in the real world because a function can be executed by itself without being part of an expression:

```
* Function executed by itself.
c_func( <parameter list> )
```

is the same as

```
* Function executed with a DO.
DO c_func WITH <parameter list>
```

The following C program illustrates _ret():

```
/*********
*  C_FUNC.C
*
*  Syntax: DO C_FUNC
*  Notes : Alternate syntax could be C_FUNC() which may
*          have, but does not require, the _ret()
*          function.
*********/

#include "extend.h"

CLIPPER c_func()
{
    .
    .  <code goes here>
    .
    /* return nothing to Clipper when called by DO */
    _ret();
}
```

The _ret() function can be called as a procedure from ASM programs by adding an underscore and eliminating the parentheses as follows:

```
call __RET
```

No stack manipulation is required.

_retc() — Extend Function

Syntax: _retc(char * <string>)

Action: Returns a character string to the calling program.

Return: <expC> string at the specified address.

Detail: The _retc() function allows an external program to return a character value to the calling program. The parameter for this function is a pointer representing the address of the character value in memory. The following C program illustrates _retc():

```
/*********
*  CHAR.C
*
*  Syntax: CHAR( <C string> )
*  Return: <C modified string>
*********/

#include "extend.h"

CLIPPER char()
/* do not use C parameters */
{
   /* declare variables */
   char *instr, *ret;
   int i;
   unsigned int len;

   /* check syntax */
   if ( PCOUNT==1 && ISCHAR(1) )
   {
      instr = _parc(1);   /* set pointer to parameter */
      len   = _parclen(1)+1;     /* get string length */

      /* allocate memory for return string */
      ret = _exmgrab( len );

      /* check memory allocation */
      if ( ret )
      {
         /* process string, one character at a time */
         for ( i = 0; i < len; i++ )
         {
            if ( <condition> )
               ret[i] = instr[i];
         }

         /* add null string terminator */
         ret[i] = '\0';
```

```
          /* return new string to Clipper */
          _retc( ret );

          /* free allocated memory */
          _exmback(ret, len);
       }
       else
          /* never executes - there is no NULL pointer */
          _retc( "Allocation Error" );
    }
    else
       _retc( "Syntax Error" );
}
```

The _retc() function can be called as a procedure from ASM programs by adding an underscore and eliminating the parentheses as follows:

```
mov    dx, &lt;segment&gt; ; DX:AX points to the return string
mov    ax, <offset>
push   dx
push   ax
call   __RETC
add    sp, 4
```

_retclen() Extend Function

Syntax: _retclen(char * <string>, unsigned <length>)

Action: Returns a character string with embedded nulls to the calling program.

Return: <expC> string of a given length beginning at the specified address.

Detail: The _retclen() function allows an external program to return a character value containing embedded nulls to the calling program. The parameter for this function is a pointer representing the address of the character value in memory and a string length. Same as _retc(), but lets you specify a length when there may be embedded null characters in the string. The following C program illustrates _retclen():

```
/*********
*  CHAR.C
*
*  Syntax: CHAR( <C string> )
*  Return: <C modified string>
*********/

#include "extend.h"

CLIPPER char()
/* do not use C parameters */
{
   /* declare variables */
   char *instr, *ret;
   int i;
   unsigned int len;

   /* check syntax */
   if ( PCOUNT==1 && ISCHAR(1) )
   {
      instr = _parc(1);   /* set pointer to parameter */
      len   = _parclen(1)+1;     /* get string length */

      /* allocate memory for return string */
      ret = _exmgrab( len );

      /* check memory allocation */
      if ( ret )
      {
         /* process string, one character at a time */
         for ( i = 0; i < len; i++ )
         {
            if ( <condition> )
               ret[i] = instr[i];
         }

         /* add null string terminator */
         ret[i] = '\0';
```

```
            /* return new string to Clipper */
            _retclen( ret, len );

            /* free allocated memory */
            _exmback(ret, len);
         }
         else
            /* never executes - there is no NULL pointer */
            _retc( "Allocation Error" );
      }
      else
         _retc( "Syntax Error" );
   }
```

The _retclen() function can be called as a procedure from ASM programs by adding an underscore and eliminating the parentheses as follows:

```
mov    dx, &lt;segment&gt;     ; DX:AX points to return string
mov    ax, <offset>
mov    cx, <length>
push   cx
push   dx
push   ax
call   __RETCLEN
add    sp, 6
```

_retds() — Extend Function

Syntax: _retds(char * <date string>)

Action: Returns a date value to the calling program.

Return: <expD> date at the specified address.

Detail: The date string is a format of "YYYYMMDD".

The _retds() function allows an external program to return a date value to the calling program. The parameter for this function is a pointer representing the address of the date value in memory. The following C program illustrates _retds():

```
/*********
*  DATES.C
*
*  Syntax: DATES( <D date> )
*  Return: <D date>, blank if syntax error.
*  Notes : Received and manipulated in C as a string in
*          the format: "CCYYMMDD"
*********/

#include "extend.h"
#define  DSBLANK  "00000000"  /* blank date for error */
#define  DSLEN    8           /* date string length */

CLIPPER dates()
/* do not use C parameters */
{
   /* declare variables */
   char *instr, *ret;
   int i, len = DSLEN+1;

   /* check syntax */
   if ( PCOUNT==1 && ISDATE(1) )
   {
      instr = _pards(1);  /* set pointer to parameter */

      /* allocate memory for return string */
      ret = _exmgrab( len );

      /* check memory allocation */
      if ( ret )
      {
         /* process date string, one char at a time */
         for ( i = 0; i < DSLEN; i++ )
         {
            ret[i] = instr[i];
         }
```

```
            /* add null string terminator */
            ret[i] = '\0';

            /* return new date string to Clipper */
            _retds( ret );

            /* free allocated memory */
            _exmback(ret, len);
         }
         else
            /* never executes - there is no NULL pointer */
            _retds( DSBLANK );
      }
      else
         _retds( DSBLANK );
   }
```

The _retds() function can be called as a procedure from ASM programs by adding an underscore and eliminating the parentheses as follows:

```
mov    dx, &lt;segment&gt; ;DX:AX points to return date string
mov    ax, <offset>
push   dx
push   ax
call   __RETDS
add    sp, 4
```

_retl() — Extend Function

Syntax: _retl(integer)

Action: Returns a logical value to the calling program.

Return: <expL> equivalent of the specified integer (.T. = 1, .F. = 0).

Detail: The _retl() allows an external program to return a logical value to the calling program. The following C program illustrates _retl():

```
/*********
*  LOGICAL.C
*
*  Syntax: LOGICAL( <L condition> )
*  Return: <L true or false>
*********/

#include "extend.h"
#define  FALSE  0       /* error always false */

CLIPPER logical()
/* do not use C parameters */
{
   /* declare variables */
   int in;

   /* check syntax */
   if ( PCOUNT==1 && ISLOG(1) )
   {
      in = _parl(1);         /* get incoming parameter */
      in = <condition>;      /* process condition */
      _retl( in );   /* return new logical to Clipper */
   }
   else
      _retl( FALSE );
}
```

The _retl() function can be called as a procedure from ASM programs by adding an underscore and eliminating the parentheses as follows:

```
mov    ax, <integer>  ; zero is false, one is true
push   ax
call   __RETL
add    sp, 2
```

_retnd() **Extend Function**

Syntax: _retnd(double)

Action: Converts a double to a numeric and returns it to the calling program.

Return: <expN> of the specified double.

Detail: The retnd() function allows an external function to return a double to the calling program as a numeric value. The following C program illustrates _retnd():

```
/*********
*  DOUBLE.C
*
*  Syntax: DOUBLE( <N double> )
*  Return: <N double>
*********/

#include "extend.h"
#define  ERROR  -1.00    /* error value is usually -1 */

CLIPPER double()
/* do not use C parameters */
{
   /* declare variables */
   int in, ret;

   /* check syntax */
   if ( PCOUNT==1 && ISNUM(1) )
   {
      in = _parnd(1);        /* get incoming parameter */
      ret = in;              /* process number */
      _retnd( ret );  /* return new number to Clipper */
   }
   else
      _retnd( ERROR );
}
```

Note that working with doubles in C requires either linking in the Microsoft alternate floating point library or using undocumented Clipper internal functions.

The _retnd() function can be called as a procedure from ASM programs by adding an underscore and eliminating the parentheses as follows:

```
; AX, BX, CX, DX contain double as four words
mov     ax, <first word>
mov     bx, <second word>
mov     cx, <third word>
mov     dx, <fourth word>
push    ax
push    bx
push    cx
push    dx
call    __RETND
add     sp, 8
```

_retni() — Extend Function

Syntax: _retni(integer)

Action: Converts an integer to a numeric and returns it to the calling program.

Return: <expN> of the specified integer.

Detail: The retni() function allows an external function to return an integer to the calling program as a numeric value. The following C program illustrates _retni():

```
/*********
*  INTEGER.C
*
*  Syntax: INTEGER( <N integer> )
*  Return: <N integer>
*********/

#include "extend.h"
```

```
#define  ERROR  -1        /* error value is usually -1 */

CLIPPER integer()
/* do not use C parameters */
{
   /* declare variables */
   int in, ret;

   /* check syntax */
   if ( PCOUNT==1 && ISNUM(1) )
   {
      in = _parni(1);       /* get incoming parameter */
      ret = in;             /* process number */
      _retni( ret );  /* return new number to Clipper */
   }
   else
      _retni( ERROR );
}
```

The _retni() function can be called as a procedure from ASM programs by adding an underscore and eliminating the parentheses as follows:

```
mov    ax, <integer>
push   ax
call   __RETNI
add    sp, 2
```

_retnl() **Extend Function**

Syntax: _retnl(long)

Action: Converts a long integer to a numeric and returns it to the calling program.

Return: <expN> of the specified long integer.

Detail: The retnl() function allows an external function to return a long integer to the calling program as a numeric value. The following C program illustrates _retnl():

```
/*********
*  LONG.C
*
*  Syntax: LONG( <N long> )
*  Return: <N long>
*********/

#include "extend.h"
#define  ERROR  -1        /* error value is usually -1 */

CLIPPER long()
/* do not use C parameters */
{
   /* declare variables */
   long in, ret;

   /* check syntax */
   if ( PCOUNT==1 && ISNUM(1) )
   {
      in = _parnl(1);          /* get incoming parameter */
      ret = in;                /* process number */
      _retnl( ret );  /* return new number to Clipper */
   }
   else
      _retnl( ERROR );
}
```

The _retnl() function can be called as a procedure from ASM programs by adding an underscore and eliminating the parentheses as follows:

```
mov    ax, <first word>     ; AX, BX contain long
mov    bx, <second word>    ;   as two words
push   ax
push   bx
call   __RETNL
add    sp, 4
```

Appendix A

This appendix lists Clipper's keywords by their functional category.

Array

Character

Comparison

Compile

Configuration

Conversion

Database

Date

Debug

Display

Environment

Error

Extend

External

File

Help

Index

Input

Language

Link

Logical

Memory

Menu

Network

Numeric

Operating System (OS)

Output

Program

Search

TRHELP

Appendix B

This appendix lists Clipper's keywords by their type in the language.

Command

Function

Info

Keyword

Operator

Parameter

Procedure

Program

Symbol

Index

B

C

D

E

F

N

O

P

Q

R

S

T

Tom Rettig's HELP™

Pop-up Quick Reference Software

- Time saver: puts information on your computer where you need it most
- Easy to use: familiar menus & hot keys, nothing new to learn
- Portable: carry single diskette instead of heavy manuals
- Comprehensive: contains full text and code from this book
- Executable options: stand-alone, parent, and resident
- Output options: write into editor, print, and leave screen image
- Data files available for dBASE III & IV, FoxBASE, Clipper, Quicksilver, dBXL, and Tom Rettig's Library
- Make your own data files to document your application

Choice of Database Experts

"Tom Rettig was among the first to document and conventionalize the dBASE language. His new Help system puts that experience and expertise at your fingertips." — *Wayne Ratliff, creator of dBASE*

"The best tool is always the one designed specifically for the job. Tom Rettig's HELP eases the learning curve of dBASE, SQL, and other high-level languages." — *Adam Green, Educator*

"After looking at all the major points, there is only one logical conclusion to draw: when you're programming in Clipper and you need assistance, you want Tom Rettig's HELP!" — *Steve Straley, Author*

"For all around quality and design integrity, Tom Rettig's HELP is the champ. It's chock-full of thoughtful features I just can't do without." — *Comparative review with Norton Guides by Marc Schnapp for Data Based Advisor*

Reader & Data File $119.95 • Extra Data Files $69.95 • Data File Maker $199.95

To order or request more information, contact:

9300 Wilshire Boulevard, Suite 470
Beverly Hills, CA 90212–3237
Telephone: (213) 272–3784

Telex: 499–6426 RETTIG • MCI Mail: TRA • CompuServe 75066,352